2/04

FILMMAKERS SERIES
edited by
ANTHONY SLIDE

Hitchcock and Poe

The Legacy of Delight and Terror

Dennis R. Perry

The Scarecrow Press, Inc.
Lanham, Maryland, and Oxford
2003

SCARECROW PRESS, INC.

Published in the United States of America
by Scarecrow Press, Inc.
A wholly owned subsidiary of The Rowman & Littlefield Publishing Group, Inc.
4501 Forbes Boulevard, Suite 200, Lanham, MD 20706
www.scarecrowpress.com

PO Box 317
Oxford
OX2 9RU, UK

British Library Cataloguing-in-Publication Information Available

Library of Congress Cataloging-in-Publication Data

Perry, Dennis R.
  Hitchcock and Poe : the legacy of delight and terror / Dennis R. Perry.
     p. cm.
  Includes bibliographical references and index.
  ISBN 0-8108-4822-8 (alk. paper)
  1. Hitchcock, Alfred, 1899—Criticism and interpretation. 2. Poe, Edgar
Allan, 1809–1849—Criticism and interpretation. I. Title.
PN1998.3.H58P46 2003
791.43'0233'092-dc21   2003008249

⊗™ The paper used in this publication meets the minimum requirements of
American National Standard for Information Sciences—Permanence of
Paper for Printed Library Materials, ANSI/NISO Z39.48-1992.
Manufactured in the United States of America.

To Mary Lyn

Contents

             "The Man of the Crowd" and *Rear Window*

Chapter 8   Romantic Obsession: Return to Transcendence   157
             "The Fall of the House of Usher" and *Vertigo*

Chapter 9   Humor and Horror: Collapsing into Unity   185
             "Ligeia" and *The 39 Steps*

             Annotated Bibliography   209

             Index   217

             About the Author   00

~

Preface

In Alfred Hitchcock's *Strangers on a Train* (1951), two seemingly different men cross tracks. The film unsettles the viewer as it becomes clear that the two men share common problems, frustrations—and guilt. This study of Edgar Allan Poe and Alfred Hitchcock seeks to identify common ground between two artists with different backgrounds who practiced different art forms. In many ways, as the saying goes, they attended different schools together. Born in America in 1809, Poe was the child of literary romanticism. Hitchcock was born in England ninety years later and was the child of cinematic modernism. Nevertheless, their aesthetic paths crossed and their common artistic goal transcended the gulf of a century: both perfected ways of terrorizing readers and audiences through precise narrative forms born of a set of common obsessions. Crisscross!

Though Hitchcock made a long statement about Poe's importance in his artistic development, though as a young man he wrote stories similar to Poe's, and though several of his films are remarkably parallel to Poe's tales in both theme and situation, Poe did not influence Hitchcock in any materially traceable way in any particular film. I have no evidence, for instance, that he wrote "Ligeia" in the margin of *Vertigo's* shooting script. Nor do I assert that Poe is the director's most important influence. Clearly Hitchcock has a number of important artistic fathers, Poe among them. Yet there is an unusually high degree of artistic affinity between the two artists, as Hitchcock himself acknowledged: "Edgar Allan Poe and I certainly have a common point. We are both prisoners of a genre: 'suspense.'"[1] In his 1964 foreword to a Swedish edition of Poe's tales, Hitchcock continues to discuss his association with Poe in terms of genre: "For a good many years I have been called the 'King of the Thriller.'" But "I must acknowledge that this renowned author is the genre's undisputed genius."[2] Thus we have Hitchcock's testimony of his affinity with Poe in words and on film. In this study I will define the broader range of Poe's "legacy" to Hitchcock as reflected in his films more fully than it has been done previously. The chapters in this volume analyze themes common to both artists by comparing a tale and a film with shared plot and character orientations. This strategy is plausible because Hitchcock was involved in every aspect of the creation of his films, including the development of the screenplay.

I first connected Poe and Hitchcock when I noticed the similarities between "Fall of the House of Usher" and *Vertigo* with their double Madeleines who both mysteriously die and return. Beyond situational and name correspondences, I also noted a certain surreal quality and a common emphasis on doubling, perverseness, voyeurism, obsession, and mystery. In both works I strongly sensed the wonder and awe of the sublime that links the tales and their creators. This shock of recognition led to years of studying the extent of their sublime and obsessive affinities. Although the idea of linking Poe and Hitchcock is not original with me, I only became aware of other critics' work as I pursued my own discovery. Previous observations have been limited mostly to passing insights or an examination of one common strain or another. Scholars made many connections between Poe and Hitchcock before and after my article in *Literature/Film Quarterly*, "Imps of the Perverse: Discovering the Poe/Hitchcock Connection" (1996). Several notable Hitchcock scholars have commented on various affinities that link the artists in a host of interesting ways (see the annotated bibliography at the end of this book). Mine has been the pleasure and challenge of documenting in detail a set of narrative and narrational concerns common to Poe and Hitchcock. I think of this volume as a culmination of the linking impulse between Poe and Hitchcock that began with the first book-length study of Hitchcock's films by Rohmer and Chabrol in 1957.

This study will not radically alter specific interpretations of Hitchcock's films. Rather, it is broader and more impressionistic, the intent being to alter the degree to which we recognize what we already know of Hitchcock's films in terms of their aesthetic likenesses to Poe's purposes, philosophy, techniques, and passions. Discovering that someone has a twin mystifies and enchants our perception of the person. In the case at hand, recognizing Hitchcock's affinities with Poe makes looking at Hitchcock's films again like Hawthorne's description of looking at an enchanted moonlit room through a mirror:

> Glancing at the looking-glass, we behold—deep within its haunted verge—the smouldering glow of the half-extinguished anthracite, the white moonbeams on the floor, and a repetition of all the gleam and shadow of the picture, with one remove farther from the actual and nearer to the imaginative.[3]

This brings us to Hawthorne's point about the effect of literary romances on the reader. As we look at Hitchcock through Poe's haunted mirror, we see him "one remove farther" from the modern, well-lit surfaces of his films that disguise the moonlit romance in their deep structures. In some important ways, as Poe's artistic twin, Hitchcock can be seen more clearly as the romantic he is. While Leitch's study revealed him as the game master, Brill's the mythmaker, and Cohen's the Victorian, I assert that Hitchcock is in every sense a romantic.[4] No single study can ever capture all facets of such a complex artistic personality, but it can aspire to highlight at least one.

Since these "twins" are separated by nearly a century, their resemblance is more like artistic genealogy. Artistically and psychologically speaking, Poe is like the great-great-great-grandfather whose portrait hanging in the ancestral halls resembles Hitchcock. Poe's art is Hitchcock's inheritance, a legacy of how to delight audiences with terror. It is a specific approach, mostly eschewing horror and revulsion in favor of psychological suspense, subjectivity, guilt, and fear. It is an art of obsession and fetishes, of shocks and surprises, of moods and atmospheres.

The legacy includes an emphasis on narrative structure over realistic explorations of character, technique and impression over ideas. Hitchcock inherits a belief in art for art's sake, which he interprets as "pure cinema." The exciting episode, the dramatic shot, and the careful molding of suspense into frenzy takes precedence over making an audience think. Poe put into Hitchcock's plump genes a passion to dazzle and frighten audiences at the same time.

After all has been said and done on this subject, what remains, and what makes a book like this possible, is the inexplicable passion Poe and Hitchcock shared to enrich their narratives with imagery and details that infinitely reflect each other in ways that infinitely multiply perspectives and perpetually interest mass audiences and scholars alike. Through their attention to detail, together with unforgettable characters, situations, and images, both made artistic integrity and popular success into congenial grave fellows. Just as the details in their individual stories reflect each other, so their stories intertextually reflect each other. What follows in this study is like the train yard in *Strangers on a Train*, with its dozens of tracks going in all directions. Poe's and Hitchcock's infinite lines of track crisscross, continually revealing surprising, delightful, and terrifying convergences.

Notes

1. From a 1960 interview reprinted in Sidney Gottlieb, ed., *Hitchcock on Hitchcock: Selected Writings and Interviews* (Berkeley: University of California Press, 1995), 145.

2. Foreword to *Edgar Allan Poe: Sallsamma historier* (Stockholm: Raben & Sjogren, 1964), 7.

3. *The Scarlet Letter*, ed. Ross C. Murfin, Bedford Case Studies Series (Boston: Bedford, 1991), 46.

4. See Thomas Leitch, *Find the Director and Other Hitchcock Games* (Athens: University of Georgia Press, 1991); Lesley Brill, *The Hitchcock Romance: Love and Irony in Hitchcock's Films* (Princeton: Princeton University Press, 1988); Paula Marantz Cohen, *Alfred Hitchcock: The Legacy of Victorianism* (Lexington: University of Kentucky Press, 1995).

~

Acknowledgments

Like films, books are collaborative projects. I wish to thank Hitchcock colleagues Ken Mogg and Thomas Leitch for sharing their expertise and considerable time in reading portions of this book. I'm indebted to Ken Egan for his enthusiasm and insights as the book progressed. My thanks as well to my Brigham Young University English Department colleagues for helpful and encouraging criticisms, and the students of my Hitchcock and Poe course for their fresh and stimulating ideas. And my appreciation goes to colleagues at the University of Missouri-Rolla for support and friendship during the conception of this study. A special thanks to my graduate assistant, Genevieve Larsen (and to the BYU English Department for providing her), for her alert editorial comments, computer competence, excellent research, and unflagging hard work. Finally, my infinite gratitude to my best friend and wife, Mary Lyn, for everything, including her patience and skill in repeatedly editing and retyping this book.

Permissions have graciously been given by the *Hitchcock Annual* and the Poe Studies Association for reprinting parts of bibliographic articles appearing as the following:

Perry, Dennis R. "Annotated Checklist of Edgar Allan Poe Connections to Alfred Hitchcock." *PSA Newsletter* 27, no. 2 (1999): 7–9.

———. "Bibliography of Scholarship Linking Alfred Hitchcock and Edgar Allan Poe." *Hitchcock Annual*, 2000–2001, 163–73.

CHAPTER ONE

~

Introduction: Hitchcock and Poe

In this first book-length study of the aesthetic relationship between Edgar Allan Poe and Alfred Hitchcock, I explore Poe's influence on important aspects of the "Hitchcock touch." I use the term "influence" rather loosely here and throughout the study, aware of how thorny influence studies are. As Bernard DeVoto slyly noted, "Source-hunting is the most profitless of literary occupations."[1] A more appropriate term is probably "affinity," since the similarities clearly exist, though we can't know exactly how they got there. Hitchcock read Poe intensely in his teens and later declared that "without wanting to seem immodest, I can't help but compare what I try to put in my films with what Poe put in his stories: a perfectly unbelievable story recounted to readers with such a hallucinatory logic that one has the impression that this same story can happen to you tomorrow."[2]

From that early experience, whether consciously or not, Hitchcock continued using Poe as a resource of ideas, though Poe's most considerable narrative legacy to Hitchcock is the expert crafting of emotional responses in audiences. The key to that legacy is the concept of the sublime, the simultaneous experience of delight and terror, which becomes the hallmark of both their narrative styles. As Hitchcock discovered from reading Poe, "fear . . . is a feeling that people like to feel when they are certain of being in safety" (143). Since *Eureka* (1848) is a template for Poe's use of the sublime, as well as for his imagery and structures, I use it as an organizational and interpretive metaphor by which to examine Hitchcock's cinematic use of Poe, both as disciple and heretic. After all, as Jean Douchet affirms, "is not inversion our filmmaker's favorite system?"[3] In this introduction I will examine the case for and against a significant relationship between Poe and Hitchcock, and summarize Poe's *Eureka*, showing how it reveals some of the aesthetic convergences of Poe and Hitchcock, particularly in terms of the sublime.

Obviously, to compare a filmmaker with a writer poses some "fit" problems. To level the aesthetic playing field I will make the auteurist argument that Hitchcock was the central, controlling creative force behind his films, thus defining him with Poe as an author. Despite the significant contributions of screenwriters, cameramen, and composers, and despite working in several different major studios, Hitchcock always managed to put his personal signature on his films, making his name synonymous with a unique type of suspense thriller. His style is as recognizable as he is in his cameos. According to Sterritt, "As much as any major filmmaker ever has, he channeled the talent of his collaborators and the temper of his times into coherent narrative/aesthetic patterns dictated by his own deepest instincts."[4] In discussing his relationship with the cinematographer, for example, Hitchcock stated that "the cameraman knows me well enough to know what I want—and when in doubt, I draw a rectangle, and then draw the shot out for him."[5] Sometimes, ironically, the exception proves the rule in how Hitchcock got what he wanted from his collaborators.[6] Hitchcock was intimately involved in most of his productions from the beginning. He explains his working method to Peter Bogdanovich:

I work many weeks with [the writer] and he takes notes. And I describe the picture for the production designers as well. *Marnie* has all been finished as far as the layout of the picture, but there's no dialogue in it. I would say I apply myself two-thirds before he writes and one-third after he writes. But I will not and do not photograph anything that he puts in the script on his own, apart from words. I mean any cinematic method of telling it—how can he know it? On *North by Northwest* Ernie Lehman wouldn't let me out of the office for a whole year. I was with him on every shot, every scene. Because it wasn't his material. (6)

In addition to his amazingly coherent style, despite constant experimentation, he had the power through much of his career to make major production decisions. Although some of the properties he chose to film were themselves influenced by Poe in one way or another, his choosing them demonstrates another aspect of his authorial control. As Robin Wood so reasonably put it, "A complete account of any one of the great Hitchcock films would have to see it as the product of an intricate network of influences, circumstances of production, collaborations, happy confluences. But at the center of that network is—must be—a particular creative personality."[7] In short, being the author of his films puts Hitchcock on common ground with Poe as a fellow storyteller.

One justification of a study such as this is given by David Sterritt, who notes that there are few clues in the Hitchcock chronology to indicate the source of his inspirations or why they developed as they did. "It becomes all the more necessary, therefore, to identify and assess the transpersonal forces that made themselves felt in his work despite his passion for personal control" (*Films of Alfred Hitchcock,* 3). Other important literary influences on Hitchcock include Dickens, Buchan, and Priestley, but Hitchcock implies Poe's singular importance in his desire to tell certain kinds of stories: "very probably, it's because I like Edgar Allan Poe's stories so much that I began to make suspense films" (143). Poe's influence on Hitchcock seems to have begun with the sixteen-year-old East Londoner's sympathetic emotional connection to the troubled American writer: "I read first, at random, his biography, and the sadness of his life made a great impression on me. I felt an immense pity for him because, in spite of his talent, he had always been unhappy" (143).[8] A rather lonely boy himself, Hitchcock became obsessed with Poe's tales, enjoying the kind of joy and refuge in reading that characterizes romantic youth: "When I would come back from the office where I worked, I would hurry to my room, take a cheap edition of his *Tales of the Grotesque and Arabesque,* and begin reading." This daily supping from Poe was the real genesis of Hitchcock's creative life. Reading Poe seems to have taught Hitchcock core principles of what to narrate and how: "I still remember my feelings when I finished 'The Murders in the Rue Morgue.' I was afraid, but this fear made me in fact discover something that I haven't since forgotten. Fear, you see, is a feeling that people like to feel when they are certain of being in safety" (143).

Though Hitchcock may not have realized it, he echoes Poe's sentiments in "The Lake": "Yet that terror was not fright, \ But a tremulous delight—" (ll.13–14).[9] In essence, this paradox of the sublime, this double vision that pervades all of Hitchcock, seems to derive from his experiences reading Poe.

Further maturation of this idea becomes the creative epiphany that guides his work—the realization that the contradictory pleasures of delight and terror can be engendered and modulated by specific artistic techniques that involve audiences in his films in complex ways. He sums up his affinity with Poe, appropriately, in terms of the genres of suspense, mystery, and terror they shared: "We are both prisoners of a genre: 'suspense.' You know the story that one has recounted many, many times: if I was making 'Cinderella,' everyone would look for the corpse. And if Edgar Allan Poe had written 'Sleeping Beauty,' one would look for the murderer" (145). The first manifestation of Poe's influence on Hitchcock came during his days as newsletter editor at Henley's. He published several short tales that are clearly, if not exclusively, influenced by Poe.[10]

Beyond Hitchcock's statements on Poe, certain affinities between them, personal and aesthetic, are apparent. Both, for example, combined in their work a nearly equal interest in the emotive expressiveness of art and the rigor of rational structure. While Poe loved puzzles, cryptography, and chess problems (he invented the analytic detective story), Hitchcock studied engineering, once kept track of shipping schedules, and came to film through technical journals on cinema. Not coincidentally, both were rational and articulate about their art, utilizing elaborate planning in order to elicit powerful audience responses. In terms of personal proclivities, each had a dark sense of humor, was obsessed with the ambiguities inherent in experience, and honed to perfection a circumscribed set of narrative frameworks around themes such as ratiocination, voyeurism, inexplicable predicaments, doubles, perverse self-destruction, and idealized women. Just as Poe transmutes "Morella" into "Berenice" and "Ligeia," Hitchcock updated *The 39 Steps* (1935) into *Saboteur* (1942) and *North by Northwest* (1959). As storytellers, both are self-conscious as well as self-reflexive. Poe writes of his school days in England ("William Wilson"), while Hitchcock explores his own propensity for making over his leading ladies (*Vertigo*).

From another perspective, Poe and Hitchcock were similar in what they didn't do. Since ideas distract from their aim of engendering emotional reactions, neither was aesthetically interested in politics, and both preferred creating schematized romances that don't aspire to realistic character development.[11] Rather than aim for verisimilitude, their tales tend to be dreamlike, episodic, and highlighted by brilliant set pieces. Finally, the magnitude of their continuing mass appeal is unprecedented, as is their extensive influence. Various studies demonstrate Poe's influence on seemingly everyone from Arthur Conan Doyle to Claude Debussy.[12] Hitchcock's imitators are also legion, ranging from the more subtle quotes by Spielberg and Scorcese to the more obvious borrowings of Stanley Donan and Brian DePalma.[13] Among critics and biographers Poe and Hitchcock have generated the kind of enthusiastic, personal criticism other writers and directors can only dream of: Hoffmann's *Poe Poe Poe Poe Poe Poe Poe* and Conrad's *The Hitchcock Murders* are ardent homages and personal responses combined in a critical stew.[14] Such enthusiasm abroad led to a particularly fascinating career convergence. Both were primarily popular with mass audiences, though rejected as serious artists until discovered and religiously championed by French artist/critics—Baudelaire for Poe and Truffaut for Hitchcock.

Recognition of Poe's influence is key to understanding aspects of Hitchcock's work. In his message from the conference director on the occasion of the 1999 centennial celebration of Hitchcock at New York University, Richard Allen divides Hitchcock scholars into those who highlight the comic dimensions of the director and those who "stress the darker side of Hitchcock's universe, his links to Poe, Baudelaire, and expressionism."[15] Not surprisingly, the idea of analyzing Poe's influence on Hitchcock's films was first broached by French critics Rohmer and Chabrol in a book-length study of Hitchcock's films in 1957. They refer to Poe several times in passing, noting at one point a visual echo of Poe's maelstrom in the runaway carousel in *Strangers on a Train*.[16] Perhaps picking up the idea from his friends, fellow French film critic turned filmmaker Francois Truffaut also notes links between Hitchcock and Poe as "artists of anxiety."[17] By far, "The Purloined Letter" provides the most numerous occasions for comparison, often facilitated by another French perspective, the psychoanalytic theory of

Jacques Lacan. In addition, a few citations are attacks on Poe or Hitchcock, referring to one in order to reinforce criticism of the other.

While all of these citations support the case for an affinity between Poe and Hitchcock, a case can also be made against it. Studies like mine, which isolate the significance of a particular strain in Hitchcock's work, are necessarily selective. I don't, for example, try to find connections between "Three Sundays in a Week" and *To Catch a Thief* (1955) or between "Hans Phaall" and *Rich and Strange* (1932). Some differences between Hitchcock and Poe are so obvious that they hardly require listing. For one thing, there is little parallel in Hitchcock to Poe's outrageous satires and satirical dialogues. For another, Hitchcock's modern mise-en-scène, logical plot development, generally admirable protagonists, and happy Hollywood endings find little affinity with Poe's gothic settings and horrifying endings. Hitchcock himself is ambivalent: "Was I influenced by Edgar Allan Poe? To be frank, I couldn't affirm it with certainty. Of course, subconsciously, we are always influenced by the books that we've read" (142). As he does with all his predecessors, he minimizes Poe's influence by including it in the vast unconscious resources from which all creativity springs: "The novels, the painting, the music, and all the works of art, in general, form our intellectual culture from which we can't get away. Even if we want to!" (142). If Hitchcock contradicts himself in both claiming and denying affinity with Poe, he, like Whitman, contains multitudes of them. It is one of the characteristics of his genius that he synthesizes his art from so many sources, uncovering serious, light, dark, romantic, and modern sides of his aesthetic personality. Despite Hitchcock's protesting too much, the films speak for themselves. While some aspects of Hitchcock are not Poe-esque, many aspects clearly are. Such is perhaps the major assertion this book seeks to demonstrate.

In sum, Hitchcock's need to appear original and in complete conscious control of his art ironically echoes Poe in "The Philosophy of Composition," as he explains how every aspect of "The Raven" was created by rational rather than intuitive processes. Hitchcock's ambivalence about Poe's influence is what ultimately makes that influence so significant to the director's work. Poe represented for Hitchcock two things: Poe used a set of themes and techniques that Hitchcock also explores, as well as gothic horror conventions Hitchcock wanted to avoid. Thus Poe's influence on Hitchcock is paradoxical, based on both acceptance and resistance. This paradox is the creative catalyst that provokes Hitchcock's need to be original and stay a step ahead of audience expectations, as in the crop duster sequence in *North by Northwest*. This scene is an interesting case in point. While similar in the dynamics of its suspense and imagery to the pendulum scene in Poe's "Pit and the Pendulum," it has been so effectively displaced outdoors into the realm of the ordinary that Hitchcock would seem justified in claiming that the sequence does not resemble Poe. Of course, on the surface he is right. And most would not notice a similarity (I've never read of the link being mentioned). Under the surface, however, the sequences are nearly identical in terms of suspense, character situation, unseen political forces controlling the fate of the protagonists, and the protagonists' resourceful means of escaping death. Hitchcock's displacement of this Poe sequence typifies Hitchcock's creative use of Poe. While Hitchcock is an amalgamation of all his influences, he heavily borrows themes and images from Poe, molding them into elegant and modern cinematic expression. Such modification of Poe sources is an important aspect of the "Hitchcock touch." Other modifications of Poe that will be examined in this study include the self-destructive hubris of the murderers in *Rope* and "The Tell-Tale Heart," the unnerving hauntings by doubles in *Strangers on a Train* and "William Wilson," and the obsessive evocation of a dead lover in *Vertigo* and "Ligeia."

Despite these surface differences and in addition to the many convergences of plot, character, and theme, it is the deep structure of the relationship between storyteller and audience that clearly links Hitchcock to Poe. For both, delight and terror were heightened by the explicit artificiality of their narratives, often located in the irony and fantastic events of the plot. Audience delight is found in the artist's awareness of manipulating them in novel ways in a stale genre. Hitchcock's and Poe's art is like a thrill ride, but a decidedly complex and intellectual one. Audiences are both challenged and rewarded. Hitchcock, for instance, goes beyond the typical Hollywood film in *Rear Window* when Jeff is attacked by Thorwald. The usual way would be for Thorwald to burst in and attack Jeff immediately. Contrariwise, Hitchcock has Jeff fight back ingeniously with flash cubes, lending elements of surprise and charm to an otherwise routine encounter. Poe too engages us with surprises in "The

Tell-Tale Heart." Rather than have the murderous narrator merely "get caught" in the end, he loses an animated struggle with an irresistible impulse to self-destruct. Thus, in a sense, Poe and Hitchcock are linked not only by a common genre, but with extraordinarily similarly inventive genius that drives them to create unforgettable situations and images.

By avoiding gothic settings and adding explicit humor to his horror, Hitchcock avoids seeming as much like Poe as he actually is. In terms of Harold Bloom's "anxiety of influence,"[18] Hitchcock "corrects" Poe and thus establishes himself as a strong artist, despite the powerful early impressions Poe made on him. However, Hitchcock maintains other aspects of Poe, perhaps less noticeable, even to himself. First, he reflects Poe's subjective center, replacing the mad narrators with his point-of-view camera. We see *Vertigo* narrated through Scottie's eyes just as genuinely as "Man of the Crowd" through its narrator's. Second, Hitchcock, like Poe, creates memorable episodes and set pieces in the tradition of romance fiction, making them the center of his narrative structures. Hitchcock often came up with the episodes before he had a complete story. Third, Hitchcock focuses on manipulating audience responses on a sophisticated level through bait and switch maneuvers that maintain a sublime struggle between delight and terror. Poe accomplished this along the fine line between terror and irony; Hitchcock avoided the expected by transferring guilt and encouraging questionable audience sympathies. Finally, with Poe, he explored in depth a set of themes and strategies that became his hallmarks.

In order to get at these areas of narrative junction throughout the study, I argue for the centrality of *Eureka* in making clear the common concerns of Poe and Hitchcock. Poe's *Eureka*, originally a long lecture delivered in 1848 and later published as *Eureka: A Prose Poem*, is a difficult work to summarize. Purporting to be both intuitive science and romance, the subject is "to speak of the *Physical, Metaphysical, and Mathematical—of the Material and Spiritual Universe; of its Essence, its Origin, its Creation, its Present Condition, and its Destiny.*"[19] What follows is necessarily only a bare-bones outline of a dense treatise that speculates on infinity, the origin of solar systems, star clusters, the form of the Milky Way, the size and shape of the universe, and orbital revolutions, together with assessments of various competing theories, philosophical speculations, and much more. My concern in the following summary is to highlight the aspects of *Eureka* that seem most relevant to a comparative study of Poe and Hitchcock. Poe begins by describing his project in metaphor, asking us to imagine someone atop Mount Etna "whirling on his heel" in order to "comprehend the panorama in the sublimity of its *oneness*" (6). Similarly, his examination of the universe is meant to create in the reader a comprehensive "impression" of its totality, both in time and space. After a long discussion justifying his methodology of intuitive science in which he champions bold speculators like Kepler and Humboldt while satirizing the more circumspect Aristotle (Aries Tottle) and Bacon (Hog), Poe launches into a detailed descriptive analysis of the creation, progress, and destiny of the universe.

In the beginning, so to speak, God created the universe as a single infinitely large particle, perfect in its unity. Poe describes this as the natural state of the universe, and of atoms that are naturally inclined to join together. In a move inexplicable except to the divine will, God then divided his universe into an infinite number of fragments that began to diffuse in all directions from the original center. Implicit in this description are two conflicting principles, attraction (positive) and repulsion (negative), which are identified respectively with gravity and electricity. Like the contemporary "big bang" theory, Poe suggests that the diffusing force which fragmented the original particle pushes the fragments out from each other as well as from the center, representing a dominance of the repulsive force over the attractive, despite the natural tendency of atoms to attract. Thus the universe is composed of matter and matter is composed of positive and negative forces in conflict. At a certain epoch, this negative diffusive force will dissipate and a gradually increasing return to the original unity will begin. At that time the attractive force of gravity will reassert itself fully as every atom in the universe will begin rotating in an intergalactic vortex until everything—including galaxies, solar systems, planets, and living beings—collapses together upon the invisible center of origin. Moreover, this process is endlessly cyclical: "the processes we have here ventured to contemplate will be renewed forever, and forever, and forever; a novel Universe swelling into existence, and then subsiding into nothingness, at every throb of the Heart Divine" (134). Concerning our role in this reunification, Poe informs us that this Heart Divine "*is our own*," that collectively we are part and parcel of the deity.

In addition to the "scientific" perspective in *Eureka*, Poe himself refers to this scenario in literary terms, calling it God's plot. It is "but the most sublime of poems" in which "Poetry and Truth are one" (124). He compares its perfection of form to a "work of human art" in which the "*dénoûment* is awkwardly brought about," rather than "springing out of the bosom of the thesis . . . part and parcel of the fundamental conception of the book" (129). As an original but indirect form of literary criticism, *Eureka*, along with his other critical statements, has been rightly taken by scholars as a key to understanding his art. With others I trace the narrative uniqueness of Poe to *Eureka*, agreeing with those who find Poe's cosmological narrative central to understanding Poe's fictional narratives.[20] *Eureka's* structure, like both the biblical story of creation/fall/redemption or the classic Hollywood narrative of equilibrium/disruption/reequilibrium, is a kind of macrocosmic, master narrative design, one characterized by the peculiar narrative obsessions of Poe and, whether consciously or not, of Hitchcock.

I have organized the book's chapters around these obsessions in order to highlight Poe's and Hitchcock's affinities as storytellers as well as around the cyclical structure of *Eureka*. Thus chapter 2 concerns ratiocination, Poe's term for the process of analytically solving a crime. The emphasis is on reason, clarity, and order as Poe's detective stories and Hitchcock's *Murder!* are compared. The underlying reasonableness of the world of the detective story becomes a microcosmic parallel to the original unity of the universe. Chapter 3, about the apocalypse, suggests the moment of cataclysmic shattering of the original oneness into diffused fragments. Poe's "Masque of the Red Death" and Hitchcock's *The Birds* are the representative texts. Chapter 4 looks at inexplicable predicaments, representing the state of the disoriented and diffusing fragments, analogous to the paradoxes of all earthly life. "The Pit and the Pendulum" and *North by Northwest* present characters in a succession of insoluble problems—the antithesis of chapter 2. Chapter 5, on doubles, reflects the fact that each fragment/person, once part of the same whole, is therefore a double of all others. "William Wilson" and *Strangers on a Train* concern this theme. Chapter 6, about the imp of the perverse, explores the struggle described in *Eureka* between the healthy positive and self-destructive negative impulses in all things. "The Tell-Tale Heart" and *Rope* are representative texts. Chapters 7–8, on voyeurism and romantic obsession, touch on the intense desire of fragments to unite, though prevented by repulsive forces that create complex psychological tensions. Voyeurism texts include "The Man of the Crowd" and *Rear Window*, while romantic obsession is reflected in "Ligeia" and *Vertigo*. Finally, chapter 9 is on humor, signifying a return to unity, comedy replacing tragedy as positive attractive forces dominate the negative. I examine again "Ligeia" and *The 39 Steps* in terms of the struggle between humor and horror as analogous to the struggle between positive and negative forces.

Obviously this organization is just as fantastic and artificial as the stories of Poe and Hitchcock and, like any scheme, has pros and cons. On the one hand, this organization obscures the way these themes overlap. *Psycho*, for example, deals with detective work, inexplicability, doubles, and voyeurism, among other things. "Ligeia" also concerns romantic obsession, voyeurism, doubles, the imp of the perverse, and inexplicability. I have chosen works that deal centrally with the subject of the chapter but demonstrate some of the overlapping strategies as well. On the other hand, this organization has the virtue, by macrocosmic analogy, of linking Poe's cosmology to the local characters, situations, and themes in the tales and films. Another significant reason for using *Eureka* to organize this study is its relation to the sublime, the concept of delight and terror that is Hitchcock's chief lesson from the master. Poe's literary purpose in writing *Eureka* seemingly was to create the ultimate expression of the sublime. His repeated use of the terms "sublime," "sublimity," "awful," "Majestic," and "grandeur" expresses the inconceivable vastness, symmetry, and beauty of a universe that is at once delightful and terrifying. Edmund Burke's description applies well to the works of Poe and Hitchcock: "Whatever is fitted in any sort to excite the ideas of pain, and danger, that is to say, whatever is in any sort terrible . . . or operates in a manner analogous to terror, is a source of the sublime."[21] Echoing what Hitchcock realized from reading Poe, Burke writes that "when danger and pain press too nearly they are incapable of giving any delight, and are simply terrible; but at certain distances, and with certain modifications, they may be, and they are delightful, as we everyday experience" (A *Philosophical Enquiry*, 40). When Poe creates a powerful "impression" in the souls of his readers and Hitchcock makes his audiences scream with delight, surprise, and terror simultaneously, they are practicing the sublime.

Burke listed several sources of the sublime, including *power* (fear of a superior force), *difficulty* (extremely complex predicament), *obscurity* (darkness, fogginess, confusion producing a sense of isolation and help-lessness), and *privation* (isolation, silence, solitude, darkness). These, of course, are easy to correlate with the works of Poe and Hitchcock. For example, fear of power is central to both "Pit and the Pendulum" and Roger Thornhill's encounter with a hostile crop duster. The mariner's "Descent into the Maelstrom" and Alicia's poisoning in *Notorious* are classic cases of extreme life-or-death difficulty. Privation is evident in the unbearable silence in Poe's tale "Silence" and in the unnerving si-lence as Bruno stalks Guy in *Strangers on a Train*. These categories of the sublime correlate with most of the chapters: apocalypse with fear of power and difficulty, inexplicable predicament with difficulty, doubles with difficulty and obscurity, imp of the perverse with difficulty and power, and voyeurism and romantic obsession with privation. By de-sign, the first chapter (ratiocination) and last chapter (humor) are or-dered as counterpoint, affirming the often overlooked positive strains in Poe and Hitchcock—another important convergence emphasizing the "delight" part of Poe's legacy to Hitchcock.

In conclusion, while this book is far from comprehensive in tracking down details that might be applied to their artistic relationship, it does suggest new insights into Poe's role in creating the Hitchcock touch. Viewing Hitchcock in the context of his interest in Poe makes us more aware of the dimensions of Hitchcock's eclectic creative style—how he rearranges and displaces particular images, situations, and themes, transforming them and developing their potential in new contexts for the audience's gaze. Hitchcock's partial denial of Poe's influence shows his fear of our gaze, of our seeing what is meant to be hidden or re-pressed. Along these lines there is a telling image in John Ballantine's surreal dream from *Spellbound* that reflects Hitchcock's fears. Ballantine describes himself playing cards with a bearded man to whom he deals a seven of clubs on a table full of ominously long shadows that point to his guilt. The bearded man then turns his cards over, which are blank, and says "I win." The blank cards, suggesting Ballantine's amnesia, lead to the appearance of the proprietor of the 21 Club, a faceless man who angrily threatens the bearded man—connecting guilt and amnesia by locating the faceless man as Ballantine's irritated conscience. Eventually in the film the faceless man is revealed as the murderous Dr. Murchison, whom Ballantine saw kill Edwards. For Ballantine to relieve his guilt by becoming Edwards himself, Murchison's identity had to be repressed. Thus Murchison and Edwards become doubles of Ballantine. Just so, Poe plays a similar role in Hitchcock's films. He is the father/double who must be denied, whose face, only when hidden by a mask, allows the son to exist independently. Hitchcock is aware of Poe, but only as in a dream, a presence that is denied as it bursts like a bubble out of consciousness upon rational reflection. Hitchcock's aesthetic classicism will not allow the dark romantic unconscious, perhaps activated originally by Poe, to assert itself as a creative resource, particularly if the center of that creative unconscious is other than himself. Like Poe in "The Philosophy of Composition," Hitchcock stresses the rational aspects of his creative processes.

In short, Poe helps us see the carefully disguised gothic romanticism denied by the ordinary surfaces of Hitchcock's films, which in turn helps explain his ambivalence toward Poe's influence. The shadow of Poe lurking in Hitchcock's unconscious may have led to his very conscious avoidance of the gothic and romantic trappings in which Poe's work is steeped, enabling the master of suspense to find himself creatively. Yet, however repressed Poe became in Hitchcock's art, however modern and removed the films seem from nineteenth-century concerns, Hitchcock could never escape the gravity of the dark obsessions he shared with Poe, nor the need to explore them. Like Ballantine in *Spellbound* and Scottie in *Vertigo*, Hitchcock's dreams, which he made into films, grew out of a haunted memory, out of a past filled with Poe-esque shadows that terrorized and delighted him as an artist and a man.

Notes

1. *Mark Twain's America* (Boston: Houghton Mifflin, 1967), 244. Ulrich Weisstein, in his excellent *Comparative Literature and Literary Theory*, trans. William Riggan (Bloomfield: Indiana University Press, 1973), summarizes some of these problems as theorists have tried to define them. Both influence and affinity are dangerous methods of literary study because they tend to be so subjective and impressionistic, and as Jean Marie Carre noted, one is "frequently forced to deal with intangibles." Ihab Hassan finds it unfortunate that

"the concept of influence "is called upon to account for any relationship, running the gamut of incidence to causality, with a somewhat expansive range of intermediate correlations" (29). J. T. Shaw adds the problem of distinguishing direct from indirect influence (30). With so many obstacles to such a study, how does one maintain a sound methodological footing and not slip into the "bottomless pit of mere speculation" (7)?

2. In Sidney Gottlieb, ed., *Hitchcock on Hitchcock: Selected Writings and Interviews* (Berkeley: University of California Press, 1995), 143. Unless otherwise noted, all Hitchcock quotations are from this book.

3. Jean Douchet, "Hitchcock and His Public," in *A Hitchcock Reader*, eds. Marshall Deutelbaum and Leland Poague (Ames: Iowa State University Press, 1986), 12.

4. David Sterritt, *The Films of Alfred Hitchcock* (Cambridge: Cambridge University Press, 1993), 2. See also Gilberto Perez, *The Materialist Ghost: Films and Their Medium* (Baltimore: Johns Hopkins University Press, 1998), 7–9. Sterritt uses Hitchcock as a major example of the director as artist and commercial filmmaker.

5. See Peter Bogdanovich, *The Cinema of Alfred Hitchcock* (New York: Museum of Modern Art, 1963), 4.

6. Donald Spoto, *The Dark Side of Genius: The Life of Alfred Hitchcock* (New York: Ballantine, 1983), 547–48. Henry Mancini blew it by trying to write a "Hitchcock" score, which isn't what Hitchcock wanted. He wanted a Mancini score.

7. Robin Wood, *Hitchcock's Films Revisited* (New York: Columbia University Press, 1989), 216–17. Other defenders of the auteurist theory in Hitchcock's case—with qualifications—include Gilberto Perez (*The Materialist Ghost*, 3–7), Truffaut, of course (*Hitchcock*, 12–14), and slightly less enthusiastically, Leslie Brill (*The Hitchcock Romance*, xiv).

8. The biography he read is likely John H. Ingram, *Edgar Allan Poe: His Life, Letters, and Opinions* (London: John Hogg, 1880). Ingram and the publisher are English and the tone is very sympathetic, meant to correct earlier negative assessments of Poe. The account of Poe's last days is written with particular compassion.

9. From Thomas Ollive Mabbott, ed., *Collected Works of Edgar Allan Poe: Poems*, vol. 1 (Cambridge: Harvard University Press, 1969). Unless otherwise noted, all quotations from Poe's fiction and poetry will be from this edition.

10. See Patrick McGilligan, "Alfred Hitchcock: Before the Flickers," *Film Comment*, July–August 1999, 22–31. He uncovers and reprints for the first time a number of stories Hitchcock wrote as editor of the *Henley Telegraph*.

11. While scholars are beginning to explore these areas, ideology clearly takes a backseat to sensation in the works of Poe and Hitchcock. For recent work on Poe's interest in his times, see Shawn Rosenheim and Stephen Rachman, eds., *The American Face of Edgar Allan Poe* (Baltimore: Johns Hopkins University Press, 1995). For Hitchcock and his times, see Robert J. Corber, *In the Name of National Security: Hitchcock, Homophobia, and the Political Construction of Gender in Postwar America* (Durham, N.C.: Duke University Press, 1993).

12. For studies of Poe's influence on others, see Lois Davis Vines, ed., *Poe Abroad: Influence, Reputation, Affinities* (Iowa City: University of Iowa Press, 1999); Jack Sullivan, *New World Symphonies: How American Culture Changed European Music* (New Haven: Yale University Press, 1999); Benjamin Franklin Fisher IV, ed., *Poe and Our Times: Influences and Affinities* (Baltimore: Edgar Allan Poe Society, 1986); and Joan Delaney Grossman, *Edgar Allan Poe in Russia: A Study in Legend and Literary Influence* (Wurzburg: Jal-Verlag, 1973).

13. Ken Mogg, *The Alfred Hitchcock Story* (Dallas: Taylor, 1999), 158.

14. Daniel Hoffmann, *Poe Poe Poe Poe Poe Poe Poe* (New York: Avon, 1972); Peter Conrad, *The Hitchcock Murders* (London: Faber & Faber, 2000).

15. Richard Allen, *Hitchcock: A Centennial Celebration*, conference brochure, Department of Cinema Studies, Tisch School of the Arts, New York University, October 13–17, 1999, 4.

16. Eric Rohmer and Claude Chabrol, *Hitchcock: The First Forty-four Films*, trans. Stanley Hochman (New York: Frederick Ungar, 1979), 112.

17. Francois Truffaut, *Hitchcock* (New York: Touchstone, 1966), 15.

18. Harold Bloom, *The Anxiety of Influence: A Theory of Poetry*, 2d ed. (New York: Oxford University Press, 1997).

19. Edgar Allan Poe, *Eureka: A Prose Poem* (Amherst, N.Y.: Prometheus, 1997), 5.

20. Joan Dayan, *Fables of Mind: An Inquiry into Poe's Fiction* (New York: Oxford University Press, 1987); J. Gerald Kennedy, *Poe, Death, and the Life of Writing* (New Haven: Yale University Press, 1987); David Halliburton, *Edgar Allan Poe: A Phenomenological View* (Princeton: Princeton University Press, 1973); and Richard Wilbur, "The House of Poe," in *The Recognition of Edgar Allan Poe*, ed. Eric W. Carlson (Ann Arbor: University of Michigan Press, 1970), 254–77.

21. Edmund Burke, *A Philosophical Enquiry into the Origin of Our Ideas of the Sublime and Beautiful*, ed. James T. Boulton (London: Routledge & Kegan Paul, 1958), 39.

CHAPTER TWO

~

Ratiocination: Original Unity

Hitchcock's relationship to the detective genre that Poe is credited with inventing has always been ambiguous. On the one hand he is blatantly against the whole idea:

> For seventeen years I have been making pictures described alternately as thrillers, dark mysteries, and chillers, yet I have never actually directed a whodunit or puzzler. Off hand this may sound like debunking, but I do not believe that puzzling the audience is the essence of suspense.[1]

On the other hand, he admits that his films have a "touch of murder and an air of mystery" about them (114). Interestingly, Hitchcock mentions the "Murders in the Rue Morgue" as particularly important in his own development, learning that fear can be fun when you know you are safe. Hitchcock synthesized both Poe and his successors in the field of mystery thrillers to create an original approach focused on suspense rather than on intellectual crime puzzles. Hitchcock never set aside important lessons he learned from Poe; as Herb says in *Shadow of a Doubt* about detective heroes as a whole, "You can say what you like about Sherlock Holmes, but that Frenchman beats them all."[2]

Among its many phases of development, the universe in *Eureka* begins in harmonious order, though embedded with attractive and diffusive

17

forces. These forces are in balance until, inexplicably, the diffusive force strikes an uneven balance which causes apocalyptic fragmentation that increases separation and diffusion of the fragments. Within this overarching Eurekan narrative framework, the detective tale functioned as Poe's fantasy of arresting the irrational forces of diffusion through reason. But, as J. Gerald Kennedy notes, all of Poe's fiction comes back to concern over reason versus irrational feeling.[3] In the detective story, however, reason triumphs most convincingly. With his new genre Poe exercised his fascination with puzzle solving, cryptograms, and conundrums by applying it to narrative, indulging in the pleasing dream, so untrue in his own experience, that order could rein in chaos. His detective stories exist in the Eurekan interstices between the end of harmony and the beginning of fragmentation.

As the widely recognized creator of the detective story, Edgar Allan Poe has directly or indirectly influenced virtually every detective, mystery, sensation, and thriller writer since his time. This applies, of course, to Alfred Hitchcock, whose films are also both directly and indirectly influenced by several of Poe's narrative formulas. Like Charles Dickens, who knew of Poe and his innovations but developed his crime fiction in his own original directions, Hitchcock added his own touches of pure cinema to the genre. Despite the continuous modifications to Poe's detective story, many of which profoundly influenced him, Hitchcock continued to look back toward Poe's approach in terms of the doubleness of the sublime, maintaining a link between the detective and the gothic-horror tale. Poe and Hitchcock approached the challenge of creating sublimity within the limits of an essentially intellectual genre by exploring (1) the ambiguity between reason and intuition in a world where the line between reality and illusion is blurred, (2) the doubleness of characters, and (3) theatricality. Because questions of the ambiguity of reality and identity are characteristic of the theater, these become a central thematic and narrative undercurrent of the detective stories of Poe and Hitchcock. Violence and eccentric characters, suspense and interest are developed as characters slip in and out of various roles, stage theatrical traps, and thus manipulate reality and illusion. This chapter will examine these overlapping concerns by comparing the Dupin tales mainly with Hitchcock's *Murder!* (1930), *Dial M for Murder* (1954), and *Spellbound* (1946).

While Poe synthesized several source texts to develop the detective story, the result in terms of genre has been the most ubiquitous constant in popular literature since his time.[4] In his five tales of detection and mystery ("The Murders in the Rue Morgue" [1841], "The Mystery of Marie Roget" [1842–1843], "The Gold Bug" [1843], "Thou Art the Man" [1844], and "The Purloined Letter" [1845]), amazingly, Poe touched on most of the approaches to follow: the sensational thriller, analytical exercise, classic detective story, puzzle/code-based story, and small town murder mystery. Poe was also a pioneer in making the least likely suspect the guilty one, having the crime's perpetrator plant false clues, and employing ballistics evidence. Despite these dazzling innovations, the single most influential element Poe created was the character of C. Auguste Dupin, the analytic genius who became the prototype for Sherlock Holmes and most subsequent puzzle solvers of detective fiction.[5] Dupin, a fallen aristocrat who resides with the unnamed narrator of his adventures in "a time-eaten and grotesque mansion, long deserted . . . and tottering to its fall in a retired and desolate portion of the Faubourg St. Germain," becomes the first detective hero of literature and the first series hero in literature.[6] As a man of imaginative intuition—the key to his analytical genius—Dupin and his narrator friend are recluses who live in artificial darkness each day because it "suited the rather fantastic gloom of [their] common temper" (532). In these circumstances they meditate, read, and speak away their time in analytical fancies. The narrator's descriptions of Dupin's analytical acumen, including his capacity to read minds through inspired observation, becomes what Leroy Panek names in these stories a "general thesis on genius."[7] In fact, two of the three Dupin stories are introduced with lengthy explanations of the superior type of analysis the hero engages in.

Dupin's analytical method involves careful and creative scrutiny that simplifies elements of a problem and uncovers information that, though hidden, is observably on the surface. Growing out of romantic philosophy, Poe distinguishes between ingenuity and analysis, associating the former with the fancy, the latter with imagination. In the process of explaining his methods to his friend, Dupin identifies his reasoning with poetry, claiming it as the source of his analytical powers. However, Poe embodies this method differently in each of the three

Dupin tales. In "Murders in the Rue Morgue," in which a mother and a daughter are inexplicably and horribly murdered, Dupin makes observations at the scene of the crime that contradict police observations, makes deductions about who could have entered, escaped, and handled the bodies in the peculiarly violent way displayed, and finally stages a theatrical mousetrap to affirm his conclusions that the murderer was none other than an orangutan. In "The Mystery of Marie Roget," Dupin engages in literary interpretation by closely reading various newspaper accounts in order to sort through correct and incorrect assumptions.[8] "The Purloined Letter" offers a third application of imaginative analysis as Dupin identifies himself psychologically with his criminal counterpart. By accurately measuring the intelligence of his adversary, who stole and hid a letter, Dupin, without leaving his apartment, is able to intuit how the "hidden" letter is actually in plain sight.

Born in 1899, Hitchcock was fascinated, like the rest of England at the time, with true crime as well as crime fiction. Like Dickens, Hitchcock attended the Old Bailey, watching trials and storing up materials. He went to the Black Museum at Scotland Yard, a sort of police chamber of horrors, and read accounts of crime in the Sunday papers. He eventually amassed a large library of criminal cases and never tired of such famously gruesome murderers as Christie, who strangled eight women for sexual satisfaction and then buried them under the floorboards (reminiscent of Hitchcock's *Frenzy* and Poe's "The Tell-Tale Heart"). Although, as we have seen, Hitchcock reveals elements in his films from many of the detective writers noted above, he always claimed that "fear in the cinema is my special field" (118). Despite these various influences, Hitchcock never forgot the Poe thrillers that so affected him in his youth. Significantly, in Hitchcock's homage to Poe he explicitly mentions "Murders in the Rue Morgue" and "The Gold Bug," tales of crime and mystery that continued to resonate for him. When Hitchcock said that he "can't help but compare what I try to put in my films with what Poe put in his stories" (143), among the things he meant certainly included Poe's doubleness of vision. Ketterer notes that for Poe everyday reality is deception, that the limits of seeing reality were "basic to Poe."[9] This certainly describes many scenes in Hitchcock's films, where people (Uncle Charlie, Eve Kendall, the Draytons) or situations (Armstrong's defection, the saboteur's wealthy charity ball, Mr. Memory's performance) are not what they seem. Hitchcock's double vision, like Poe's, led him to create a slippery world in which reality and dream, guilt and innocence, art and life, and the creative and resolvent are often indistinguishable. Such doubleness creates a suspenseful atmosphere that reflects the delight and terror of the sublime, the literature of unsettling schizophrenia in which one's worst fears become perversely exhilarating.[10] Like Poe, Hitchcock provides his audiences with enjoyable terror and safe horror. He has a therapeutic view of fear: "Our nature is such that we must have these 'shake-ups,' or we grow sluggish and jellified" (109). But he also notes that this approach has its limitations: "You want them to get off the switchback railway [roller coaster] giggling with pleasure: like the woman who comes out of a sentimental movie and says, 'It was lovely. I had a good cry.'"[11]

Elements from Poe's *Eureka*, his manifesto of the sublime consciousness, link the detective story back to his horror stories. Note the pattern Poe established, as described by Magistrale and Poger: "in both horror and detection individuals and the human community itself are threatened by a destructive agency. To counterbalance its influence, reason and ratiocination are employed to discover the identity of the murderer. The murderer is then banished, and order is restored."[12]

Poe's detective tales fit this pattern as Dupin's analytical prowess disentangles ambiguous clues to vanquish the various threats to order. But, as John Irwin notes, "Murders in the Rue Morgue" includes elements from Poe's horror tales. For example, "the irrational assault on a mother and daughter by a male animal within a locked room was a continuation of that violence against the female double by a male figure trapped within the symbolic womb of the family/home in the dying women stories."[13] Like the horror tales, the detective tales represent a threat to reason itself—without Dupin crimes become insoluble and the forces of chaos dominate. Herein is the crux of the difference between Poe's detective stories and his tales of terror. While *Eureka* describes a fragmentation and final reunification of the original unity of the universe, only the detective stories in Poe's canon consistently restore order.[14]

Sounding as if he were discussing *Eureka*, Irwin calls this restoration of order the "figuration of the womb fantasy across the three Dupin stories [in which] one can detect a clear trajectory running from a physical sense of return to origin to a mental one" (319). Through Dupin's god-like mind, the powers of perverse self-destruction are held at bay, chaos is checked, and harmony is restored. In that sense, embodied within the story itself is the sense of safety that Hitchcock says is the pleasure of the horror tales, perhaps accounting for their popularity. In his horror tales Poe supplies the terror while the reader must sometimes work hard to supply a sense of well-being. With his detective story, however, Poe supplies both the "horror" of chaos unleashed and the well-being of containing it.

The central character of Poe's tales of ratiocination, C. Auguste Dupin, with his sublime double vision, provides the link between the Poe and Hitchcock mysteries. The double nature of the detective, which is associated closely with the double nature of reason itself ("the creative and the resolvent"), is introduced by Poe's narrator as he describes how Dupin seems to go into a trance during the analytic process. The creative side of Dupin seems to be the analytical process of inspired observation; the resolvent side is the transcendence achieved when solving a puzzle. The resolvent is the result of Dupin's meditating in the dark, busying his soul "in dreams" (533), enabling him, free of distractions, to reduce a puzzle's terms to its lowest forms until he is finally free from the bonds of earthly reason, associated here with standard investigative methods—the initial steps in Dupin's analytic process. Thus the resolvent Dupin uses facts to transcend rationality; he becomes frigid, his eyes vacant, and his voice rising. In an interesting tie-in with the horror tales, the narrator suggests that perhaps these symptoms are the product of "a diseased intelligence" (533). Because analysis is associated with madness, we, like the narrator, are awed by Dupin. This is partly because Dupin's mind renders ambiguous all theories of the rational, leaving, as Ketterer observes, "the difference between order and chaos . . . merely a 'perspective anomaly'" (xiv). While one admires his superior ratiocinative abilities, they are so unusual that delight is tempered with a measure of terror—not unlike watching a magician saw a woman in half. Hoffman notes that since Dupin's reasoning partakes of the irrational, it is higher, tapping into a preconscious dream mind of associativeness.[15] In returning from this strange state triumphant and unscathed, Dupin's analytical process somewhat mirrors the *Eureka* cycle by beginning in one state, moving into another, and finally returning again. He leaves his secure and orderly state, enters into the chaos and fragmentation of a seemingly insoluble case, and returns having imagined and enacted a reordering of the world. In fact, Dupin is like *Eureka's* god who created the universe and at whose inscrutable will its fragmented and diffused parts return together.

Because even Dupin can't rely on his ratiocinative powers alone to solve his cases (though he tries to in "The Mystery of Marie Roget"), theatricality becomes part and parcel of the ratiocinative process and of the narrative pleasure in recounting his analytical steps. Loisa Nygaard has noted that detectives like Dupin and his successors, because they are detached from life to a significant degree, make ratiocination a game.[16] She might more accurately have suggested that they make ratiocination like a stage play. True to his double nature, Dupin resorts to theatrical methods to complete his cases in "Rue Morgue" and "Purloined Letter." In the former, he places an ad concerning the orangutan, luring its owner into an apartment where he confronts him. He pretends to have discovered and captured the creature, drawing the sailor into admitting his ownership. For the sailor this bit of theater becomes a slippery business, as Dupin and the narrator shift from his innocent helpers to dangerous, armed antagonists who force a confession from him. In another example of theatrical surprise from "Thou Art the Man," a grand guignol-like mousetrap is created when the narrator sends a wine cask to murderer Charles Goodfellow. When he opens the cask, the corpse rises and seems to say, "Thou art the man," inducing the murderer's instant confession.

In the "Purloined Letter" Dupin's stagecraft is most thoroughly displayed. Early on, he pretends to go along with the prefect in criticizing poets as fools. Later, upon the prefect's second visit to discuss the location of the stolen letter, Dupin pretends not to have it. After he lets the prefect express his frustration, Dupin begins asking about the promised reward and then chides the prefect that he has not exerted himself "to the utmost in this matter" (982). He continues to forestall the conclusion by telling a parable of the need to seek advice, finally reducing the prefect to declare, "I am *perfectly* willing to take advice, and to pay for it." Dupin then brings his little drama to a climax by drawing a checkbook from his drawer, stating that "you may as well fill me up a check for the amount mentioned. When you have signed it, I will hand you the letter" (983). After a long, suspenseful pause, the prefect signs the check and Dupin produces the letter. Having kept back his discoveries, letting the mystery of the stolen letter remain incomprehensible, Dupin uses theatricality to punctuate his cleverness by perfectly manipulating his audience. Dupin not only solves incomprehensible mysteries but creates them in the process, an interesting double movement that gives further dimension to the two sides of Dupin's nature. As when he seems to read the narrator's mind in "Rue Morgue," Dupin uses the unexpected to create for the narrator, and for us, a world where magic things can happen. The rational equivalent of Israfel, he is himself an artist of the highest caliber, in essence embodying the narrative structure of surprise that is characteristic of the detective story.

Dupin's final theatrical wizardry in "Purloined Letter" is no less dazzling when he visits Minister D— wearing dark glasses and pretending to have weak eyes so that he can scan the room unnoticed and detect the whereabouts of the stolen and openly disguised letter. He returns later and stages a ruckus on the street outside to draw D— to the window, allowing Dupin to replace the stolen letter with a facsimile. Again he punctuates the effect of his drama with a climax by enclosing in the facsimile a verse from *Atree et Thyeste* that will remind D— that Dupin had promised to be avenged for a wrong D— had done him previously. The incredible feat in fathoming D—'s hiding place is his utter accuracy in pinpointing the coordinates between D—'s dual nature as both mathematician and poet and then predicting exactly where such a person would hide a letter of the type stolen in order to evade police scrutiny and yet keep it handy.

Thus, in his ratiocination tales, Dupin has a dual nature, and his theatrical special effects make the world a double realm between reality and theater, linking the intellectual with the sublime (even the genre itself is slippery, hovering between sketch and tale). This sense of uncertainty about the state of the world and its potential slipperiness, as well as Dupin's double nature and ratiocinative genius, provide sublime elements of surprise, suspense, and wonder in the tales, yet Poe always concludes with the comforting assurance that justice triumphs.

Murder!

While Rohmer and Chabrol call *Murder!* (1930) an "absolutely classic detective plot," Thomas Leitch points out that little attention is focused on the investigative process.[17] Nevertheless, Hitchcock's hero in the film, Sir John, utilizes Dupin's methods, especially his theatricality, in solving crimes. Other themes and situations from Poe's tales of ratiocination also emerge, such as the doubleness of individuals and situations that makes appearance and reality ambiguous. These issues are subsumed in the film under the running motif of acting and the theater. As in Poe's "Rue Morgue" and "Purloined Letter," a female victim, Diana Baring, is at the center of the case. The investigations are conducted using intuition, imagination, and theatrics. In addition, the "detective," Sir John Menier, like Dupin, is an amateur, a prominent actor/playwright whose imagination surpasses the routine analytical methods of the unimaginative police. As in "Rue Morgue" analyzing how a high window could be accessed by the murderer becomes a key clue in the mystery, and like "Purloined Letter" the answer—in this case the murderer—is in plain sight all along, since the murderer, Handel Fane, is clearly seen but disguised as a policeman. Like Dupin, Sir John meditates, reads people, sees the significance of evidence overlooked by the police, and uses a dramatic mousetrap to elicit a confession from the murderer. In addition to these parallels, the sublime slipperiness of reality is suggested through the double aspects of Sir John, the ambiguity between reason and intuition, and the fine line between reality and drama. In this film set in the world of the theater, all the world is indeed a stage and practically "all the men and women merely players."

Like Dupin, Sir John is presented as a unique character set apart by his wealth, breeding, and, importantly, artistic talent as actor, playwright, and producer. Dupin too is an aristocrat (though a poor one), which, with his extraordinary talents, sets him apart. The theatricality of his character is echoed by the camera's presentation of him. Sir John's appearance in the film is coyly delayed, he being the last juror in the Baring murder trial to be noticed by the camera, which has been slowly circling the jury. When the camera finally reveals him, we discover that he is the eccentric one, the only juror who is not in a hurry and who has concluded that Diana Baring is innocent. When attention is drawn to him, he states that he is not a businessman, theatrically announcing himself as "a poor actor," a title suggesting that he makes a career out of being a double of himself. Though he does all he can to defend Diana Baring, he is ultimately unable to move the jury/audience to reconsider and is bullied into going along with a guilty verdict. He is next introduced, like Dupin, in his "cloistered intimacy,"[18] through a series of shots that takes us from outside his home in Berkeley Square to the outer doors, doorbell, elevator, front door, living room, and finally into his bathroom. These images serve as curtains opening the next act in Sir John's passion.

These shots also suggest our deeper approach into Sir John's mind as we are led into his meditations about the jury trial, as he looks at himself in the mirror while shaving. Punctuating the doubleness suggested by this scene, Hitchcock shows Sir John's mirror reflection and the back of his head and shoulders in the foreground, giving the impression of two people talking together. While this scene, like the later mousetrap scene, has roots in Shakespearean soliloquies, it also links Sir John to Dupin's meditative side. In some sense Sir John's tryst with his other self in the mirror is like the trance Dupin enters during his "Bi-Part" "resolvent" phases. Sir John also seems in another world as he ponders the details of the case. The case in *Murder!* like those of Dupin's, presents Sir John with difficulty in the sublime sense of a seemingly insurmountable problem. The case has been heard and judged, and the sentence of death pronounced, and all Sir John has are intuitions that fall flat with the rest of the jury. While shaving, Sir John hears a flawed and incomplete radio report of Diana's case. Like the newspaper reports in "Murders of the Rue Morgue" and "Mystery of Marie Roget," such reports suggest the mundane analytical powers of the masses and the press establishment. Wagner's overture to *Tristan and Isolde*, which follows the news, reflects Sir John's awareness of growing feelings for Diana, and its crescendos punctuate his intuitive revelations about the overlooked significance of the brandy at the crime scene and the fact that someone else must have been in the room to commit the murder. In essence, Sir John's entranced mind is guided by the intuitive logic of Wagner's music. In his trancelike state at the mirror Sir John experiences a change, separating his passive and active, his perplexed and purposive selves, discovering an inner resolve to rescue Diana Baring because an SOS radio story inspires him. Additionally, he is moved by his love for the imprisoned actress, a side of himself he only finally acknowledges during his self-interview at the mirror. Love becomes a transcendent spur behind his investigation, empowering his intuition and guiding his thought. In his trance, Sir John resembles the "resolvent Dupin." Sir John's intuition also feeds on mundane facts and is based on the fact that he, like Dupin, identifies with the crime victims, in this case fellow thespian Diana Baring.

Throughout *Murder!* Hitchcock incorporates other doubles to emphasize the dream world of the theater. Even the trial itself is presented as a play, a fanfare accompanying the title, "Rex vs. Diana Baring." Sir John's own double nature as actor and playwright is confirmed as he adds "detective" to his list of theatrical selves. This role is part of his "new play," which he equates with his investigation. It requires him to do things a wealthy man like him wouldn't normally do, including consorting intimately with the lower-class Markhams. As theatrical managers, they can grant Sir John access to people and places associated with the murder. The idea that Mr. Markham is actually one of his doubles is visually reinforced with the cut from Sir John's living room to Markham's home, revealing them both wearing similarly striped robes. Here Hitchcock foreshadows the striped circus tent at the end of the film, reinforcing a further doubling of the circus and the theater, and also suggests the "acts" all are called on to perform in this film. Sir John's association with the Markhams often becomes humorous as he brings the Markhams up to his level ("we artists") and purposely uses the wrong spoon during lunch to avoid embarrassing Mrs. Doucie Markham, who uses a teaspoon to eat her soup. Tania Modleski accurately points out that in addition to writing his play about the murder case, his acting in a way to include the Markhams is applying techniques of his art to life.[19] In an amusing early scene in which the police are questioning Diana's acting troupe from backstage during the performance (fittingly, of a farce), we see many costume changes, which suggest the slipperiness of identity in the world of this film. Among these changes is Handell Fane taking off a policeman's uniform while another actor dons an identical police costume (which, while we don't yet realize it, reveals the murderer's disguise). Fane himself, who we

later learn is the murderer, is repeatedly doubled in his various guises—
actor, trapeze artist, pure Caucasian, and female impersonator.

Fane is also the most significant of Sir John's doubles; they are reminiscent of Dupin and Minister D——. Among other similarities to Sir John,
Fane loves Diana. Even their behavior reflects each other, both moving
and speaking slowly and deliberately, suggesting both real and "feigned"
good breeding. Their doubleness is tested with Sir John's suggestion that
they collaborate on his play, *The Inner History of the Baring Case*, which of
course Fane also does in the note he leaves behind after committing suicide. During the mousetrap scene, Fane proves to be a worthy adversary.
He avoids giving himself away and plays off of Sir John's trap by insisting
he needs a poker to get into the part for which he is reading. Like Sir John,
he is an actor, slipping in and out of various roles as needed. Finally, Sir
John's circus-striped robe links him to Fane, in another reflection of the
theater. As in "Purloined Letter," the doubling of detective and criminal
introduces moral ambiguities, particularly the transfer of guilt. In this case,
Sir John is unable to convince the jury of his intuition about Diana's innocence, making him partly responsible for her predicament, reflecting
Fane's deeper guilt at not rescuing Diana by confessing his crime.

The ambiguity between reason and intuition that underlies Poe's
Dupin stories is highlighted in the jury scene. For example, one woman
agrees with the psychoanalytic defense that Diana was in a "fugue state"
and acted without knowing what she did. Another woman juror suggests that if that were true and Diana were released, then the jury would
be responsible for other possible murders she might commit due to her
"dual personality." While the jury accepts this reasoning, obviously it is
based on pure speculation. Other jurors also confuse the issue, one feeling there is too much responsibility placed on them and another finding Diana so "perfectly ripping" that he can't imagine a "girl of that
sort" murdering anybody. Such opinions are soundly put in their place
as the foreman notes that the world can't be run on sentiment and that
how "the young lady" appeals to one is irrelevant to the "case at hand."
The foreman becomes a foil for Sir John. Like Sir John, he is well-
spoken and intelligent, a natural leader. But unlike Sir John, he is a
practical, not particularly sensitive businessman who is quick to reject
anything that is not based on apparent facts. He is solid, respectable,
and seemingly wiser than most of the others.

The early proceedings of the jury, and how they are framed by Hitchcock, make Sir John's hesitancy to vote guilty suspect: his reasons, in the context of the other weak ones, seem equally unimpressive. He claims, for example, that he is "convinced" Diana is telling the truth, that he has been "impressed" with her behavior. He offers no evidence for these statements; they rely on his intuitive sense of what she could and couldn't do based on his feelings alone. Sir John claims that his intuitions are deeper than those of the earlier juror who found Diana "ripping," but they don't necessarily seem so. In fact, when told that Fane's testimony was of no use since "he was so obviously in love with the prisoner," Sir John looks up quickly with the shock of self-recognition, suggesting to us that he too has tender feelings for the prisoner. This certainly throws his intuition into doubt as we are immediately reminded that the one juror who likes Diana was told that an ugly woman would likely have little chance with him. We are not certain that Sir John himself would be hesitant to condemn Diana were she less attractive. Even worse, Sir John justifies his perspective on his experience as an actor and playwright:

> My time on the stage would be shortened if I had not for years trained myself to . . . apply the techniques of life to the problems of my art. But today, ladies and gentleman, that process is reversed. I find myself applying the techniques of my art to a problem of real life, and my art is not satisfied.

As in "Rue Morgue" and "Purloined Letter," which emphasizes poetry over mathematics, the analytic imagination is here identified with art.[20] These unscientific remarks bring the jurors to their feet to surround Sir John and bombard him with questions of facts that he cannot satisfactorily answer. As the jurors in unison repeatedly asks him, "Any answer to that, Sir John?" they become a Greek chorus praising the fact-based method of analysis shared by the public, the court, and the press. Sir John, like Poe's Dupin, has challenged assumptions, except that he is not yet prepared to prove his impressions. In these scenes Hitchcock raises the issue of what is acceptable evidence and, specifically, if and when intuitive impressions are justified.

Although Sir John's investigation proceeds to demonstrate the uncertainty of impressions, it increasingly confirms that his are correct.

The uncertainty of impressions, as in "Rue Morgue," is demonstrated in hearing voices and making assumptions about them. Diana's landlady says that she had heard none but women's voices on the night of the murder, but when Sir John leaves the room and imitates a woman's voice, the landlady is fooled (as are we), obviously demonstrating the unreliability of such assumptions. His case is based on the idea that apparent facts are often built on assumptions, their value depending on how imaginatively read. For example, that Diana smelled of alcohol convinced the jury that she had drunk the brandy. However, Sir John raises the question that perhaps she merely smelled of dinner wine. Also, since no other person was known to be in the room when the murder took place, it is assumed by the court and jury that no one was there. Sir John suggests that another person may have been there, but *who* remains unknown. In each case, facts prove less reliable than intuition. Finally, when Sir John realizes that the policeman seen disappearing after the crime was an impersonator, he proves once and for all the unreliability of appearances. If we had any doubts about Sir John's approach, we certainly are given pause about the certainty with which we process things we see—especially in Hitchcock's film.

Finally, the images of the theater further suggest the ambiguity of reality and illusion. With so many doublings, actors, and costume changes, *Murder!* is a veritable house of mirrors in a carnival where images only seem real. As in Poe's Dupin tales, Hitchcock puts an emphasis on the gaze, which, as Modleski notes, is related inherently to detective stories (31). Not surprisingly, the film begins and ends with deceptive images. The opening scenes show a clock tower chiming from the end of the street, followed by a scream and a series of windows opening and people trying to see what the ruckus is all about. These people suggest spectators at a play trying to get a better look at the stage from an obscure balcony seat. As it will turn out, since the first policeman seen is the murderer in disguise, the entire scene becomes a bit of theater and the people are quite rightly assuming the role of audience. In fact, with the film's "audience," we are deceived early in the scene as Hitchcock's shooting script arranges the shot of a woman's silhouette changing: "a glimpse of a silhouette of a beautiful figure and profile on blind. As the latter goes up we find to our disappointment that it is the angry face of an unattractive woman."[21] Hitchcock maintains this perspective as the murder investigation and Sir John's mousetrap play become synonymous. The film's ending also proves to be something other than it seems as the camera retreats from what appears to be the last scene of the film, but is actually the end of a play starring Sir John and Diana Baring. Thus the concluding scene is both the end of the film and the end of Sir John's play, which had been one all along. The deceptions at the end and the beginning of the film thrust the audience into the position of the reader of the Dupin stories—a state of sublime uncertainty about the nature of reality. As Modleski states of the film, "at the heart of the film is the fear that theater may so infuse and confuse reality that proper distinctions and boundaries by which make sense of life no longer hold true" (32).

Many of the sequences in *Murder!* are mounted theatrically. During the opening scenes, once the neighbors get inside the scene of the crime, Hitch shows us a theatrical tableau: Diana sits entranced with the murdered Edna Druce at her feet with silent spectators looking on. The camera accommodates our curiosity by making a circular tour of the scene, moving from the policeman down Diana's body to her limp hand, fire poker on the floor, prostrate body of Edna, and back up to the policeman. Ironically, the policeman is pointing a light on Diana as if the appearances in the room and their meaning were reliably clear. In effect, it becomes a stage light that merely clarifies appearances. Such use of circular camera work is common to the film, circumscribing space like a stage and linking various elements of the film together, suggesting again the slippery nature of the identity of things. For example, Hitchcock's circular pan around the jury table suggests the problem of pinpointing truth, going around and around the jury as the jury does the truth of the case. Just as in the circular camera movement at the crime scene noted above, circularity avoids truth by going around it. Sir John is attempting to get at the center itself, based on his faith that truth involves more than hovering around seemingly obvious facts. The image of circularity leads to the circus climax with its rings. It is here, when first at the circus, that Sir John conceives, or at least reveals, his mousetrap scheme to trap Fane.

Before the mousetrap scene is introduced, Hitchcock combines a melodramatically suspenseful series of shots in cyclical repetition, telescoping time, as Sir John searches for Fane and his investigation begins to enclose the culprit. The round of shots moves sequentially from a weather vane (William Rothman suggests the vane is an emblem of Fane [or feign])[22] to a high-angle shot of Diana's circular pacing, to the shadow of a circular noose that is slowly rising up a wall.[23] In addition, the spinning vane itself reinforces the circular imagery. Diana's pacing reminds us how she has been stepping around Fane throughout the case. If he isn't found, her neck, instead of his, will fill that circular hangman's noose. Hitchcock accelerates the pace of the shot series, as well as our suspense, until a voice-over reveals that Fane has been found working at the circus. We then see Sir John and Markham at the circus watching Fane's trapeze act, which is illuminated by searchlights that surround him in circular light. In essence, Fane has stepped out of the closet into center ring to be scrutinized. The full-circle plot of detective tales, bringing things back into order in the end, reflects the reuniting of the diffused fragments of Poe's universe. The quickening pace of the ending of this montage cycle reflects the increased rotary speed of the vortical gathering of universal fragments in God's Eurekan plot.

Sir John is led to Fane because of Diana's slip that he was half-caste. Realizing instantly that trying to maintain his secret motivated Fane's murdering Edna, Sir John's shock of recognition becomes a similar emotional high point for the film to the horrified narrator in "Rue Morgue" learning from Dupin that the hair specimen found at the L'Espanaye room isn't human. Both moments create a sense of strangeness and otherness, further amplified in the film by Fane's cross-dressing. In addition to this plot movement connecting Fane and the ape, they are also connected through their incredible athleticism. Dupin realizes early on, based on the window latch and locked door, that nothing human could have accessed the room. Similarly, on finding the sink in Fane's dressing room damaged, Sir John realizes that someone with the extraordinary strength of a trapeze artist could climb out the window and do the seemingly impossible trick of accessing Diana's house without touching the ground. Like Poe's tale, the film resolves its case with a spectacularly weird and unguessable circumstance that is at once surprising and uncanny.

The major theatrical event in the film comes as Sir John brings Fane in supposedly to read for his new play, *The Inner History of the Baring*

Case, but really intends to force a confession. As Sir John suggests to Markham, this mousetrap scheme comes from Hamlet's attempt to prove his uncle's guilt in a play within a play. This is a third level of play within play, since Sir John's investigation/play is also a play within Hitchcock's film. Here Hitchcock is harking back to Poe as well as to Shakespeare, since in both "Rue Morgue" and "Purloined Letter" Dupin traps his prey with customized theatrical scenes that reveal the truth of his analyses. While Hitchcock begins the film as a whodunit, these last twenty minutes become a suspense thriller. This is a pattern he will follow in films like *Rebecca* (1940) and *Vertigo* (1958), which start out as one thing and become another.[24]

In the important play scene in *Murder!*, the line dividing appearance and reality becomes very fuzzy. The mousetrap takes place in Sir John's office, which is decorated with massive columns that fittingly remind us of the classical frame of a proscenium arch—the perfect setting for the little drama he has set up for Fane. The room also features a polar bear rug that suggests Sir John's predatory role as cat to Fane's mouse. As Fane theatrically enters and Sir John explains that he has written a play about the Diana Baring murder case, their conversation is filmed without cuts, the camera moving back and forth between the two. This important image, like the circle, has appeared several times already, particularly at Sir John's interview with Diana in prison and in Fane's trapeze act. In this instance, the back-and-forth camera suggests the life-and-death struggle between these competitive actors, both pretending to be something they are not, with the added complication of Sir John's triple role as playwright, actor, and spectator of Fane's reactions to being cast as Edna Druce's murderer. Sir John attempts to cause Fane to break down psychologically and emotionally by equating him with the murderer in his play ("*You* make *your* entrance"). In other words Sir John is trying to get Fane to cross the line from play to reality. Reality becomes hard to distinguish from "imagination," a word used often and conspicuously during the scene: the brandy was not "exploited with sufficient imagination"; and instead of using a real poker for the reading, Fane is told he must "use [his] imagination." Sir John's statement that the police have little sense of drama, not exploiting the brandy angle better, alerts Fane that Sir John *has* sufficient imagination to have figured out the case. Fane's request for a real poker to play the scene, as Rothman has pointed out, would give him some chance to es-cape the office by force (86). Like Minister D— in "Purloined Letter," whom Dupin knows to be "desperate" and capable of killing him, Fane is dangerous and willing to kill to protect himself and his secret. Ironi-cally, at this point, Sir John, rather than a poker, offers Fane a pencil, the weapon he has used to write this mousetrap.

Play and reality—and Hitchcock's thriller—converge at the climac-tic moment when Sir John reads from the script Edna's unfortunate line, "he's a half . . ." Hitchcock jump-cuts to a high-angle view of the two looking at their scripts in an unbearably shocking and silent mo-ment that seems to reenact the moment of the murder, which left Di-ana Baring in shocked silence. Quickly the script is turned to a blank page, and with Sir John we are held in suspension, awaiting a climac-tic turn of events.

Later, back at the circus, Sir John's forestalled denouement finally plays out. Ending the film at the circus is appropriate, since it is the place for exotic extremes in performance, reflecting Fane's roles as both woman and murderer. As he goes back and forth on the trapeze bar, his shadow centers in the circular searchlights that illuminate his act. The back-and-forth of the trapeze act emphasizes the trap Fane finds himself in. Just as he can go in only those two directions, no matter where he goes, Sir John will be there—not only to accuse him of murder but to reveal his half-caste secret. Fane is also caught between two ambiguities: his desire to flaunt himself as actor, circus performer, female imperson-ator, and his need to hide himself and keep his secret from others. His need to expose himself is reinforced by the circular imagery of the cir-cus, its rings, lights, and the circular headdress of Fane's costume. His need to hide is shown most clearly as he swings back and forth and sees in his mind's eye Sir John and Diana staring at him—the two people who know his secret. Fane has the last word in his defeat, however. He creates a surprise ending to Sir John's play by hanging himself during his act and leaving a confession note behind that will save Diana Baring from the noose. While circus fans enjoy safe thrills, suicide is too much and sends them into hysteria (as Hitchcock's killing of the boy in *Sabo-tage* a couple of years later will also do). Thus Fane adds taboo enter-tainment to his violations (murder, cross-dressing, sexuality, and race). The tensions Fane experiences in living with all of his dualities—white and black, man and woman, actor and circus performer—embodies the psychomachia described by Poe in *Eureka*, causing fragmentation, diffusion, and finally psychological breakdown. His various roles finally defy categorization, as Modleski notes, making Sir John a restorer of social boundaries in solving the case.[25]

The case is thus solved, giving Sir John, finally, a response to the jury's repeated question, "Any answer for that, Sir John?" Like Dupin, Sir John has solved a case in a way that differs from the one taken by the public, courts, and press. He sees deeper by applying the techniques of his art to a problem of life. His "sense of drama," a knowledge of character and correct casting, consistent motivation, and a playwright's knowledge that all which appears to be is not, enables him to use peculiar analytic tools imaginatively exploiting possibilities that routine police and jury methods overlook or dismiss ("We are the experts of highbrow shockers, Markham"). Likewise, his dramatic orientation enables him to set the crucial mousetrap to solve the case. Like Sir George, Sir John has heroically slain the dragon that threatens the fair maiden and everyone else, pulling order and reality out from the brink of racial, sexual, and theatrical chaos.

The film's many circular images take us back to the cyclical development of the universe in Poe's *Eureka*. There reality slips in and out in endless cycles between harmony and reason, fragmentation and madness. The world, like the circus, is a place of jeopardy, full of death-defying feats that supply sublime thrills. As in the theater and in the circus, with its "acts," little in the film is stable or reliable. Even more than the theater, circus "acts" effectively reflect the fragmentation of the universe, in which no continuous narrative is attempted.

Dial M for Murder

Another Hitchcock film having characteristics of the detective tale is *Dial M for Murder* (1954), which harks back to issues in Poe's ratiocinative tales but turns some of them on their head. The interest here isn't on finding out who committed a crime, since that is shown clearly, but in watching would-be murderer Tony Wendice as he reacts and adapts to the police investigation. Adapted by Frederick Knott from his popular stage play, the film offered a ready-made and sure-fire property

to recoup Warner Bros. losses from *Under Capricorn* (1949) and to pro-
mote Warner's 3-D experiments. However, these practical reasons were
not the only ones attracting Hitchcock to the play. Elements similar to
his own style—such as the claustrophobic setting (*Lifeboat* and *Rope*),
doubles (*Shadow of a Doubt* and *Strangers on a Train*), a horrifically
graphic death scene (*Spellbound* and *Rope*), object-centered plot (a key
in *Notorious* and a rope in *Rope*), and the mousetrap motif (*Murder!* and
Stage Fright)—made it even more enticing. As Rohmer and Chabrol
correctly comment, despite being an adaptation, *Dial M* is "quite Hitchcockian."[26] Of course, these Hitchcockian elements are also Poe-esque,
and the numerous adaptations of Poe's detective elements in the play
undoubtedly attracted Hitchcock as well. For example, *Dial M* is cen-
tered around a female victim of violence and blackmail, reminiscent of
the brutalized females in "Rue Morgue" and the blackmailed queen in
"Purloined Letter." Inspector Hubbard's switching keys under Tony
Wendice's nose to set up his mousetrap resolution to the case is also like
"Purloined Letter." In addition, Tony and Hubbard both electrify others
with their surprise revelations in the manner of Poe's Dupin. Although
it was commercially attractive, Hitchcock chose to film *Dial M* for much
the same reason he did *Vertigo*—it was tailor-made for him. Finally, beyond the fact that *Dial M* came with Poe and Hitchcock elements firmly
in place, Hitchcock made important modifications to the play, enabling
him to bring in his own thematic concerns.[27]

The plot of *Dial M* is interesting because it goes beyond Poe's one-
on-one confrontation between Dupin and a single antagonist. Hitchcock exploits a three-way battle for analytical wit and theatrical dominance between Inspector Hubbard, mystery writer Mark Halliday, and
would-be murderer Tony Wendice. They are pitted against each other
not only mentally but artfully as playwrights who, like Sir John and
Fane, concoct competing scenarios of the murder case before them.

Hitchcock's twist on Poe is that he makes the police inspector—the
establishment figure with his old, proven methods—the genius who ultimately outwits the clever would-be murderer and the writer to solve
the crime. (Hitchcock reverts to his usual Poe-esque denunciation of
the police in his next film, *Rear Window*.) *Dial M* opens and closes with
the protective image of the ever vigilant bobby standing guard on the
streets of London. However, knowing that Hitchcock has little affinity

for authority figures—especially the police who supposedly locked him up as little boy for five minutes at his father's behest—we can't take these images at face value. The rank-and-file police are generally not presented in a positive light, even in *Dial M*. First, they are easily duped by Tony, who plants evidence against his wife that they accept without question. Later, Inspector Hubbard has to prevent one policeman from foppishly carrying Margot's purse on his wrist: "You clot! You can't go out in the street like that. You'll be arrested." In fact, Inspector Hubbard is portrayed as quite apart from the ordinary policeman. He has intelligence, taste, breeding, and a tremendous ego: on recognizing an oversight of his, for example, he comments that "even I didn't guess that at once. Extraordinary!" Also like Dupin, he thoughtfully smokes a pipe. Hence, the images of the protective bobby that open and close the film are more ironic than sincere, highlighting the fact that only an especially brilliant and civilized detective like Hubbard can match wits with Wendice. The regular policemen would have let him kill his wife right under their noses—since it seems to be in front of the Wendices' flat that we see the vigilant neighborhood bobby (booby?) stationed.

Hubbard is also pitted against mystery writer Mark Halliday. This becomes ironic in the context of Poe's detective tales, in which Dupin extols the poet's imagination as the superior means of analysis (though Halliday is a pulp writer and not a poet). While Halliday comes close to figuring out how Tony planned the crime, he leaves out some crucial details and fails to note Tony's suspicious behavior. In an obvious allusion to discussion in "The Purloined Letter" of analytically playing draughts—a game that requires keen observation of opposing players— Halliday admits that he is a "lousy bridge player." In the context of Poe's correlation of game playing and analysis, it is clear that Mark is one-dimensional, understanding the mechanics of crime but not the motivations of real people. While Mark claims as a writer to put himself "in the criminal's shoes" (one of Dupin's crucial talents), in real life he is blinded by assumptions. Inspector Hubbard proves the superior analyst in two ways: (1) he worries about the details more deeply and (2) he suspects everybody, including Tony. Mark's oversight of Tony's potential guilt creates a tense scene that is reminiscent of the mousetrap scene in *Murder!* between Sir John and Fane. As Mark explains to Tony that he should confess to plotting Margot's murder, he actually figures out nearly every detail of Tony's plan. However, his failure to imagine Tony's guilt makes the potential mousetrap ineffective. Indeed, as Inspector Hubbard later states, "They talk about flat-footed police-man. May the saints protect us from the gifted amateur."

Ultimately, Hubbard, Halliday, and Tony all use Dupin's technique of anticipating the thinking of others, although differently and with varied results. In designing the crime Tony anticipates the reactions of Swann very accurately, as well as those of the police. When Swann suggests that Tony is smart, he replies that "I've just had time to think things out, put myself in your position." When the police come to investigate Swann's death, Tony plants clues that not only anticipate, but manipulate police thinking. Making himself a criminal designing a crime, Mark uses the method in his writing. Of course, he also uses this method effectively in imagining what Tony might confess to free Margot. Finally, Inspector Hubbard traps Tony by anticipating his thinking: "He will put two and two together and use the key under the stair carpet." The use of anticipating others' thoughts is also part of the theme of appearance and reality. Each character becomes an actor in a play within a play of his own composition. Tony's play is the murder plot in which Swann is cast as star. In his own play Tony acts the part of the faithful and innocent husband. With Swann, he pretends at first to want to be shopping, then walks Swan through the part of murderer, and then while he is on the phone Swann walks through a rehearsal himself. For his part, Halliday acts as Margot's platonic friend, when he is actually her illicit lover. And Detective Hubbard acts as if he were uninterested in the facts of the case, often looking up distractedly to say "hmm?" when given seemingly important information. Like Dupin with Minister D——, Hubbard knows the value of pretending to know nothing. This later enables him to prepare the final theatrical he concocts to test Margot and Tony and thus solve the crime.

The parallel roles of Hubbard and Tony to Dupin and Minister D—— are remarkable. In addition to the likeness Hubbard bears Dupin, Tony is quite like Minister D—— in being a cunning and ruthless sophisticate who outwits the average policeman with only half trying. And like D——, he steals his wife's love letter and uses it to blackmail her. Later, just as Dupin had stolen D——'s stolen letter and replaced it with another, Hubbard steals Tony's key. He does so by sending Tony to the window to check on Halliday, reminiscent of the distraction Dupin created to take D— to the window while he exchanged his facsimile for the real letter.

All of this suggests how difficult it could be to distinguish appearance from reality in the world of this film. But the deeper theatrical ambitions of Hubbard, Tony, and Mark make reality even more slippery and the film's suspense all the more gripping. In fact, the film can be divided into a series of plays that continually collide with each other. The first is by Mark and Margot; following their adulterous affair, they pretend to be mere friends for Tony's sake. Unfortunately for them, Tony skips a tennis tournament to follow them and watches their backstage performance through a window as they are cooking spaghetti. This, as well as Mark's love letter purloined from Margot's purse, leads him to create his own scenario and recast their parts. Luring Swann to his flat under false pretenses, Tony begins his play by casting the crooked Swann in the role of murderer in his play by blackmailing him.[28] After giving appropriate background to the story behind the play, Tony blocks out the action in his flat. Hitchcock's overhead shot follows Tony as the entire murder is laid out. Later, when Margot spoils the murder by killing Swann, Tony enters into another playwriting phase revision. Having failed to murder his wife, he arranges details so that she will be convicted of murdering her blackmailer. To this point, Tony seems in firm control of the police and of his own destiny.

Mark, however, offers a competing version of things on the eve of Margot's execution. Having figured out that Margot can be saved if Tony will essentially own up to what he has in fact done (though Mark doesn't know that he has done it), he attempts to recast Tony's play with him as the murderer. Visually, the scene closely parallels Tony's blocking out the murder for Swann as Mark walks Tony through the plan. When Inspector Hubbard arrives, with the opening scene of his own play, he seemingly supports Tony's contempt for Mark's rewrite. Hubbard's first act, but the film's last, ostensibly involves details of money Tony is spending, but in reality is about getting into the flat and switching keys with him and getting him to pick up Margot's things at the police station. The complexity of three simultaneous scenarios colliding in these scenes is dizzying: Tony pretending he is sympathetic with Mark despite having evidence of Margo's guilt; Mark now knowing Tony is the murderer (after finding the briefcase full of money) but being unable to prove it; Hubbard pretending to be there on some routine police matter while actually feeling Mark is right.

The real contest involves who can improvise a revision the most effectively. Mark came to the apartment with his rescuing scheme but realizes Tony's guilt on finding the money he hid for paying Swann. Tony, when confronted with this new evidence against him, turns it all on Margot, that the money was there because she was to pay off Swann. The quick-wittedness is dazzling—like having three Dupins trying to outwit each other. This battle of wits becomes consciously competitive as Tony challenges, "Go on Mark, make your move."

Hubbard, of course, proves to be the real Dupin of the story since his mousetrap prevails in the end. This trap is so cleverly set that Tony himself uses the key and walks right into it. Even he becomes confused by the unending twists in the world he himself made slippery by turning it into an ever complicating mystery. Hubbard, like Dupin, disentangles the chaos Tony starts and returns the fragments back into the whole. Notwithstanding, a strange note is sounded in the film, which seems ultimately positive. Before the murder, Mark warns Tony that perfect murders are only perfect on paper; in real life things never turn out as you think they will. And in the end, Tony explicitly concedes the point ("As you said Mark, it might have worked on paper . . ."). But this actually raises the question about whether the world is as unpredictable and slippery as the shifting fictional ones our three antagonists create. Thus the sublime is created not only in the murder scene or in the intellectual prowess of the antagonists, but in the implications about life itself poised on the edge of chaos, creating the need for ineffective bobbies to stand guard. Had not Tony made the mistake of spreading all of that money around his neighborhood, the forces of chaos, in the form of Margot's extinction and Mark's sorrow, certainly would have prevailed. Another aspect of the sublime in *Dial M* is our ambiguous connection to Tony, whom Hitchcock makes somewhat sympathetic. After all, he is charming and his wife has been unfaithful (Hitchcock certainly punishes her in the film). Typical of many Hitchcock films, *Dial M* makes the audience uncomfortable identifying with characters.

With the detective tale, both Poe and Hitchcock dip our big toes into the icy waters of chaos and terror, drawing them out again before we fall all the way in. The forces of violence, crime, and confusion are presented only to be disentangled and rendered ultimately harmless by reason. Interestingly, the forces of chaos are overcome as detectives employ their own illusions of ambiguity, theatricality, and doubleness. Most importantly, intuition, rather than purely scientific reason, becomes the means to discerning the irrational impulses that lay behind criminal behavior. As Dupin explains about discovering where Minister D— had hidden the letter: "I knew him, however, as both mathematician and poet, and my measures were adapted to his capacity, with reference to the circumstances by which he was surrounded. I knew him as a courtier, too, and as a bold *intriguant*. Such a man, I considered, could not fail to be aware of the ordinary political modes of action" (988). Whatever poetic genius provided D— with his concept for hiding the letter in plain sight also provided Dupin with the means of discovering his secret. Hence we have two sides of the same impulse, reflecting the doubleness of the Eurekan universe itself with its attractive and diffusive impulses in tension.

In addition to theatricality, doubleness, appearance versus reality, and analytical methods, Hitchcock, like Poe, layers his stories with much more than meets the eye. John T. Irwin writes of Poe: "In 'The Gold Bug,' for example, Poe uses the cryptographic writing of Captain Kidd's note (a physical writing that is literally invisible until heat is applied to the scrap of parchment) to evoke the invisibility of a text's meaning compared to the visibility of its writing."[29] Similarly Hitchcock layers his films with details that critics have yet to exhaust the significance of, suggesting his complicated vision of reality. It took French critics to peel away the apparent limits of Hitchcock's "mere" commercial product from his more complex art. The same process has developed around Poe's writings. It is these layers, these more complex stories, that lead to the darker affinities between Poe and Hitchcock beyond the detective story.

Notes

1. Sidney Gottlieb, ed., *Hitchcock on Hitchcock: Selected Writings and Interviews* (Berkeley: University of California Press, 1995), 113. Unless otherwise noted, all Hitchcock quotations throughout this volume are taken from Gottlieb's book.

2. The "Frenchman" could mean Dupin, the most famous of French detectives. The other obvious choice is Hercules Poirot, though this would be ambiguous since he is Belgian. Joe's subsequent comment that "bubbles don't necessarily

kill a person" seems a non sequitur, referring to Dorothy Sayer's *Unnatural Death* (1927).

3. J. Gerald Kennedy, "The Limits of Reason: Poe's Deluded Detectives," in *On Poe: The Best from American Literature*, eds. Louis J. Budd and Edwin H. Cady (Durham, N.C.: Duke University Press, 1993), 172–73.

4. Voltaire, Vidoq, Shakespeare, and Sophocles' *Oedipus Rex* are all cited as contributors to the development of the detective story.

5. While Doyle made his own contributions, he openly acknowledged his debt to Poe: "Where was the detective story until Poe breathed the breath of life into it?" (A. E. Murch, *The Development of the Detective Novel* [New York: Greenwood, 1968], 83). He further said that "Poe's masterful detective, M. Dupin, had from my childhood been one of my heroes" (Leroy Lad Panek, *An Introduction to the Detective Story* [Bowling Green, Ohio: Bowling Green University Press, 1987], 77).

6. "The Murders in the Rue Morgue," in *Edgar Allan Poe: Tales and Sketches*, vol. 1, ed. Thomas Ollive Mabbott (Urbana: University of Illinois Press, 1978), 532. All subsequent references to works by Poe will refer to this edition unless otherwise specified.

7. Leroy Lad Panek, *An Introduction to the Detective Story* (Bowling Green, Ohio: Bowling University Press, 1987), 277.

8. Poe is trying to become Dupin himself, as the case is based closely on the actual murder of Mary Rogers in New York City.

9. David Ketterer, *The Rationale of Deception in Poe* (Baton Rouge: Louisiana State University Press, 1979), xii, 1.

10. On Hitchcock's doubleness, see Leslie Brill, *The Hitchcock Romance: Love and Irony in Hitchcock's Films* (Princeton: Princeton University Press, 1988), 73–74. He sees both irony and romance in Hitchcock's vision in tension—at once opposite and identical. Richard Allen, "Hitchcock, or the Pleasures of Metaskepticism," in *Alfred Hitchcock: Centenary Essays*, eds. Richard Allen and S. Ishi Gonzales (London: BFI, 1999), 222, responds to Brill, claiming that he privileges romance, which reduces the tension Brill claims. Allen defines Hitchcock's doubleness as a mixture of irony and romance; Hitchcock "at once affirms the reality of appearances and affirms the 'fiction' or romance appearances serve to sustain, yet, at the same time, calls into question the reality of appearances, and by doing so undermines the 'fiction' or romance of exposing its fictiveness."

11. Alfred Hitchcock, BBC interview by Huw Wheldon in "Monitor," *The Listener*, August 6, 1964, 190.

12. Tony Magistrale and Sidney Poger, *Poe's Children: Connections between Tales of Terror and Detection* (New York: Peter Lang, 1999), 4.

13. John T. Irwin, *The Mystery to a Solution: Poe, Borges, and the Analytic Detective Story* (Baltimore: Johns Hopkins University Press, 1994), 318.

14. Two exceptions in Poe are "The Pit and the Pendulum," in which order is restored deus ex machina in the end, and "Descent into the Maelstrom," which like a detective tale restores order through the careful observation and analysis of the protagonist in getting out of the whirlpool.

15. Daniel Hoffmann, *Poe, Poe, Poe, Poe, Poe, Poe, Poe* (New York: Avon, 1972), 107–8.

16. Loisa Nygaard, "Winning the Game: Inductive Reasoning in Poe's 'Murders in the Rue Morgue,'" *Studies in Romanticism*, 33 (1994): 225.

17. Eric Rohmer and Claude Chabrol, *Hitchcock: The First Forty-Four Films*, trans. Stanley Hochman (New York: Frederick Unger, 1957), 27; Thomas Leitch, *Find the Director, and Other Hitchcock Games* (Athens: University of Georgia Press, 1991), 66–67. Maurice Yacowar claims that *Stage Fright* (1950) and *Trouble with Harry* (1957) are the only other whodunits Hitchcock made (*Hitchcock's British Films* [Hamden, Conn.: Archon, 1977], 123).

18. David Halliburton, *Edgar Allan Poe: A Phenomenological View* (Princeton: Princeton University Press, 1973), 237.

19. Tonia Modleski, *The Women Who Knew Too Much: Hitchcock and Feminist Theory* (New York: Methuen, 1988), 32.

20. Ketterer, *Rationale of Deception*, 242.

21. Page 3 of shooting script, quoted in Yacowar, 130.

22. See William Rothman, *Hitchcock: The Murderous Gaze* (Cambridge: Harvard University Press, 1982), 84.

23. This sequence echoes the earlier shot series in the jury room when Sir John is surrounded and the following dialogue is essentially repeated a number of times: (1) Sir John is told a fact that condemns Diana, (2) at which another juror says "That's right," (3) followed by the jury in unison chanting, "Any answer for that, Sir John?" (4) to which Sir John answers wearily, "Not at the moment."

24. See Susan Smith, *Hitchcock: Suspense, Humor, and Tone* (London: BFI, 2000), 17, 35–36.

25. Modleski, *Women Who Knew Too Much*, 26, 36.

26. Rohmer and Chabrol, *Hitchcock*, 120.

27. See Peter Bordonaro, "*Dial M for Murder*: A Play by Frederick Knott/A Film by Alfred Hitchcock," *Sight and Sound* 45, no. 3 (1976), for a thorough examination of how Hitchcock makes Tony more sympathetic while adding emphasis to Margot's adulterous guilt. The result complicates the play and problematizes audience response to the characters.

28. Leitch points out that the flat becomes a series of traps: for Swann, then Margot, and finally for Tony himself (163).

29. Irwin, *Mystery*, 320.

CHAPTER THREE

~

Apocalypse:
Crises of Fragmentation

The apocalypse in Poe and Hitchcock begins where the ratiocination stories end, at the breaking up of the rational and predictable universe. Just as the detective stories concern themselves with explaining apparently inexplicable reality, the apocalyptic stories tell of reality coming apart and the failure of human will and reason to put it back together. In *Eureka*, Poe describes how the original oneness of the universe is forced into "the abnormal condition of *Many*."[1] While unity implied homogeneity within the one, diffusion suggests "differences at all points from the uniquity and simplicity of the origin" (*Eureka*, 28). This moment of fragmentation and diffusion in the apocalyptic phase defines the frenzy of collapse in many of Poe's tales and Hitchcock's films. Sanity becomes madness, sense nonsense. The ability to analytically discern unified patterns evident in a condition of stable unity and sameness (as in the ratiocination tales) is replaced by panic in an atmosphere of rapid and violent flux. In this chapter I will explore how Hitchcock creates an audience-centered apocalypse in *The Birds* in terms of both biblical imagery and dissonances, including the irreconcilable coexistence of humor and horror as an objective correlative of sublime delight and terror. Despite the many dark scholarly assessments of the film, reading *The Birds* in the even darker context of Poe's

"Masque," together with Hitchcock's special use of apocalyptic imagery and humor, makes the film lighter and more optimistic than generally reckoned.

Poe's and Hitchcock's vision in "The Masque of the Red Death" and *The Birds* is thoroughly apocalyptic, both artists building suspense toward an impending disaster. From the shattering breakup of the unified universe and its fragmented and diffusive aftermath to the multigalactic vortex when the universe collapses back into its original unity, *Eureka*'s impending disasters are reflected microcosmically in many of Poe's tales and poems, representing, if not the collective end of the world, then the microcosmic catastrophe of an individual character. Douglas Robinson defines apocalyptic literature in theological scholarship as the future being unveiled in the present and the encroachment of a radically new order into a "historical situation that has disintegrated into chaos."[2] Thus human weakness brings on and leads to the ultimate chaos of apocalypse. So often in Poe's tales, madness is the human weakness that brings on shattering changes. Such works as "The Fall of the House of Usher," "William Wilson," "The Black Cat," "Morella," "Ms. Found in a Bottle," "Ulalume," "The Raven," *The Narrative of Arthur Gordon Pym*, and "The City in the Sea" foreshadow an impending disaster that inevitably occurs. In addition to "The Masque of the Red Death," more explicit collective apocalyptic works include "King Pest," "Mellonta Tauta," "Al Aaraaf," *Eureka*, and others. The latter three, including "Mesmeric Revelation," allude to the cyclical creation and destruction of the earth or the universe and the underlying longing in Poe's work that Wilbur describes as his insistent theme of transcending the creative, emotional, and physical limits of mortal existence.[3] Thus virtually all of Poe's more serious work is at least subtextually apocalyptic. For the narrator of "Ligeia," Roderick Usher, Prince Prospero, and others, this universal spectacle is experienced in their individual lives. The essence of Poe's art is imagining the potential end of one way of being abruptly moving to another, whether insanity, sleep, or death. But this thematic dimension is only half of the apocalyptic story, since Poe invariably subverts the structural conventions of serious gothic art. Poe raises issues about what his art is by invoking an inevitable double aspect that G. R. Thompson calls "romantic irony,"[4] undercutting the gothic theme with ironic subtexts.

While *The Birds* is Hitchcock's only explicitly apocalyptic film, Hitchcock agreeing with Peter Bogdanovich that it is a "vision of Judgment Day,"[5] it isn't his only one, nor his only way of telling an apocalyptic story. In a recent article, Christopher Sharrett proposed that *The Birds* (1963), as well as *Psycho* (1960), is a forerunner to apocalyptic films of the 1960s such as *Bonnie and Clyde* (1968) and *The Wild Bunch* (1969). Like them (and Poe), these Hitchcock films subvert our ideas about what a "work of art should represent."[6] *The Birds* generated an interpretive feeding frenzy because, as Thomas Leitch has noted, it is "the only Hitchcock film to have generated radical discrepancies in interpretation."[7] The endless speculations about the film are generated primarily by (1) the inexplicability and violence of the bird attacks, (2) the seemingly loose relationship between the attacks and the human drama, and (3) the film's apparently inconclusive ending.[8] While these aspects of the film certainly point to dark purposes, the hopeful—and even humorous—signs in the film have been generally slighted or misunderstood. Attempts to take account of all sides of the complex geometry of *The Birds* are provided a helpful image in Poe's *Eureka*. In explaining how the mind can "receive and . . . perceive an individual impression" of the universe, Poe uses the following metaphor: "He who from the top of Aetna casts his eyes leisurely around, is affected chiefly by the *extent* and *diversity* of the scene. Only by a rapid whirling on his heel could he hope to comprehend the panorama in the sublimity of its *oneness*" (6). Such a panoramic view helps reveal more fully the effect of Hitchcock's sublime dissonances in *The Birds*. The darker and lighter aspects taken together in an apocalyptic context, particularly echoing Poe's similar use of biblical prophecies and visions of the end of the world in "Masque," show that just as a millennial dawn follows the inevitable destruction, so Melanie Daniels and the Brenner family have cause for hope, despite the chaos in the world.[9]

Much of Hitchcock's work, like Poe's, is implicitly apocalyptic. His many spy films, for example, suggest frightening threats against Western civilization. In *The 39 Steps* (1935), *Sabotage* (1936), *Foreign Correspondent* (1940), *Saboteur* (1942), *Lifeboat* (1943), *North by Northwest* (1959), and *Topaz* (1969) the home front is threatened by foreign intrigue. Through sabotage, murder, kidnapping, and war (as in *Foreign Correspondent* and *Lifeboat*), Hitchcock creates an atmosphere of counting down to an apocalypse with suggestive signs of the times. *Foreign Correspondent* ends with war crashing down on Johnny Jones (Joel McCrea) as he reports to American listeners during the London blitz. However, Hitchcock prefers his war films to emphasize the impact of disaster as it affects individuals rather than societies. Hence, these stories are often about the protagonists becoming increasingly involved in the plots of their enemies and becoming aware of the depth of corruption in unexpected places (e.g., *North by Northwest*). In this sense, some of these films are apocalyptic in exactly the way Sharrett suggests, subverting our views of America and how it is represented on film. In films about the apocalypse of the individual, the protagonist experiences his or her world falling apart before entering a "radically new order of being." In *Shadow of a Doubt* (1943), *The Man Who Knew Too Much* (1956), and *Marnie* (1964), for example, disaster is foreshadowed early on and fulfilled in the course of the film. Hitchcock's films are regularly fueled by the imaginative catastrophe, playing on audience fears (especially during World War II and the Cold War) of the very real possibility of the ground falling out from under them. But even more to the point in this chapter are Hitchcock's experimental films (*Lifeboat*, *Rope*, *Rear Window*, and *Psycho*), which challenge genre conventions and conventional space limitations. Anticipating the unique approach used in *The Birds*, these films put audiences through unparalleled cinematic ordeals outside the comfortable Hollywood formulas of the time.

While Poe's imagery resulted from a life of personal disasters, Hitchcock's apocalyptic imagination was fueled by his moment in history. Born in 1899, Hitchcock lived through World Wars I and II, the Korean and Vietnam Wars, the Cold War, and the worldwide financial depression of the 1930s. The eruption of chaos and its potential to change everything was real and immediate for him and his generation. As JoAnn James observes, "the maelstroms of the twentieth century have given contemporary urgency to a new apocalyptic literature."[10] Following the earthshaking events up to and including World War II, Hitchcock lived through an unsettling period immersed in Cold War fears of annihilation. Susan Sontag notes that

> the trauma suffered by everyone in the middle of the 20th-century [made] clear that, from now on to the end of human history, every person would spend his individual life under the threat not only of individ-

ual death, which is certain, but of something almost insupportable psychologically—collective incineration and extinction which could come at any time, virtually without warning.[11]

As a Roman Catholic, if a lapsed one, Hitchcock would have been aware of the apocalyptic visions of Mary, particularly the Fatima secret message concerning Russia that led many Catholics in the 1950s and 1960s to understand the Cold War as a religious apocalypse.[12] Beyond the nuclear threats of the period, there was the danger of an ecological holocaust that Rachel Carson warned of in *Silent Spring* (1962). In other areas of political and popular culture during the 1960s, it became obvious that America had come to the unsettling end of the "liberal consensus," punctuated by the Vietnam and civil rights protests. These protests suggested radical ideas that were echoed in anthems to a new world to come (like Bob Dylan's "The Times They Are A-Changing" [1963]). Soon Barry McGuire's "Eve of Destruction" (1965) and the Doors' "The End" (1967) took these ideas to further apocalyptic extremes. *The Birds* appeared in the middle of a period when violent change had already taken wing—Hitchcock merely literalized it. *The Birds* was released among mainstream films that also echoed apocalyptic themes: Dr. No (1962), *The Manchurian Candidate* (1962), *Four Horseman of the Apocalypse* (1962), *Dr. Strangelove* (1964), *Fail Safe* (1964), *Behold a Pale Horse* (1964), and *Seven Days in May* (1964).

In the decade before *The Birds* the fear of atomic holocaust was evident everywhere, particularly in B movies about giant atomic-revived monsters (*Beast from 20,000 Fathoms* [1953], *Them* [1954], *Godzilla* [1956]), apocalyptic disasters (*When Worlds Collide* [1951], *World Without End* [1956], *The Day the Sky Exploded* [1961]), postapocalyptic life (*The Day the World Ended* [1956], *Panic in the Year Zero* [1962]), alien invasion films (*The Day the Earth Stood Still* [1951], *Invaders from Mars* [1953]), and realistic nuclear dramas (*On the Beach* [1959], *The World, the Flesh, and the Devil* [1959]).[13] Peter Biskind sums up the imaginative impact of these films in the 1950s and how unique they were to their time:

> But in sci-fi, the emergencies were much more serious than they were in war films. They jeopardized the future of the race; they were not national, nor even international, but planetary. The vast scale of destruction also differentiated sci-fi from the horror films of the thirties and forties that

preceded them. In *Frankenstein* (1931) and *Dracula* (1931), the scale of misfortune was small, a few villagers mugged by a monster, a little blood let by a vampire. But films like *When Worlds Collide* (1951) or *War of the Worlds* (1953) were suffused with what Susan Sontag called the "imagination of disaster," fear of the cataclysmic destruction of civilization, mayhem of an unimaginably higher order than we had ever seen before, the beginning of the end of life-as-we-know-it.[14]

Although *The Birds* is cinematically unique, it is thematically a product of its unsettled times.

While much of this cinema of worldwide disaster sets the imaginative stage for Hitchcock's supreme apocalyptic vision in *The Birds*, Poe's "Masque of the Red Death" anticipates Hitchcock with a dramatic framework of inexplicable sublimity and imagery for exploring the apocalypse in a manner distinct from contemporary cinematic conventions of science fiction. As Christopher Sharrett points out, few such science fiction films "address problems deeply rooted in human psychology or the constitution of civilization" ("Myth," 39). Horror films, however, are more apocalyptic in "offering a powerful critique of fundamental assumptions of much American art, including concepts such as 'human nature' heretofore treated as self-evident and sacrosanct by all genres" ("Myth," 40). From this perspective Sharrett proposes that *The Birds* raises issues about our ideas of what film art "should represent." As a literary horror precedent, down to its specific plot details, theme, and biblical allusions to end-of-the-world prophecies, Poe's "Masque of the Red Death" is echoed in *The Birds*. Like the Poe tale, including a devastating and deadly plague sweeping the land and throwing all into chaos, Hitchcock's characters try to hole up in a fortress and wall out the plague. Life in the "Masque" fortress is punctuated by the frightening chiming of the clock in the black room, while *The Birds* is punctuated by increasingly disturbing bird attacks, likewise causing eerie, confused, and terrified silences. Finally, unsuccessfully walling out the threat from without, both stories reach a climax in a final encounter that subdues the central character. In both tales, these aspects of the narrative obtain a sublime aura of apocalyptic magnitude through the imagery of biblical prophecies concerning conditions at the end of the world.

"The Masque of the Red Death"

While criticism of "The Masque of the Red Death" has often focused on its many possible sources, including etiquette books, the tale has not been analyzed in terms of biblical prophecies of the end of the world—including Douglas Robinson's analysis of the tale within the context of the apocalypse. Patrick Cheney's article on the use of the Bible and *The Tempest* in "Masque" suggests that Poe ironically reverses the mythic pattern in the Bible, depicting "the triumph of [the] agents of destruction over man."[15] In Cheney's version, the Red Death is the Antichrist, denying "Christ his power of resurrection" ("Poe's Use," 36). Further, the Red Death "replaces Christ as the shaping force of reality" ("Poe's Use," 38). Finally, Cheney downplays the significance of biblical imagery through most of the story: "Poe's use of biblical symbolism does not become particularly noteworthy until the last paragraph" ("Poe's Use," 34). While an interesting take on the tale, Cheney's study doesn't go far enough. He emphasizes narrative shape at the expense of biblical details that, in fact, challenge his idea that the story only ironically reverses biblical patterns. But even here, while the Bible is central to Cheney's reading, the apocalypse is not. I will argue that the apocalypse is a most important aspect of the biblical imagery in Poe's tale, and that it is a displaced refiguring of the Bible in dramatic and symbolic terms that reinforces traditional readings of the apocalypse, as well as inverts them. And, importantly for this chapter, pulling in two directions at once prefigures a pattern in *The Birds*.

The setting in "Masque" is reminiscent of a common apocalyptic pattern in the Bible. For example, Jesus tells his disciples what will precede his second coming by comparing the people to those during the time of Noah who ate, drank, and married "until the day that Noah entered into the ark" (Matt 24:38). He also tells the parable of the rich man who builds a barn for his goods and selfishly tells himself, "Soul . . . take thine ease, eat, drink, and be merry" (Luke 12:19). This parable is narrated with a cosmic irony that is reflected in "Masque" when the narrator ironically says of Prospero's plans: "All these and security were within. Without was the 'Red Death'" (671). Like the rich farmer of the parable, who is told that "this night thy soul shall be required of thee" (Luke 12:19–20), Prospero dies at the peak of his pleasure and security, as we knew he would. Also equating personal and collective apocalypse, an important biblical source for "Masque" is Daniel 5, where King Belshazzar meets his untimely death while making "a great feast to a thousand of his lords" and "drinking wine before the thousand" (v. 1). His doom is sealed when he has the "golden and silver vessels," which Nebuchadnezzar had taken out of the temple in Jerusalem, brought out "that the king, and his princes, his wives, and his concubines, might drink therein" (v. 2). Committing blasphemy, Belshazzar foreshadows Prince Prospero's attempts to defy mortal and divine limitations by walling out death itself. Belshazzar further seals his doom by idolizing the "gods of gold, and of silver, of brass, of iron, of wood, and of stone" (v. 4). For his part, Prospero ignores the needs of humanity and worships pleasure and his own "magnificent . . . yet august taste" (670). The end comes in stages as Belshazzar sees a message on the wall written by a disembodied hand, which causes the king's merry countenance to change: "and his thoughts troubled him, so that . . . his knees smote one against another" (v. 6). Like the sounding of the clock in "Masque," the writing on the wall stops the revelry cold, and Belshazzar seeks someone to interpret the writing, ultimately finding Daniel. Unlike the mysterious and silent masked figure in "Masque," Daniel is a more vocal messenger of death to the king. He first accuses the king of defiant pride and lifting himself "against the Lord of heaven" (v. 23). Daniel then interprets the writing on the wall as a message from God, declaring that Belshazzar has been found wanting and that his kingdom will be divided and given to the Medes and Persians. The chapter then ends (as in "Masque") when "that night was Belshazzar the king of the Chaldeans slain" (v. 30).

The fact that Poe's "Masque of the Red Death" presents the apocalypse as a day of wrath and widespread death confirms, as much as it ironically reverses, biblical patterns. As one prophet puts it, "the day of the Lord is great and very terrible; and who can abide it" (Joel 2:11). Others note that the day of the Lord comes in "perilous times" (2 Tim 3:1) and is a day "his wrath is come" (Rev 6:17). Further, that day "comes upon you unawares" (Luke 21:34) and is a day of "darkness" (Matt 24:29). On this day, all will be "desolate" (Ezk 35:15) as the Lord comes to "destroy sinners" (Isa 13:9) and "sever the wicked" (Matt 13:49). Other references reinforce Poe's awareness of scripture in writing "Masque." The Bible defines the wicked as those "choked by the riches and pleasures of life" (Luke 8:14). Poe presents his characters as worldly courtiers, under the influence of Prospero, allegorically trying to escape death altogether. Specific biblical imagery that Poe draws on fills in the allegory. Such biblical images as a bloody sea (Rev 16:3), heat/fire (Rev 16:8), and darkness (Rev 16:10) provide image patterns for Poe. Reflecting the "wonders of blood and fire" (Joel 2: 30), the sun "blackened and the moon turned to blood" (Rev 6:12), and a "consumption decreed that shall overflow" (Isa 10:22), Poe creates settings for the "Masque" such as braziers of fire, blood red lighting in the black seventh room, and a plague.

Poe's numerology in "Masque" also echoes biblical patterns. The plagues in John's apocalypse, for example, are associated with the number seven, the number of successive rooms in Poe's tale. Just as the plagues represent an apocalyptic countdown, so the rooms Prospero and the revelers pass through to pursue the Red Death ironically become the countdown to their end. Invariably, interpreters of the tale associate the seven colored rooms with Shakespeare's "seven ages of man." However, as John represents the sealed portions of the book, each signifies not the ages of men individually but collectively, and the sixth seal reveals events preceding the end of the world, including earthquakes, darkness, and stars falling from heaven (vv. 12–13). In chapter 5, the apostle describes a book on the throne of God with seven seals, followed by a vision in which he sees Christ as a slain lamb with seven horns and seven eyes, "which are the seven Spirits of god sent forth into all the earth" (v. 6). Without trying to unpack these images with too much specificity, I would note that like the fearful striking of the clock in "Masque," the opening of the seventh seal is accompanied by awed silence. Also foreshadowing the clock, chapter 8 describes seven angels with seven trumpets, each of which precipitates a new disaster, functioning as a celestial clock measuring earth's final hours.[16] Of course, the end in "Masque" only occurs when Prospero and death go through all seven rooms. Like the seals on the book, the angled architecture conceals one room (or time period) from another, leading inevitably to the ultimate silence and death of the seventh room. Importantly, linking the rooms in "Masque" to biblical precedent, the seals in Revelation are also associated with a succession of colors in a vision of white, red, and black horses (6:4–8).[17]

Finally, while Cheney links the Red Death to the Antichrist, the biblical record uses similar terms to Poe's in describing Christ himself at the second coming. The Red Death wears vesture and countenance "dabbed in blood" ("Masque," 675) and comes like a "thief in the night" (1 Thess 5:2). Most tellingly, with his coming he brings death to all of the wicked (2 Thess 2:8). Similarly, Christ is described at his second coming as wearing "dyed garments" that represent the blood he shed during his own sacrificial death (Isa 63:1). He also displays the evidences of his death, including the wounds in his hands (Zech 13:6). Allegorically, then, the tale depicts Christ returning to regain dominion of the world from the real Antichrist, Prospero, whose dreamlike kingdom of selfish revelry is "found wanting." Hence, instead of being an ironic reversal of Christ, the figure of the Red Death fulfills biblical prophecy of Christ's coming in terrible wrath to destroy the wicked and end the temporary reign of Satan. Poe's tale can be read as an allegorical reframing of the biblical story. What leads to the ironic reading is that Poe stops short of the millennial dawn that Scripture indicates will follow the apocalyptic holocaust. However, since Poe's tale focuses exclusively on Prospero and his wicked courtiers, the tale doesn't exclude salvation elsewhere. Hitchcock's apocalypse includes a hopeful dawn.

The Birds

The Birds, which Fellini called "an apocalyptic poem," exemplifies the moment of fragmentation described by Poe in *Eureka* in its situations and characters. *Eureka*'s "characters" and the "plot" in which they are embroiled provide glimpses into making sense of events in the film, which critics find ambiguous viewed in isolation. *Eureka*'s characters are the diffused fragments of the universe, which differ in size, kind, form, and distance from each other (*Eureka*, 29–30). These characters are both repulsed by and attracted to each other. The attraction is Newtonian gravity while the repulsion is electricity, which is "*manifested* only when bodies of appreciable difference, are brought into approximation" (*Eureka*, 34). Reflecting these patterns, Melanie's arrival in Bodega Bay manifests a repulsive response from Annie, Lydia, and others. Melanie's obvious charms elicit jealous suspicion from Annie, while her notoriety ("jumping naked into fountains") puts Lydia off.

From this perspective, the bird attacks function as a violent chorus, or objective correlative reflecting the intensity of the repulsive forces unleashed. While such a relation between the bird attacks and character tensions has been recognized before, *Eureka* reminds us that the repulsive forces are only part of a larger narrative cycle:

> The repulsion, already considered as so peculiarly limited in other regards, must be understood, let me repeat, as having power to prevent absolute coalition, *only to a certain epoch*. Unless we are to conceive that the appetite for Unity among the atoms is doomed to be satisfied never; unless we are to conceive that what had a beginning is to have no end—a conception which cannot *really* be entertained, however much we may talk or dream of entertaining it—we are forced to conclude that the repulsive influence imagined will, finally, under pressure of the Unitendency . . . shall be the superior force . . . and thus permit the universal subsidence into the inevitable, because original and therefore normal, One. (*Eureka*, 32)

Here Poe explains the narrative (as well as physical) logic underlying "God's plot," suggesting that the diffusive power eventually must dissipate and allow the fragments to reunite. Susan Lurie's psychoanalytic perspective shortsightedly emphasizes the negative implications in which, so to speak, the diffusions taking place in the film involve "the disenfranchising and exorcism of the mother, the placement of the desired woman in the place of the helpless child, the punishing of female desire, [and] the mutilation of the love object."[18] However, the cyclical Eurekan structure suggests that the process of reunification is equally evident as barriers between Melanie and Mitch, Annie, and Lydia successively break down, a process finally completed by the end of the bird attacks. Hence the complex dynamic in the film involves simultaneous attraction and repulsion of characters that builds to the apocalyptic climax. As detailed in the biblical prophecies, the film reflects the ultimately positive apocalyptic purposes.

The visual and situational details in *The Birds*, as in "Masque," echo the Bible to reinforce its apocalyptic themes. As in "Masque," *The Birds* reflects Joel's prophecy of "wonders in the heavens, and in the earth, blood, and fire, and pillars of smoke" (Joel 2:30). These images are particularly evident during the mass attack on the town, as we become front-row witnesses of the horror unleashed by the apocalyptic chaos of the birds: several fires, smoke, uncontrolled horses, cars, and fire hoses, and a bloodied man unsuccessfully trying to defend himself from attacking birds. Other scenes from the film continue these images, including the smoke on the horizon Mitch and Melanie see as they board up the house, the fire seen from the bird's-eye view, and the blood graphically lining the dead Annie's face, running from Dan Fawcett's empty eye sockets, oozing from Mitch's embattled hands, and staining Melanie's once patrician face. The work of the Red Death, then, becomes that of the birds breaking through windows, pecking at wooden doors, attacking with vicious determination (Rev 6:17). They seem the very embodiment of the "vengeance" Isaiah notes as the divine motive for destroying the world (Isa 34:8), particularly considering Hitchcock's hints that the bird attacks were some sort of revenge on mankind by nature.

One of the most overtly apocalyptic sequences in the film comes during the attacks on the school and town. In both attacks the visual emphasis on the birds massing, scattering, and attacking suggests the work of the seven angels characterizing the "day of the Lord's vengeance." In the Bible, angels are God's ministers of divine and terrible justice, swooping down with plagues of fire, smoke, blood, destroying trees, grass, waters, and people as directed (Rev 16). The fact that Melanie is unaware of the birds massing in the schoolyard affirms the Bible's theme of how the destruction at the end of the world will be an unpleasant surprise, coming as a thief in the night. As the birds gather on the jungle gym and later high above Bodega Bay, like the biblical angels they seem to be operating with purpose "out of the temple which is in heaven" with a "sharp sickle" to reap the earth (Rev 14:15–17). The ensuing attack on the running children, and later on the town, is the very image of prophesied destruction:

> And I saw an angel standing in the sun; and he cried with a loud voice, saying to all the fowls that fly in the midst of heaven, Come and gather yourselves together unto the supper of the great God.
> That ye may eat the flesh of kings, and the flesh of captains, and the flesh of mighty men. (Rev 19:17–18)

As the birds again begin to reap, they instill so much irrational fear in Melanie that she runs outside the safety of the café to seek shelter in an exposed phone booth. Like a diver in a shark cage, Melanie should have a perfect view of the total breakdown of order surrounding her. But her vision blurs as the hose splashes on the glass, obscuring the chaos surrounding her. Melanie's panic is shown in shots of her twisting frantically in the phone booth as if in a trap. Finally, Mitch takes Melanie back inside the café where the once complacent Bodega folk are in shock, again in fulfillment of Isaiah who prophesied that "the haughtiness of men shall be made low" (Isa 2:17). This is particularly true of Mrs. Bundy, whose scientific arrogance has been reduced to ashes. Following these scenes, Melanie and the Brenners hole up in their farmhouse and seem alone in the world, the film becoming the simple survival drama Daphne du Maurier originally wrote. Hiding in their boarded-up house, terrified and helpless, these survivors hide from the bird plague as best they can, echoing Prospero and his courtiers: "they shall go into the holes of the rocks, and into the caves of the earth, for fear of the Lord . . . when he ariseth to shake terribly the earth" (Isa 2:19).[19] Fittingly, at its fall, Babylon is described as "a cage of every unclean and hateful bird" (Rev 18:2). The bird attacks, which come as unexpectedly as "thieves in the night" also follow apocalyptic numerical protocol as there are seven attacks that we actually see in the film.

Melanie Daniels's prophetic surname and ambiguous characterization especially invokes association with biblical imagery. "Choked with her riches and pleasures" (Luke 8:14), living the idle and useless life of a rich playgirl, Melanie is identifiable allegorically as the whore of Babylon (Rev 17).[20] Lydia, referring to her as a "girl like that" whose name can't be kept out of the news, informs Mitch of Melanie's jumping into a fountain in Rome: "the newspapers said she was naked." Like the "great whore," Melanie "sitteth upon many waters" (Rev 17:1) as she rides in a motorboat and hails from that "city by the bay." In admitting to Mitch that she ran around with a "pretty wild crowd" and that "it was easy to get lost" in Rome, she confesses her sexual freedom, among the most damning sins of the great whore (Rev 17:2). While Melanie is not arrayed in scarlet and purple and an abundance of precious stones (Rev 17:4), she does dress luxuriously, flaunting a fur coat and driving an expensive sports car. And as for dwelling on "seven mountains" (Rev 17:9), hilly San Francisco becomes a suitable California stand-in for Babylon, making her a worldly outsider in the small coastal hamlet. Like the daughters of Zion in the last days, Melanie too seems "haughty, and walk[s] with stretched forth neck and wanton eyes, walking and mincing as [she] go[es]" (Isa 3:16). While many citizens of Bodega Bay eye her with wonder, if not suspicion, the hysterical woman in the café virtually equates Melanie with wickedness:

> Why are they doing this? They say when you got here the whole thing started. Who are you? What are you? Where did you come from? I think you are the cause of all this. I think you're evil! EVIL![21]

Melanie certainly functions as a harbinger of evil. Linked to the bird attacks, she is often the first to notice impending attacks (she is the first person attacked in the film, she sees the first sparrow in the fireplace, she is one of the first to see the birds attacking the schoolchildren, she is the one who notices the seagull outside the café, and she is the one to notice the noise in the attic that leads her upstairs).[22] The other shocked people huddled in the back hall of the café during the bird attack and look fearfully and suspiciously at Melanie. Finally, in becoming the last victim of the birds, like her biblical counterpart, Melanie is brought down in "torment" (Rev 18:9–10). She who was the epitome of wealth and elegance, and haughtiness, becomes a helpless and bloody catatonic, as it were, smitten "with a scab," as Isaiah warns (3:17). If Melanie isn't really as bad as the targets of biblical prophecies, she is an ambiguous figure for the audience, one with whom it is difficult to identify. Perhaps we, like Lydia, are not reconciled to her until her purifying "final ordeal" dismantles all artifice, making her helpless and in need of care and love. Like the Red Death, Melanie, a mysterious stranger, is associated with the plague and is accused of being responsible for it.

Unlike Poe's "Masque," which ends as "Darkness and Decay and the Red Death [hold] illimitable dominion over all," Hitchcock's apocalypse offers light and hope, a millennial aftermath to follow the apocalyptic terrors: "for a small moment have I forsaken thee," yet "with great mercies will I gather thee" (Isa 54:7). Hitchcock, like God, literally provides "a highway" by which Melanie and the Brenners escape (Isa 11:16). The Brenners' situation, to all appearances, fulfills other prophecies that finally the "inhabitants of the earth will be burned and there will be few men left" (Isa 24:6)—at least we only see a few in the end as the "the earth is at rest and is quiet" (Isa 14:7). While "Masque" ends in the silence of death, *The Birds* ends in the silence of relief and possible rebirth. These hopeful millennial suggestions, which are most strongly alluded to at the end of the film, are supported throughout with humor.

Many readings of Hitchcock's *The Birds* present the gulf between the light (human relationships) and dark elements (bird attacks) of the film as supporting evidence for the view that meaninglessness itself is the point, despairing of further interpretive precision.[23] I argue, however, that comic and horrific apocalyptic elements in *The Birds* form a complete fabric of tonal and thematic dissonance that is resolved in the film's generally positive conclusion. These dissonances include the quotidian and the fantastic, love and hate between Mitch and Melanie ("I loathe you"), peaceful lovebirds and attack birds, and the ambiguous double aspects of Lydia's motives and Melanie's role. Perhaps most jarring of all is the tonal dissonance between humor and horror, which echoes the other ambiguities. On the eve of the shoot, after evaluating the script, Victor Pritchett expressed to Hitchcock some reservations about tone, arguing that "a light comedy and a terror tale . . . do not weld together."[24] Despite Pritchett's objections, Hitchcock maintained this dissonance as a central, if problematical, aspect of the film's design.

Despite interruptions of horrific and shocking violence, *The Birds* has a pervasive comic tone. Not only are there the famous set pieces like the leaning lovebirds in Melanie's car and the comic prophet in the café ("It's the end of the world!"), but the film is populated with minor comic actors like Ruth McDevitt (bird shop owner), Richard Deacon (man in the elevator), Doodles Weaver (boat rental man), and John McGovern (the gently perplexed general store proprietor). These character actors appeared most often in light television and Disney movies and provided a light and reassuring feel to much of the film despite its horrific sequences. However, they also make viewing the film an unsettling experience. This blend of comic and horrific elements gives the film an artificial quality, a constant reminder that as Hitchcock once reassured Ingrid Bergman, "It's only a movie." Not only is the comedy undercut by the violence, but the violence is undercut by the comedy, exemplified in the absurd trio of still reaction shots of Melanie interspersed with shots of fire following a gas trail toward the inevitable explosion. As an audience we don't know how to interpret such a construction of images, except that it defies our expectations of both comedy and horror. Hitchcock's trailer for the film, whatever its weaknesses may be, captures this strange blend of comedy and horror, as his television introductions had (in relation to the somber events in the teleplays themselves), and indicate how basic his British black humor is to the effect he is after. Accompanied by a light comic score, Hitchcock describes the history of bird abuse at length until he is interrupted by the ominous sounds of birds and a terrified Tippi Hedren scrambling into the room warning that the birds (*The Birds*) are coming.[25]

Melanie is an important focus for the dissonances in the film between humor and horror, creating further audience uncertainty through the unlikely blend of her characterization. As the shallow playgirl with an identity crisis, her lightly notorious reputation and antics little support the apocalyptic weight her character is called to carry in the film. She is presented at first in San Francisco as a comic heroine straight out of a 1930s romantic comedy, leading to what soon becomes a comedy of manners when she arrives as a most unlikely and overdressed visitor to unglamorous Bodega Bay.[26] This in uneasy contrast to her role as the mysterious stranger figure and "evil" harbinger of the bird attacks connected to the most horrific aspects of the film. But if Melanie seems an unlikely plague, so Bodega Bay itself is a comic reduction of Babylon with its less-than-evil complacency.[27]

Hitchcock's black humor is also expressed through visually amusing aspects of the bird attacks themselves. These anomalies complicate our experience as an audience, creating guilty glee in our enjoyment at the secret jokes Hitchcock almost whispers at us during scenes that are horrifying and funny simultaneously. There is the little girl under the fence mechanically kicking her legs with a gull on her neck at Cathy's party, the obviously fake terror of the child actors being chased by birds from the school, the bird-oppressed man approaching Melanie in the phone booth, and the mime terror of Melanie, Lydia, and Cathy during the climactic attack on the Brenner home. Paglia notes humor at the end of Melanie's final ordeal as Mitch pulls her out of the room: "Comically disappearing last from view are her high heels: it's the last dance for the wily witch of the West."[28] This element of the fun Hitchcock is obviously having as he annihilates Bodega Bay punctuates the film's fictionality, itself a reassuring gesture. This is Hitchcock's comic relief, a variation on Roger's and Eve's repartee while precariously hanging from Mount Rushmore in *North by Northwest*. Just as Hitchcock told us "don't worry, the birds are coming" with his preattack bird scenes, so his black humor reminds us not to worry, all will turn out right in the end.

In terms of the apocalyptic dismantling of film conventions, this audience dilemma between humor and horror is a powerful element in the viewing experience. The audience situation finds an objective correlative in Melanie's phone booth ordeal. While she is trapped in the phone booth, her vision is obscured, first by a flailing fire hose and then by birds smashing into the glass.[29] The high-angle shots of her twisting and turning in the booth, vainly seeking a way out, suggests the cinematic cage in which Hitchcock has placed his audience, preventing our access into the film, either through its character, action, or tone. This image of twisting and turning, echoed by the flailing fire hose and foreshadowed by the winding road that Melanie takes to Bodega Bay, is further echoed when Melanie twists out of her seat and into the lamp during the major bird attack on the Brenner home. During that sequence, of course, the birds can be heard but not seen. Her vision is finally ended during her "final ordeal" in the upstairs room, leaving her eyes, ironically, wide open but blind. Like the audience, she is in a state of shock, no longer able to see, or guess, what comes next. These scenes remind us of Burke's sublime in terms of "obscurity," the terror of darkness, confusion, isolation, and a sense of helplessness, and "difficulty," being caught in an extremely complex and overwhelming predicament. Such states of mind describe the condition the characters and audience increasingly feel as the film relentlessly unfolds.

The film's apocalyptic dissonances are resolved in the hopeful imagery at the end of the film: the clouds are parted by a dawning sun, the family escapes the birds, and the camera focuses in on the lovebirds that Cathy insists on bringing along. These are all signs of peace—like the dove after Noah's flood. As Hitchcock himself notes, "love is going to survive the whole ordeal" and "that little couple of lovebirds lends an optimistic note to the theme."[30] The dove, which also becomes a sign of the Holy Ghost at Christ's baptism, is the ultimate lovebird and symbol of rebirth. Donald Spoto's claim that the film "simply stops" inconclusively is akin to choosing the least plausible of Hawthorne's multiple endings.[31] The ending is vintage Hitchcock, though more implicitly rendered. That it coincides with Hitchcock's thinking is shown by the two rejected endings that would have suggested no narrative ending. The first, the original ending in the screenplay, has the car being attacked by birds as the Brenner group leaves town. The second has the group arrive in San Francisco to discover the Golden Gate Bridge covered with birds. Hitchcock rejected that temptingly spectacular shot for relative narrative coherence. It simply was not a Hitchcock ending to leave the world and his characters in perpetual chaos (though he often flirted with the idea). His *Eureka*-like pattern, reiterated by Lesley Brill, is one of "loss, search, recovery," providing "the deep structure for . . . all Hitchcock's films."[32] Despite the seeming incompleteness of the ending's resolution, as Jean Douchet puts it, "for [Hitchcock] creation depends on an exact science of the spectator's reaction . . . [because] he attributes a mission to 'suspense.' And this mission is cathartic."[33] The sublime is achieved in powerfully depicting survival in the midst of the relentless horror that still seems present as the soundtrack increases the bird sounds. Despite their still apparent terror, they move forward united and healed. Whether the birds will continue to attack or not is beside the point. The characters have survived intact, emotionally and psychologically. As Hitchcock once remarked about *The Birds*, "I believe that when people rise to the occasion, when catastrophe comes, they are all right.[34] While the characters find millennial peace at the film's end (at least internally), the audience can bask in the comfort of a relatively happy ending, restoring the faith in the Hollywood narrative Hitchcock temporarily upended.

Notes

1. Edgar Allan Poe, *Eureka: A Prose Poem* (New York: Prometheus, 1997), 28.

2. See Douglas Robinson, *American Apocalypses: The Image of the End of the World in American Literature* (Baltimore: Johns Hopkins University Press, 1985), xii.

3. Richard Wilbur, "The House of Poe," in *The Recognition of Edgar Allan Poe: Selected Criticism Since 1829*, ed. Eric W. Carlson (Ann Arbor: University of Michigan Press, 1970), 254–77.

4. G. R. Thompson, *Poe's Fiction: Romantic Irony in the Gothic Tales* (Madison: University of Wisconsin Press, 1973), xi.

5. Peter Bogdanovich, *The Cinema of Alfred Hitchcock* (New York: Museum of Modern Art, 1963), 44.

6. Christopher Sharrett, "The Myth of Apocalypse and the Horror Film: The Primacy of *Psycho* and *The Birds*," Hitchcock Annual, 1995–1996, 42.

7. Thomas Leitch, *Find the Director and Other Hitchcock Games* (Athens: University of Georgia Press, 1991), 226.

8. Feminist assessments of the film suggest that its message is clearly negative, going back to the hostility among the female characters and apparent punishment of Melanie by the film for her moral shortcomings. Critics from more traditional perspectives discuss the film in terms of difficulties of analysis and find it mostly ambiguous. Some find the ending hopeful of healing, while others hover between one position and another. Thus the majority find the film negative, or at best, ambiguous.

9. Camille Paglia notes that "God plays no role in this film" (33) and that through the drunk in the Tides Café the "providential view of the birds as agents of wrathful supernatural power is satirized" (71). Yet the evidence of biblical echoes must be accounted for, particularly given Hitchcock's upbringing (*The Birds* [London: BFI, 1998]). I agree that Hitchcock is making no overtly religious statement through these images; however, such images subliminally raise emotional alarms, adding substantially to the sense of global disaster.

10. JoAnn James, introduction to *Apocalyptic Visions Past and Present*, eds. JoAnn James and William J. Cloonan (Tallahassee: Florida State University Press, 1988), 2.

11. Susan Sontag, "The Imagination of Disaster," in *Against Interpretation and Other Essays* (New York: Noonday, 1966), 224.

12. See Sandra L. Zimdars-Swartz and Paul F. Zimdars-Swartz, "Apocalypticism in Modern Western Europe," in *Encyclopedia of Apocalypticism*, ed. Stephen J. Stein (New York: Continuum, 1998), 13:265–92.

13. See Stephen D. O'Leary, "Popular Culture and Apocalypticism," in *The Encyclopedia of Apocalypticism*, ed. Stephen J. Stein (New York: Continuum, 1998), 3:392–426.

14. Peter Biskind, *Seeing Is Believing: How Hollywood Taught Us to Stop Worrying and Love the Fifties* (New York: Pantheon, 1983), 102. Both Paglia and David Sterritt (*The Films of Alfred Hitchcock* [Cambridge: Cambridge University Press, 1993]) have noted where *The Birds* echoes science fiction films of the 1950s. Paglia compares Hedren's movements during the house attack to "the generic gal-turned-to-jelly of 50s screamer flicks, where women were always being delectably stalked by . . . space aliens" (80). Sterritt compares the

shot of Annie and Melanie looking out at the night sky to "a shot that might have come from a science-fiction epic of the 1950s" (127).

15. Patrick Cheney, "Poe's Use of *The Tempest* and the Bible in 'The Masque of the Red Death,'" *English Language Notes* 20, no. 3–4 (1983): 32.

16. Brett Zimmerman sees "Masque" as an architectural allegory of a clock with the seven rooms forming a half circle—like half of a clock face. "Allegory and Clock Architecture in Poe's 'The Masque of the Red Death,'" *Essays in Arts and Sciences*, October 2000, 1–16.

17. There is another suggestion of Poe's use of Revelation, as well as Ezekiel, for his apocalyptic tales in "Shadow." Not only are there seven characters hold up against the plague, but at the end of the tale the voice of the shadow speaks "not the tones of any one being, but of a multitude of beings" (206). This emphasis on the power and dimensionality of the voice echoes John's description of Christ's powerful voice "as the sound of many waters" (Rev 1:15). In Ezekiel the prophet refers to the voice of the "Almighty . . . as the noise of an host" (1:24).

18. Susan Lurie, "The Construction of the 'Castrated Woman' in Psychoanalysis and Cinema," *Discourse* 4 (1981): 61.

19. While Robin Wood (*Hitchcock's Films Revisited* [New York: Columbia University Press, 1989], 161) denies that it is reasonable to correlate the mild weaknesses of the characters with bird attacks, I argue that the attacks suggest at least the potential for guilt to an audience reared in a biblical tradition that associates punishment with sin (as riches suggest God's favor).

20. Theodore Price, *Hitchcock and Homosexuality: His 50-Year Obsession with Jack the Ripper and the Superbitch Prostitute—A Psychoanalytic View* (Metuchen, N.J.: Scarecrow, 1992), 191, 199, calls Melanie a "virgin-whore" in his taxonomy of Hitchcock female types and notes that Hitchcock's calling her a "fly-by-night" is equivalent to prostitute in British slang.

21. In "Lost in the Wood," *Film Comment* 8, no. 4 (1972): 51, George Kaplan (a.k.a. Robin Wood) suggests that the hysterical woman's outburst at the camera represents a message to the audience as much as to Melanie. While Wood doesn't note this, Hitchcock may have gotten the idea from Don Siegal's 1956 *Invasion of the Body Snatchers* where Kevin McCarthy screams "You're next! You're next!" hysterically at the camera. The comparison works thematically as well, since *Invasion* is another apocalyptic film about identity and nightmarish fears, which also unsettlingly involves audiences.

22. Paglia notices that whatever "communicable disease" is keeping the chickens from eating, Melanie "is what's really going around Bodega Bay!" (43).

23. Leitch, for example, suggests the attacks are a "gag" in their unrelatedness to the film's human drama (*Find the Director*, 229).

24. Quoted in Robert E. Kapsis, "Hollywood Filmmaking and Reputation Building: Hitchcock's *The Birds*," *Journal of Popular Film and Television* 15, no. 1 (1987): 8.

25. However, our identification problems with Melanie go deeper still. While Hitchcock took great pains to encourage identification between his new star and his audience, the results are mixed. In terms of one Hollywood genre convention, Hitchcock modifies the traditional monster movie of the 1950s by undercutting traditional authority figures—cops and docs (to use Peter Biskind's terms). He revises science fiction as he had suspense films earlier (using appealing villains, daylight settings, guilt transference, etc.). In science fiction of the 1950s, conservative films make military men (cops) the heroes, while liberally oriented films make scientists (docs) the heroes. In *The Birds*, neither type prevails. The "scientist" in this film is an eccentric old woman who is blind to the idea of bird attacks ("Ridiculous!") while the local sheriff is a head-scratching hick who is equally clueless ("That's a sparrow, all right"). Though no official military types are evident, the hawkish businessman who suggests that they "get themselves guns and wipe [the birds] off the face of the earth," he is corrected by Mrs. Bundy: "that would hardly be possible [since] the five continents of the world probably contain over a hundred billion birds." Thus a military approach is also rendered futile. Further modifying clichés, the ambiguous "heroine" is not ultimately protected from the "monster," the "hero" leaving her to face the birds alone in the end. But this subtextual deconstruction of science fiction is only a side joke next to the dismantling of the overall structure of characters and narrative logic. Despite Hedren's obvious talent and potential, she doesn't garner immediate audience sympathy and identification reserved for major stars like Grace Kelly or Audrey Hepburn, either of whom would have made *The Birds* a very different film. Audiences would have easily warmed up to them, despite the playgirl persona, as audiences did with the shallow Cary Grant character in *North by Northwest*. With Hedren audiences are being asked to identify with a woman who is subtextually identified with the whore of Babylon, placing us in the same dilemma as the citizens of Bodega Bay—we are wary and suspicious. Her negative aspects stain her comic persona, causing the audience to see her double—wanting to identify with her (since she is practically in every shot and it is through her we see the action unfold) but unable to do so wholeheartedly.

26. Raymond Durgnat, *The Strange Case of Alfred Hitchcock, or the Plain Man's Hitchcock* (London: Faber & Faber, 1974), 334–35, compares these scenes to Ernst Lubisch comedy.

27. See Kapsis, "Hollywood Filmmaking," 9–10, on Hitchcock's concerns about audience reception of Hedren and steps taken to get audiences to "warm up" to her.

28. Paglia, 84.

29. See Bill Nichols, "*The Birds*: At the Window," *Film Reader* 4 (1979), in which he describes how the audience perspective is aligned with Melanie's point of view.

30. Truffaut, *Hitchcock*, 218.

31. Donald Spoto, *The Art of Alfred Hitchcock: Fifty Years of His Motion Pictures* (New York: Anchor, 1992), 332.

32. *The Hitchcock Romance: Love and Irony in Hitchcock's Films* (Princeton: Princeton University Press, 1988), 4. While *The Birds* is not the clearest instance of the romance pattern Brill identifies in Hitchcock's films, yet, as in *North by Northwest*, Mitch and Melanie "are alienated, uncertain of their identities, and in need of mates. Each for the other fills voids and ends idleness" (21).

33. Jean Douchet, "Hitch and his Public," trans. Verena Conley, in *A Hitchcock Reader*, eds. Marshall Deutelbaum and Leland Poague (Ames: Iowa State University Press, 1986), 7.

34. Quoted in Bogdanovich, *Cinema of Alfred Hitchcock*, 44.

CHAPTER FOUR

~

Inexplicable Predicaments: Diffusion from the Center

Following the shock and terror of the apocalypse phase of the Eurekan cycle is the long and inexplicable journey of diffusion, the result of the explosive fragmentation of the original oneness of the universe. Poe describes this new condition as "*forcing* the originally and therefore normally *One* into the abnormal condition of Many," suggesting a novel and alien condition for the individual fragments. Furthermore, "the assumption of absolute Unity in the primordial Particle includes that of infinite divisibility." Thus "from the one Particle, as a centre, let us suppose to be radiated spherically—in all directions—to immeasurable but still definite distances in the previously vacant Space—a certain inexpressibly great yet limited number of unimaginably yet not infinitely minute atoms" (*Eureka*, 28). The separation of the fragments is further punctuated by their differing forms, sizes, and distances from the center. As Poe explains, while "the immediate and perpetual tendency of the disunited atoms to return into their normal Unity is implied, as I have said, in their abnormal diffusion, still it is clear that this tendency will be without consequence . . .until the diffusive energy, in ceasing to be exerted, shall leave, it, the tendency, free to seek its satisfaction" (*Eureka*, 30). Poe further suggests that a "repulsive" power, analogous to electricity, keeps individual atoms from returning to their natural state of unity. Thus on a symbolic narrative level, fragments are characters in crisis, separated and isolated, journeying into the terror of unknown and undefined regions—physically and psychologically.

In this chapter I will examine two pairs of Poe and Hitchcock works that personify this phase of the *Eureka* journey: "The Pit and the Pendulum" and *North by Northwest* (1959), as well as "Ulalume" and *Spellbound* (1945). These works feature characters on an inexplicable journey that, to one degree or another, include a number of similar elements reflecting aspects of Poe's *Eureka*: (1) earth-shattering life changes, (2) unseen manipulative powers, (3) inexplicable occurrences, (4) mysterious threats from above, (5) potential downward plunges, and (6) deus ex machina endings. The narratives are further characterized by the unnaturalness and disorientation that exemplify the diffusive stage of *Eureka*, including disruptions of coherent thought that make rational thinking or acting difficult. Related to this condition is a breathless episodic incompleteness of experience; no sooner does one problem emerge and get dealt with than a new predicament arises. Like *Eureka*'s diffused fragments, the protagonists are propelled and controlled by invisible forces into alien, often surrealistic dreamscapes. They encounter difficult and complex situations beyond their comprehension and mysterious others forcing them to adapt to new people and conditions with resourcefulness.

These inexplicable journeys are distinguished by two narrative features Poe and Hitchcock exploit to great advantage, both of which reflect aspects of the *Eureka* plot. First is the terror associated with the sublime. Like Burke's characterization of the sublime itself, these stories are based on "an idea belonging to self preservation . . . therefore one of the most affecting we have. That its strongest emotion is an emotion of distress, and that no pleasure from a positive cause belongs to it."[1] Burke's taxonomy so perfectly suits Poe's narrative approach that its influence is obvious. As in the diffusion phase of *Eureka*, experience becomes inexplicable and terrifying precisely because of the specific sublime characteristics: horrors of darkness, astonishment, obscurity, privation, vastness, and difficulty. This is the very language of predicament and inexplicability, of helplessness before incomprehensible power. Further, like the tone and effect of our four focus narratives, terror produces unnatural tension and violent emotions (*A Philosophical*

Enquiry, 134), manifesting itself in these narratives as the protagonists experience larger than life challenges. Audiences, in the relative safety of armchair or theater chair, vicariously experience the delight and terror of these protagonists' predicaments.[2]

In addition to the sublime, the second narrative feature concerns the terrors associated with psychological development. The journey through life is the source of many narrative archetypes. My focus will be on the development of the child protagonist in terms of Jung's theory of the creation of consciousness.[3] His theory propounds that when a child is born, it is one in body and soul with its mother. The process of inevitable separation of its consciousness is called differentiation, and independent exploration of unknown situations and people is a frightening experience analogous to the sublime terrors of Eurekan diffusion. Jung states that first the infant has a discontinuous consciousness that grows in awareness through separation from the mother and other frustrations incident to growth, among which is forced interaction with strangers. Slowly the infant learns to react positively to new situations and people. Jung asserts that this is partly a process of learning to separate opposites, revealing to the developing infant that life is not all perfect unity, that it is not one with the mother. The ego identity continues to develop through exploring, learning methods of adapting to the environment as well as to the behavior of others. Later this process becomes integrative, one of reconciling opposites, which eventually allows the child to merge in friendship with others besides the mother, finally love and marriage at a later stage of maturity. As "The Pit and the Pendulum" demonstrates, such processes involve shattering changes that are fraught with terror, obscure threats, and feelings of utter helplessness. Analysis of Poe and Hitchcock's predicament journeys reveals their use of this narrative pattern of Jung's differentiation, which powerfully depicts the terrors of inexplicability.

"The Pit and the Pendulum" and *North by Northwest*

"The Pit and the Pendulum" presents a protagonist in an alien setting who is continually beset with inexplicable predicaments leading him from infantile semiconsciousness to mature resourcefulness. At first he is without orientation, memory, or continuous consciousness. In this condition he is particularly subject to the sublime terrors of darkness, obscurity, privation, and astonishment. Marie Bonaparte reads this tale as an allegory of both prebirth horrors and early childhood fear of the father.[4] Her Freudian interpretation of the tale accounts for much of the protagonist's situation but misses the tale's real story—psychic development.[5] From a Eurekan perspective, "Pit" begins just as the protagonist is undergoing the last phases of the apocalyptic judgments of the Spanish Inquisition. He has just been sentenced to death, and his grasp of reality becomes tentative: "the sound of the inquisitorial voices seemed merged in one dreamy indeterminate hum" ("Pit and the Pendulum," 681). As if experiencing the inexplicably perverse divine will that decreed the fragmenting of the original universal Particle, the disoriented protagonist describes the

> lips of the black-robed judges. They appeared to me white—whiter than the sheet upon which I trace these words—and thin even to grotesqueness; thin with the intensity of their expression of firmness—of immovable resolution—of stern contempt for human torture. (681)

Then, in an apocalyptic allusion to St. John's vision, the narrator's "vision fell upon the seven tall candles upon the table" (682). While at first he finds them comforting, "slender angels" wearing the aspect of "charity," he soon associates them with the judges as "meaningless spectres with heads of flame" (682). In John's vision the candlesticks represent "the seven churches" that are under condemnation (Rev 1:20; 2:5) and are threatened with judgment by a glorified Christ. Described in terms similar to those used of the candles, his whiteness and his eyes "as a flame of fire" (Rev 1:14; 2:5).

"Pit's" psychic apocalypse caused by the Inquisition is framed in language that suggests the protagonist's regression to a state of infancy: the protagonist is continually sick with a "most deadly nausea" (682) and suffers from discontinuous consciousness. Not only were his "senses . . . leaving [him]" (681), but he experiences a surrealistic chaos of mutating forms and sounds. The inquisitors' "voices seemed merged in one dreamy indeterminate hum." He sees the "nearly imperceptible waving of the sable draperies," and finally he is engulfed in a sense of "rushing descent" (682). Of particular interest in terms of the differentiation process is the mutation of the candles from saving and charitable "slender angels" to "meaningless spectres" (682). As Jung describes the early infant's experience, "just as the child in embryo is practically nothing but a part of the mother's body, and wholly dependent on her, so in early infancy the psyche to a large extent is part of the maternal psyche, and will soon become part of the paternal psyche as well."[6] The candles at first suggest the comfort of the infant's hitherto comforting and loving oneness with the mother; however, the "meaningless spectres" become the alien others the infant must accommodate in the developmental process. This horrific change of condition in the "loss" of the mother results in a longing to return to the womb, described here as a death wish: "And then there stole into my fancy, like a rich musical note, the thought of what sweet rest there must be in the grave" (682). In the quick metamorphosis of this image, Poe suggests the psychic trauma that accompanies the paternal end of oneness in the maternal universe. Linking both the *Eureka* and infant development phases, the sense of being under the control of unseen, hostile forces is dominant, blending a terror of the unknown with the inexplicable.

Finally, concluding the Inquisition, the protagonist enters oblivion:

> the figures of the judges vanished, as if magically, from before me; the tall candles sank into nothingness! their flames went out utterly; the blackness of darkness supervened; all sensations appeared swallowed up in a mad rushing descent as of the soul into Hades. Then silence, and stillness, and night were the universe. (682)

The narrator begins his journey appropriately unconscious, a virtual infant wrenched from his once presumably comfortable life, entering an inexplicable world in which experience will provide little help.

When he awakens, he begins the journey toward ego consciousness in his attempts to comprehend the experience of his swoon: "I had swooned; but still will not say that all of consciousness was lost" (682).[7] As he later struggles to remember his experience while under his "unconscious" swoon, his description is framed seemingly by a memory of his own birth process:

> These shadows of memory tell, indistinctly, of tall figures that lifted and bore me in silence down—down—still down—till a hideous dizziness oppressed me at the mere idea of the interminableness of the descent.

After this I call to mind flatness and dampness; and then all is *madness*—
the madness of a memory which busies itself among forbidden things.
(683)

Following what seems like the passage through the birth canal, sudden
motionless follows. He next describes that "very suddenly there came
back to my soul motion and sound—the tumultuous motion of the
heart, and, in my ears, the sound of its beating" (683). Just as newborns
emerge breathless and still from the womb until brought into consciousness by the attendant, so our protagonist "suddenly" attains consciousness of his body and is awake to his inexplicable new world. The
protagonist's awakening is sudden, leaving him in a state of "mere consciousness of existence, without thought—a condition which lasted
long" (683). Another sudden jolt ushers him into the next phase:
"Then, very suddenly, *thought*, and shuddering terror, and earnest en-
deavor to comprehend my true state" (683). This begins the heroic effort of the soul to achieve fuller self-consciousness. On feeling the terror of thought and memory, he feels "a strong desire to lapse into
insensibility," rallies, and makes a "successful effort to move." This effort pays off in a fuller "memory of the trial, of the judges, of the sable
draperies, of the sentence, of the sickness, of the swoon" (684). Thus
begins a process of remembrance and connection of the disconnected
and undifferentiated images in his mind. As Jung notes, "knowing is
based . . . upon the perceived connection between psychic contents"
(*Structure and Dynamics*, 390). From here on out, the protagonist struggles against the terrors and inexplicabilities of his situation, against the
frustrations of persistent disorientation and unconsciousness, as a developing child striving to mature into a fully conscious self.

Lying on his back like an infant, not yet having opened his eyes, the
protagonist continues to struggle between a desire for oblivion and consciousness, dreading what horrors full consciousness may bring: "I
longed, yet dared not, to employ my vision" (684). When he does open
his eyes, his worst fears are confirmed: he finds himself in total darkness
that oppresses and stifles him. Such darkness perfectly reflects his fearful state of uncertainty and disorientation. As Burke notes of this sublime state, "in utter darkness, it is impossible to know in what degree of
safety we stand" (143). Utter darkness embodies the very idea of inex-

plicability and the protagonist's complete disorientation. Despite his fears, he makes an effort "to exercise my reason" by deducing his "real condition" (684). However, his fears in this early developmental stage overcome his reason. As he imagines the fearful possibilities of what the judges have in mind for him—particularly burial alive in a tomb—he once more relapses "into insensibility" (684).

Upon waking, the fear that caused him to swoon now enables him to "at once [start] to my feet" and "thrust my arms wildly above and around me in all directions" (684–85). Establishing that he has not been buried alive, he finds that his knife has been taken from him, which he hoped to use to mark a spot that would enable him to measure the dimensions of the cell. But the "disorder of [his] fancy" makes solving his dilemma seem "at first insuperable" (685). His reason soon triumphs, however, as he rips part of his serge wrapper as a marker. In striving to calculate and measure the size of the cell, he marks a new phase in his rational development. He measures the room by leaning against the wall as he walks, just as young children do when they learn to walk. Like an infant, he stumbles and falls as his energy is depleted, again falling unconscious (686). His inability to stay awake and focused on his task is typical of Jung's description of early stages of development: "at this [early] level, consciousness is merely sporadic." He further describes this discontinuous phase as "islands of consciousness which are like single lamps of lighted objects in the far-flung darkness" (*Structure and Dynamics*, 390). Our narrator's consciousness is continually interrupted by his swoons, leaving him "too much exhausted to reflect" upon waking (686).

Following his swoon, he continues his circuit of the cell with renewed strength from the food left for him. Although he eventually finds the rag marker he left, his continuing disorientation, together with occasional irregular angles, makes the shape of the cell inexplicable to him. Undaunted, he next resolves to cross the cell, taking his first steps without leaning against the wall. This again marks his developmental progress as he, like a growing child, attempts haltingly to walk by himself. In the process, he again stumbles, this time becoming entangled in his serge wrapper and falling "violently on my face" (686). He wakes to find that he has narrowly escaped falling into the infamous pit he had heard of, in which "*sudden* extinction of life formed no part of [its] most horrible plan." The pit represents the potential for regression into oblivion, a return to the womb that his growing consciousness and sense of self is struggling against. The shock and terror of discovering what his judges have in store for him causes a momentary regression as he gropes his way back to the security of the wall and the "paradise of unconscious childhood" in another swoon (*Structure and Dynamics*, 389). Jung states that such regression is part of a "mother fixation," in which toddlers (the phase at which we now find our maturing protagonist) experience a recurrent need to return to the security of oblivion and oneness with the mother (*Structure and Dynamics*, 23). Such regressions are part of the development process. To use Jung's own example of the psychic transference of energies, water that is dammed up at one point eventually finds another channel by which to move forward (*Structure and Dynamics*, 38).[8]

After this fourth period of unconsciousness, he awakes, partakes of drugged food and drink, and again enters a "sleep like that of death" (688). After an indeterminate period, he wakes and comes to a turning point, learning the answers to some of his questions. A new "sulphurous luster" now enables our protagonist to see the actual size and shape of his cell, revealing to him that he'd had a "confusion of mind" that caused him to miscalculate its size (688). Despite what he soon realizes about the real size of the room and the wall pictures, he is still sufficiently lethargic and disoriented not to notice until much later that he is now bound to a "framework of wood" (688). This development is typical of the inexplicable journey tale—just as some things are cleared up, new mysteries and predicaments appear.

He becomes aware that there is a pendulum, suspended from a figure of father time that is very slowly descending, suggesting the ultimate fear he's had in his new life. Before swooning again, he describes himself looking up "as a child," smiling at the "glittering death" (691). This struggle between thought and oblivion is the turning point in his development. He describes himself as an "imbecile—an idiot" who can hardly think clearly, alternately laughing and howling in his battle against the irresistible and relentless power of the pendulum (692). His struggle between instinct and consciousness comes to a head at this period of extremity, reflecting Jung's theory that we can thank problems for the growth of consciousness (*Structure and Dynamics*, 388): "For the first time during many hours—or perhaps days—I *thought*" (693).

His thought is his developmental breakthrough into knowing and consciousness. As Jung notes, "One can actually see the conscious mind coming into existence through the gradual unification of fragments" (*Development of Personality*, 52). In this case the fragments are the rats, the pungent meat, and the leather strap binding him to the wooden frame. While the overall experience has been and continues to be inexplicable, his psyche is no longer the mere plaything of instinct (*Development of Personality*, 54). His struggle to reach this high point of consciousness, enabling him to marshal his resourcefulness to use the rats to free him (despite the mere temporality of his freedom) embodies what Jung calls the nobility of the development process.

> Because the consciousness is constantly threatened with being overwhelmed and swallowed up by the archetypal images, that process is often understood as an heroic venture, as an heroic battle with the dragon, the unconscious, for the sake of achieving fully realized selfhood.[9]

These archetypes, such as father time (inevitable death), the demon figures on the wall (all-powerful, threatening others), and the pit (regression into infant oblivion) are all embodiments of the sublime, the overwhelming elemental forces of vastness, obscurity, and power that inspire horror and wonder simultaneously. Such are the nightmarish problems and fears of developing ego consciousness.

Among the ironies of the tale is that despite his heroic efforts to achieve consciousness and selfhood, he finds himself again helpless before the invisible manipulations of the judges as the rooms heat up and the moving walls force him toward the center of the cell to an inevitable doom down the pit: "*Free!*—and in the grasp of the Inquisition!" (695). As he is about to be forced down the pit, the protagonist regresses one final time to childhood, finding "vent in one loud, long, and final scream of despair" (697). But he is rescued at the last instant by General LaSalle. Thus in this parable of maturation Poe embodies the debilitating incoherence he later describes in the fragmention/diffusion stage of the *Eureka* journey. While this very elemental tale of terror is an archetypal retelling of the horrors of childhood, it is also the horrors of all that is potentially inexplicable, overwhelming, and terrifying in life. Without any background concerning the protagonist, readers view him as an everyman facing elementary tensions and fears between the death wish and the need to survive. Along with "Descent into a Maelstrom," this is Poe's homage to human will in the face of impossible odds. As the protagonist notes, even when curiosity and calculation are completely irrelevant and useless, he can't help trying to account for his errors in measuring his cell. As suggested in the "quotation" from Glanvill in "Ligeia," man's will reflects his divine spark and the mystery of his greatness:

> And the will therein lieth, which dieth not. Who knoweth, the mysteries of the will, with its vigor? For God is but a great will pervading all things by nature of its intentness. Man doth not yield himself to the angels, nor unto death utterly, save only through the weakness of his feeble will. ("Ligeia," 310)

Thus the mysteries of man's will is what makes him—this Eurekan fragment of God—ultimately inexplicable himself.

Like "The Pit and the Pendulum," *North by Northwest* has a protagonist, Roger Thornhill, who is violently wrenched from his ordinary life. He faces and overcomes a series of inexplicable and life-threatening challenges from hostile (often invisible) forces and gradually develops greater enlightenment in the process.[10] Both protagonists face threats from overhead and later of falling to their death. Finally, like "Pit's" narrator, Thornhill must be rescued at the last second from imminently plummeting to his death. Perhaps Hitchcock's most visually insistent reflection of "The Pit and the Pendulum" in *North by Northwest* is the crop duster's likeness to the descent of the pendulum. In both cases, the dangerous purpose of the overhead threat is at first inexplicable. Both threats are manipulated by unseen forces and come down suspensefully in a back-and-forth motion. Both involve sharp blades, though there is the added terror in *North by Northwest* of bullets from the crop duster's mounted machine guns. The differences are also striking, even opposite in terms of the setting and circumstances. Instead of being gothically confined in a dark, dank cell surrounded by rats and tied to a wooden framework, Thornhill is unrestrained and moves freely in an expansive, sunny, barren Midwestern landscape. It is this distinctive setting that both links and separates the two narratives. On the one hand, the barren dirt fields reflect the nothingness at the heart of Thornhill's char-acter—comically represented by the meaningless middle initial O. These fields, with a small stand of corn appropriately dying in one area of the landscape, seems an infertile wasteland. Thornhill, who has two failed marriages and no children to date, is himself infertile. His ad agency work is specifically about creating impressions out of nothing but words and pictures. The Midwestern wasteland also suggests his middle-age predicament, linking the film to "Pit" in terms of the motif of passing time. Just as the pendulum is suspended from a figure of fa-ther time, representing the link between time and inevitable death, so Thornhill is being assaulted by his years as he is running (literally, in this case) out of time in his current phase of development and is in the midst of what Jung calls the midlife crisis. If he is to succeed in gaining a successful personal life, he must hurry.[11]

Both "Pit" and *North by Northwest* are narratives about an inexplica-ble journey. But while "Pit" loosely allegorizes the maturation process from birth, *North by Northwest* traces a similar process in which a middle-aged man confronts diminished circumstances and attempts to apply proven means for coping with the world. Jung theorizes the midlife cri-sis as the inevitable result of facing declining powers. He compares the life cycle at this phase to the sun, which rose with youthful hope and expanding possibilities until reaching its zenith: "At the stroke of noon the descent begins. And the descent means the reversal of all the ideals and values that were cherished in the morning. The sun falls into con-tradiction with itself. It is as though it should draw in its rays instead of emitting them" (*Structure and Dynamics*, 397).

One of the problems arising during this inevitable period of change comes when there is "a more or less patent clinging to the childhood level of consciousness, a resistance to the fateful forces in and around us which would involve us in the world" (*Structure and Dynamics*, 392). A peculiar spin on this pattern comes when the parent(s) of the person is still alive: "It is as if the period of youth were being unduly drawn out" (*Structure and Dynamics*, 396). Finally, as one shrinks from "grow-ing up," entering the "afternoon years" with the false assumption that previous ideals and truths will continue to serve us well (*Structure and Dynamics*, 399), a man carrying over "childish egoism into adult life must pay for this mistake with social failure" (*Structure and Dynamics*,

400). This pattern of "neurotic disruption" helps delineate the situation and behavior of Thornhill, who finds himself trying to cope with a set of unique circumstances and predicaments. He finds his world as upside down as Poe's protagonist. His old confidence and confidence game—both of which have served him to this point—prove increasingly inadequate to plumb the inexplicability facing him now. As in "Pit," these circumstances are associated with the loss of the mother.

The opening montage of the film, as well as much of the rest of film, perfectly embodies the fragmented chaos of the universe that Poe describes in *Eureka*. The credits are projected onto the radically slanted lines of a building, suggesting a world that is out of square. The crowds of people and cars are going in every conceivable direction, each person seemingly oblivious to the rest. It's a chaotic world in which taxi rides are stolen, buses missed, nonexistent men pursued, identities mistaken, and perfect strangers try to kill you. Additionally, coincidences and surprising twists are par for the course—your mother jokes with your enemies, a crop duster tries to kill you, the police track you down, government intelligence agents sacrifice you to their spy plot, the woman who loves you sends you to your death, and the man who should make sense of all this proves to be nonexistent. In this alien world Roger Thornhill tries to make sense of his experiences. Somewhat like Alice, he finds himself in a dark wonderland where common sense, predictability, and fair play can't be found. Like the hero of "The Pit and the Pendulum," Thornhill faces a series of inexplicable tests in a world he barely recognizes that refuses to recognize him.

As the film begins, there are signs that the once supremely confident and competent Thornhill is slipping, that he is beginning his slow descent—in addition to his gray hair and obvious forty or fifty-something age. For example, he forgetfully dictates to his secretary last year's birthday message to his mother, is putting on some weight, and forgets that his secretary won't be able to contact his mother because she is at the apartment "of one of her cronies." Consequently he is nervous and distracted when he meets his clients at the Plaza Hotel's Oak Bar. A comment by one of his clients, "you may be slow in starting but there's nobody faster coming down the home stretch," suggests an alcohol problem that may be catching up with him after thousands of such schmooze sessions. Along these lines, his mother often checks his breath. In addition, other communication glitches—the hotel boy he greets coming out of the elevator is "not talkin'" with his wife and one of the clients he meets is hard of hearing—hint that Thornhill's world is changing. Such communication problems become a major sign of his midlife crisis, since Madison Avenue advertising, of course, depends on effective communication. Hence, when Thornhill is mistaken by Vandamm's men for George Kaplan, it is merely the supreme mistake that culminates all that has gone before, the sign that Thornhill's old life is over and his inexplicable journey into a potentially new identity has begun in earnest.

Perhaps the most important signifier that Thornhill is due for a midlife crisis concerns his relationship with his mother. As Jung pointed out, while parents are nearby, the period of youth artificially stretches over into middle age. Like the protagonist in "Pit," Thornhill has resisted leaving the security of his mother to progress to another level. Thornhill, who has not been able to establish a lasting, mature marriage relationship, perpetually depends on his mother as the major "significant other" in his life. As often pointed out, their comfortable intimacy suggests a counterfeit marriage—they attend the theater and dine together, and banter playfully back and forth. Like other aspects of his life, his relationship with his mother begins to unravel early in the film. Beyond his inability to get a message to her, she does not believe his story of being kidnapped and is openly scornful during his hearing. When they visit Lester Townsend's home in Glen Cove, she sides with the disbelieving police ("Roger, pay the two dollars"). Finally, in the elevator she joins the men who are trying to kill Thornhill by laughing with them. Even in their final phone conversation in the train depot, she apparently jokes that he might want to "jump off a moving plane." Her inability to take him seriously, undoubtedly based on his perpetually adolescent behavior, virtually severs their tie, metaphorically forcing Thornhill to leave the nest and depend on his own resources. His "good-bye Mother" on the phone is, for the purposes of the film, a final farewell.

The fact that he involves his mother so fully in his predicament early on points to his continuing childhood dependence on a parent (he calls her from the police station and depends on her getting them into Kaplan's room). His kidnapping, which forces him from the security of his prolonged childhood, confuses and disorders him. His disbelieving and sarcastic response to his abductors and their mistaking him for someone else is an important sign of his clinging to youthful ways of coping: "Don't tell me where we're going. Surprise me." Even his obvious amusement at his own displays of "wit" shows his immaturity. Realizing that the car door is locked, for example, he looks at one of the men and says with mocking irony, "Locked?" On receiving no response to his question, "Who's Townsend?" he sarcastically pretends he received an answer: "Really? Interesting." Not unlike a rebellious teen in the clutches of authority, he can't make himself take the situation seriously and continually baits his antagonists. His forced drunkenness humorously emphasizes his childish behavior, including staggering, singing, repeatedly lying down to sleep, and nonsensical talk at the police station: "They tried to kill me." While we don't know what might have happened had he behaved differently, his youthful egoism, in Jung's words, certainly leads to "social failure" with his antagonists as well as the police.

As Thornhill develops into a more graceful middle age, key moments following the United Nations murder echo the struggle of Poe's protagonist into consciousness. Following his apocalyptic fragmentation and diffusion, Thornhill's defining moments come (1) on the train, (2) at Prairie Stop, (3) in Chicago, and (4) in Rapid City. His movement through these spaces becomes a learning curve in which he, like the protagonist in "The Pit in the Pendulum," learns to cope with his inexplicable predicament and adapts to the often astonishing circumstances in which he finds himself.

Getting on the train to follow Kaplan to Chicago is, in a sense, the culmination of Thornhill's measuring his cell in the dark by stumbling along the walls. Like "Pit's" protagonist, who struggles against unconsciousness, Thornhill struggles with becoming fully aware that his case of mistaken identity is a deadly serious issue. Like his counterpart in the dungeon who miscalculates the size of the room, Thornhill clumsily executes his early attempts to measure his situation. By recklessly pretending to be Kaplan and entering his hotel room, he builds the case against himself and reinforces the mistake Vandamm's men make when they catch him there. He compounds his error when he goes to the United Nations and calls himself Kaplan. But there is more going on than mere recklessness. Metaphorically, he is trying out a new identity as a spy, one that could lead to independence from his mother. Jung notes that as the middle-aged person's powers begin to wane, he enters the age of "discretion" (*Structure and Dynamics*, 396), which "enforces the contraction of life" (*Structure and Dynamics*, 399). Interestingly, spies take risks but do so with care—mostly keeping in the shadows and doing their work off the radar screen. This is analogous to the graceful middle age that Thornhill must seek. At this point, however, his spying attempts have been anything but discreet—in fact, they have been clumsy. As Vandamm observes at the auction: "You disappoint me, sir. . . . What possessed you to come blundering in here like this?" Thornhill's experience on the train becomes a turning point in his development because he begins to fall in love. This becomes for him a higher consciousness he has not before experienced.

In the inexplicable predicament in which he finds himself, in an alien wonderland, love, like everything else, violates conventions of normality and is riddled with indecipherable ironies. For one thing, Eve Kendall does not behave according to the usual rules—cinematic or otherwise: she lies to protect a stranger, she is a sophisticated working woman in an era when such women are rare, and she is sexually aggressive ("It's a nice face"). A bitter irony here is that while Thornhill cringes from her honesty, she is not really honest; she works simultaneously for Vandamm and American intelligence. The supposed love she offers Thornhill is being closely monitored by Vandamm, who ultimately has Eve send Thornhill to his death at Prairie Stop. But in the world of this film, ironies abound infinitely, since Eve actually falls in love with Thornhill, the camera uncovering the cool facade she wears. The transitional superimposition of Eve's face over the Prairie Stop wasteland is a powerful visual correlative of the situation in which love finds itself in the film. Love is associated with the sterility and emptiness of fallow fields. The shot also associates love with death even more directly, the embodiment of the self-destructive perverseness permeating Poe's Eurekan universe—love that both attracts and repulses.

A further irony comes when Eve hugs Thornhill in relief that he is alive when he returns from his meeting with the crop duster. He, of course, misinterprets her gesture as another bit of acting—just as Vandamm interprets all of Thornhill's actions as theater ("What little drama are we in for today?"). But Thornhill himself gets into the act, pretending to continue being interested ("Now what can a man do with his clothes off for twenty minutes?"). Like the scene in *Notorious* in which Devlin kisses Alicia to make Alex think they are necking rather than spying, Thornhill pretends to himself he is merely acting, when actually he continues to be attracted to Eve. But Thornhill takes it another step further, immediately revealing an opposite but equal reaction with barely controlled sarcasm: "How does a girl like you get to be a girl like you?" His bitterness makes it clear that he is in love with Eve in spite of himself. These confusing emotions become the foundation of Thornhill's development beyond the shallow, middle-aged youth he has become. While the other inexplicabilities of mistaken identity and the double chase are merely intellectual problems to be solved, Eve becomes the complicating factor that ultimately leads to consciousness of a new self. Like the realization by the protagonist in "Pit," Thornhill realizes he faces moral rather than merely physical torture.

Facing the crop duster forces him to put his life on the line as he stands in front of a moving truck. Crucially, this is more than mere resourcefulness or desperation; it is an act of mature bravery and calculated risk, not unlike letting yourself be covered by rats in the faint hope that they might free you from the pendulum. In both cases, a major psychic breakthrough is required to halt the onset of time and death. He shows further daring, if a little awkwardly, in confronting Vandamm at the auction with nothing more in mind than to seek further information. While Vandamm interprets this as "blundering," Thornhill is actually improvising out of a combination of mature calculation (a surprise attack to catch the enemy off guard) and youthful brashness. However, when faced with the inevitable threat the spies improvise, he creates a "little drama" by putting on an "antic disposition" in order to bring the police and check Vandamm's power move. What looks like the imp of the perverse, is actually being "mad north—northwest" (*Hamlet*, 2.2). Thornhill has finally learned that in the world of this film, reason is less effective than a bit of irrational drama. His Madison Avenue expertise at manipulating audiences through false impressions serves him well. In short, in Chicago Thornhill learns to adapt to the new rules of the game, and he is made daringly savvy by the bitterness of romantic disillusion.

But the world is not out of surprises yet. Taken by the police from the auction, to whom he reveals himself as the "United Nations killer," Thornhill is again surprised by the inexplicable behavior of the police in driving him to the airport to meet the "professor." Learning from the professor that Eve works for American intelligence, Thornhill has a major consciousness-raising shock of recognition. At this moment, as when the protagonist in "The Pit and the Pendulum" wakes to explanatory light in his cell, Thornhill begins to see much of what has been inexplicable externally and internally. He now sees that his responses to Eve have been blindly hostile. This is evident when the plane that taxis from screen left lights half of his face only. This initial awareness of his dark side provides him with a measure of objectivity, "exposing his developing consciousness to the collective unconsciousness."[12] He is no longer totally alone, nor isolated with the mother, but sees himself in the broader scheme of things. This provides the basis of revamping the self which, according to Jung, is both "subjective and objective, individual and collective." Thornhill's maturing depends crucially, therefore, on this moment of seeing his own shadow self from the world's perspective.

The mock shooting in Rapid City, staged to convince Vandamm of Eve's faithfulness, becomes an important symbolic death for the old Thornhill. Significantly, Eve is the one who "murders" him, since she has been the major catalyst in Thornhill's development. We next see Thornhill facing Eve from a stand of trees; they have their first honest exchange, and Thornhill, his first mature love. Infatuation couldn't survive the facts that are revealed about Eve's present and past life. Eve has brought out in him a sustained tenderness and flexibility hitherto unknown. But Thornhill must face one last test in his development toward individualization.

Unwillingly sacrificing Eve to Vandamm, Thornhill is next seen in a hospital room where he is symbolically stripped to a towel and his socks. His donning the temporary change of clothes the professor brings him again signals Thornhill's change of identity. No longer sporting the ambiguous gray suit and tie that reflected his foggy morality and developmental phase between black and white, youth and graceful middle age, he now sports a white shirt and black trousers, suggesting the greater clarity and coherence of his motives. No longer preoccupied with protecting himself or attending the Winter Garden Theatre, he now journeys to the nadir of Vandamm's lair to rescue Eve. Interestingly, at this point the story itself takes on added literary coherence, becoming a displaced fairy tale of the hero rescuing the fair maid. Such black-and-white tales about good versus evil apply to the film now that the "hero" has come to himself. Previous to this he has been like Odysseus under a spell that precludes action and purpose.[13]

In essence, the Eurekan diffusion phase, represented by the developmental part of the film, ends with Thornhill and Eve falling in love. In the inexplicable phase of *Eureka*, there are no archetypes to provide deep, psychic coherence and meaning to existence. Neither Thornhill nor Eve is now alone or wandering aimlessly in a world without values or meaning. However, when Thornhill rescues Eve, his process of maturing and establishing a relationship is physically complete. In essence, the inexplicable journey has become the romance journey into the nadir of the alien world. For Thornhill, Eve becomes an anima figure, a "magnetic field" that attracts and holds fast everything pertaining to itself (*Individuation*, 123). Through her he can make sense of the world and of himself; by tapping into the collective unconsciousness, Eve brings him into contact with everyone else. The film's use of archetypal narrative patterns brings story and character into harmony, the film becoming the collective unconsciousness in which the characters exist.

In morphing into a more traditional romance, the film also departs from Poe's tale, which leaves the protagonist in his inexplicable state until his rescue. However, the heroes in both "Pit" and *North by Northwest* find themselves on the brink of a mortal fall just before being rescued deus ex machina. Climbing down the monument with Eve, Thornhill is no longer nothing. Just as the monument evokes the great figures in American history, Thornhill commits to something bigger than himself. He confesses to Eve that previous wives complained that he lived "too dull a life." The film concludes showing the transition to his mature self, now married and committed, love providing meaning and passion in a world otherwise inexplicable. In terms of the *Eureka* myth, the characters are returning to take their part in the whole—to find personal and collective wholeness. The final shot's comic sexual pun itself expresses the archetype of love and fertility in which both now participate, no longer alone chasing counterfeit phantoms.

"Ulalume" and *Spellbound*

In "Ulalume" and *Spellbound*, the *Eureka* fragmentation and diffusion phase manifests itself somewhat differently than it did as described above. In these stories the emphasis is on an inexplicable journey within the mind itself. The protagonists create disorienting dreamworlds in which they attempt to make sense of things on the basis of false assumptions. Poe and Hitchcock both practice an art of unconscious expressionism. In Jungian terms, the goal of these journeys is individuation or the integration of conscious and unconscious minds (*Structure and Dynamics*, 223). However, in that process the tendency is to mistake unconsciousness for consciousness, dream for reality. These dreamworlds reflect the states of our protagonists' unconsciousness (*Structure and Dynamics*, 263). This condition is manifested by Poe and Hitchcock in the art of expressionist display of the unconscious. Protagonists in "Ulalume" and *Spellbound* repress conscious reality, making the dream projections that they inhabit nightmarish "reaction-dreams" (*Structure and Dynamics*, 260). Such dreams are defined by Jung as trauma induced. An "autonomous part of the psyche," a "fragment" reflecting the *Eureka* fragmentation trauma itself becomes a major psychic disturbance that determines the dream (*Structure and Dynamics*, 261). Consequently, as in *North by Northwest* and "The Pit and the Pendulum," the protagonists find themselves in alien territory where reason is useless, relationships are difficult to make, and personal psychic progress becomes an obscure and painful journey. The difference here is that they create their own fragmented, diffused inner universe and need help to recover psychic unity. The situations represented in "Ulalume" and *Spellbound* are remarkably similar in terms of their deep structure, though they seem unrelated on the surface. Both narratives present protagonists who have suffered a traumatic event that leads to amnesia. In "Ulalume," the trauma is the death of the nameless narrator's lover, Ulalume. In *Spellbound*, John Ballantine witnesses the murder of psychiatrist Dr. Edwards, which reawakens the childhood guilt complex he had since accidentally causing the death of his brother. Hence one dreamworld is dominated by sorrow, the other by guilt. In both narratives the protagonists journey with a female adviser figure with whom they contend as they seek to understand the irrational phenomena surrounding them. Finally, both protagonists are emotionally volatile and both narratives focus the search for meaning around a central dream image ("imago")—the narrator's vision of the "sinfully scintillant" Astarte, the specter planet that leads him to Ulalume's "legended tomb," and Ballantine's surrealistic dream. These images both allow and prevent individuation, ultimately leading to narrative and psychic climax.

"Ulalume's" grieving narrator inhabits a dark and melancholy dreamworld that becomes increasingly, incoherently inexplicable. Here "the skies they were ashen and sober;/ the leaves they were crisped and sere—/ . . .It was night in the lonesome October."[14] This landscape is a precise projection of the narrator's own unconscious mind, which Poe establishes in the penultimate stanza: "Then my heart it grew ashen and sober/ As the leaves that were crisped and sere."[15] Even the irrational repetitions in the lines reflect the obsessive and sorrowful mind of the narrator:

> It was hard by the dim lake of Auber,
> In the misty mid region of Weir—
> It was down by the dank tarn of Auber,
> In the ghoul-haunted woodland of Weir.

These lines indicate the state of his mind as well as its psychic location midway between reality and dream. Here reality is "misty" and obscure, and as the day has faded into night and the year into October, he faces his dark night of the soul as he slips deeper into incomprehensibility. That his journey is "ghoul-haunted" suggests stock elements of the gothic nightmare, indicating the artificiality of his subjective inner landscape. That "Ulalume's" protagonist is in a dreamworld is reinforced by the poem's many echoes of Poe's "Dream-Land." As in "Ulalume," whose world is dark and lonely, with titanic woods, metaphorical volcanic rivers groaning down the "climes of the Pole," and a "dank tarn," "Dream-Land" similarly describes a dark "route obscure and lonely" near "lone waters" characterized by sublimely "titanic" woods, including a fire and ice contrast with "skies of fire" and "snows of the lolling lily." Like "Ulalume" as well, the earlier poem includes a cast of melancholy ghouls and the hope of finding the peace of reuniting with "Sheeted Memories of the Past."

One further indication that the protagonist in "Ulalume" is dreaming is that he has doubled himself in Psyche ("my Soul"), a winged female with whom he shares memories and thoughts. As they journey together they go deeper into the dream state. "These were days when my heart was volcanic/ As the scoriac rivers that roll / . . . . In the realms of the Boreal Pole." The contrast of fire and ice punctuates the trauma within his torn soul—his fiery grief that he tries to quench with the cold relief of forgetfulness. If he began the poem in the "mid region" between dream and reality, the surrealistic paradoxes of polar volcanoes indicates that his journey has taken him deeper into his dream. They take a further step when the narrator notes that they were unaware of where they were and the inexplicable significance of this night "of all nights in the year!" Although they share memories and thoughts, they are "treacherous and sere," his repressed grief signified by the dank tarn and the "ghoul-haunted woodland." Thus, as in an unstable dream, comprehension is severely limited and inexplicably powerful emotions dominate the irrational and obscure imagery of the setting.

His psychomachia assumes more specific shape in the form of a vision he sees—further indicating his full descent into dream. Significant here is the narrator's interpretive projection of his own sad feelings upon the "miraculous crescent": "She rolls through a region of sighs—/ She revels in a region of sighs." Like the protagonist in "Pit," our narrator is seeking oblivion from a mournful reality in an anima figure: "She is warmer than Dian," come to "point us . . . to the Lethean peace of the skies." Jung describes the anima as the projected image of "indescribable fulfillment" in a "real life with its laborious adaptations and manifold disappointments."[16] Dream itself, therefore, is a projection of the anima, a return to the womb—not the alternative lover the crescent is sometimes interpreted as. The "love in her luminous eyes" more properly suggests the eternal and idyllic anima than a new alternative lover to Ulalume.[17] Everything to this point in the poem has been about seeking oblivion rather than new delights. This narrator is one for whom grief has extinguished hope of conscious happiness. This "perilous image of Woman" becomes "the much needed compensation for the risks, struggles, sacrifices that all end in disappointment; she is the solace for all the bitterness of life" (*Portable Jung*, 150). Thus, moving deeper into the dream state toward total oblivion, the narrator projects in his dream, through the image of "Astarte's bediamonded crescent" the path to "Dream-Land's" "route obscure and lonely" where he can be "Out of Space—out of Time."

However, his other side, Psyche, feels "mistrust" for the star, which she senses is a prelude to renewed sorrow. Through Psyche, the narrator's soul tries to rouse himself from seeking oblivion. Her exhortation to "let us not linger!/ Ah, fly!—let us fly!" is a healthy call of his inner force to wake up and leave this treacherous dream journey. His ambiguous reply, "This is nothing but dreaming," can refer to either her fears or his dream. If it is his dream, he argues that in oblivion all sorrow is extinguished and light overcomes darkness. His trust in the crescent, its "tremulous" and "crystalline" light, is its promise of oblivion. He wishes to "bathe in" that light, submerging himself totally. Despite pacifying Psyche's "scruples and gloom," however, they inevitably arrive where all roads lead the grief-stricken: "Ulalume—Ulalume!—/ 'Tis the vault of thy lost Ulalume!" As he snaps out of his dream of unity, the trauma of fragmented loneliness again asserts itself like waking breathlessly from a nightmare. He sees his surroundings clearly now as the mournful path by which he has put Ulalume to rest. His realization is a return from the hope of reuniting with the anima, the longing for both Ulalume and the collective oneness of the original universal particle. He finds himself back in mourning: the ultimate unsolvable predicament.

Grief stricken, he again begins repressing reality, specifically his own part in manufacturing the anima vision, asking whether it may have been "drawn up" by the "pitiful, the merciful ghouls" to "bar up our way" to the tomb. Now calling the "miraculous crescent" a "sinfully scintillant planet/ From the Hell of the planetary souls," he captures the dark side of Jung's anima, the illusory and seductive (*Portable Jung*, 153). The narrator obscurely realizes that he has been duped by his own projection of the anima in the form of seductive and illusory oblivion. As in "Pit," he has been seduced by oblivion to escape reality. However, unlike "Pit's" protagonist, this narrator hasn't the will to overcome dream's illusions. In the end, he is as much in the dark as ever; his world is made perpetually inexplicable by his own refusal to face reality, the poem appropriately ending on a question. His question of the anima's origins suggests that he is beginning the journey into repression, denying that all around him is an expression of his own mind. His grief has made his world perpetually inexplicable because it is intolerable.

As in "Ulalume," the protagonist in *Spellbound*, John Ballantine, has created a fantasy world of his own to cope with his guilt for accidentally killing his brother. Like the narrator in "Ulalume," Ballantine at first finds comfort in his amnesia, assuming Dr. Edwards's identity in order to deny his death. Ballantine's amnesia-induced dream soon becomes a nightmare of feeling that he killed Dr. Edwards. Thus he cuts himself off from reality and launches himself onto an inexplicable journey: "I have no memory. It's like looking into a mirror and seeing nothing but the mirror." Ballantine's predicament, as in "Ulalume," is trauma induced, analogous to the galactic insanity of the fragmentation of the original universal particle. As Dr. Brulov notes in frustration, "You've got amnesia, and you've got a guilt complex, and you don't know if you're coming or going from someplace."

Again, as in "Ulalume," Ballantine is helped through his dream by a female counterpart, Constance Peterson, who becomes his psychiatrist and lover. In several ways the film suggests that she, like Psyche, functions as his soul. Her name suggests that she is a "constant" within him, the desire to reunite with an original psychic oneness. By Eurekan analogy, he is primarily the repulsive principle to her attractive. She is the energy to hope for resolution and eventual individuation. The attraction between them is evident when they first meet in the cafeteria through the camera's tight focus on their eyes: Constance's eyes are highlighted against the dark background. Then Constance does something that irritates Ballantine (in this case, she draws a pool with her fork on the tablecloth), indicating the balancing presence of a repulsive principle. This struggle between attraction and repulsion is typified when Ballantine on the train erupts at Constance for babbling like some "phoney King Solomon." Like the man-hating Mary Carmichael, Ballantine despises Constance's cold scientism with its "vulture eyes," as Poe describes it in "Sonnet—To Science."

This discussion has a double focus. First, Ballantine's internal struggle between attraction and repulsion is represented by his dreamworld during his several fugues. Often during these fugues Hitchcock's subjective camera shows the world as the surrealistic dream Ballantine sees. As in "Ulalume," such expressionism of the unconscious represents the inexplicable nature of postapocalyptic "reality" reflected in the mind. In terms of Hitchcock's attempts to get inside Ballantine's mind, Thomas Leitch quips that "for the only time in his career he [Hitchcock] takes the MacGuffin as seriously as his characters do" (*Find the Director*, 130). While Hitchcock's serious treatment of psychoanalysis is often denounced, it leads to some memorable shots. As with the attacks in *The Birds*, there is some sense of character development with these periodic disturbances; in this case, as in "Ulalume," they signal a deeper descent into dream. Second, I will highlight moments when the film shifts from Ballantine's point of view to that of Constance, suggesting the contrasting visions of Ballantine's conflicted mind. While Constance attempts to use scientific reasoning to reintegrate Ballantine's psyche, like the narrator of "Ulalume," Ballantine opts for irrational assumptions based on his guilty intuition that he killed Edwards. This strains their relationship and becomes the Eurekan "electricity" that prevents their uniting as a couple and his uniting as a single, rational self. Their natural variance is first evident on their picnic as she claims that love is based solely on psychic associations. On the other hand, he claims that people fall in love "for no reason at all." Constance comes to value intuition as a crucial element in her science as she and Ballantine proceed on their journey. Like Thornhill at the auction, she learns that in Ballantine's crazy world, where rules keep changing, intuition is as important as reason. Thus the narrative charts the two sides of the conflict coming together just as Ballantine reintegrates his mind.

Ballantine's inner struggle between attraction and repulsion begins as he and Constance fall in love in a dreamlike sequence utilizing close-ups of their eyes, slow motion, and a superimposed series of doors opening into pure light. After their long kiss, in one of several radical perspective shifts, Ballantine is suddenly disturbed by her robe. Again their attraction is balanced by his repulsive force as he reacts to her robe. His dreamworld is made apparent as Hitchcock's camera at first shows the lines of the robe as they actually appear. After a close-up of Ballantine's troubled gaze, the lines on the robe transform into how he sees them, as very dark tracks on a white field. Since such a transformation did not occur previously, when he reacted to the fork lines, we must assume that he is becoming more deeply immersed in his dream state, triggered by his love for Constance, which threatens his false identity as Edwards. She has "entered" his dream, so to speak, and threatens to see what's beneath it. Throughout their relationship, he hides from her powerful gaze, an interesting reversal of the usual Hollywood pattern of the male gaze.

Ballantine's next fugue state occurs almost immediately in Garms's operating room, lit in surrealistic extremes of lights and darks. The combination of panic induced by Constance's love and the linking of his and Garms's guilt complexes, causes Ballantine to feel claustrophobic. He pulls down his surgical mask and raves about opening the doors and turning on the lights. The link between Ballantine and Garms comes in part from Constance's earlier diagnosis of Garms. In this scene Hitchcock reveals Ballantine's interior world aurally as he rambles incoherently about the darkness, causing Garms to run amok. At this height of paranoia, all around him seem to be persecuting him ("You can't keep people in cells!"). Uncharacteristically relying on the verbal rather than the visual, Hitchcock lets Ballantine's ravings paint a nightmarish picture of obscure imagery—darkness, locked cells, "fools, babbling about guilt complexes!" Ballantine's only way out is to faint like the protagonist in "Pit," seeking oblivion's relief. Again, this fugue represents a further phase in Ballantine's journey, ending his counterfeit personality as Edwards. In the following scene between him and Constance her role in his journey is defined and she begins trying to penetrate his amnesia and guilt complex.

In subsequent fugues, with help from Constance, Ballantine reluctantly begins to find pieces of his psychic puzzle, though he resists waking from his dream because of his certainty that he killed Edwards. When they reach Dr. Brulov's home, the film allows us to fully enter his dreamworld. As we see the white oblivion of drinking the milk from Ballantine's perspective, the film has gone into a fugue itself, using random, extreme perspectives to suggest Ballantine's unbalanced mind. This includes viewing Brulov walking in and out of the kitchen from the point of view of the razor Ballantine holds. The dream sequence that Ballantine describes to Constance and Brulov next morning is the visual climax of the film, presenting a dreamland as fanciful as that in "Ulalume." The dream he relates perfectly reflects Ballantine's alienated mind, which is collection of fragments arranged in nonsensical, apparently meaningless patterns. "The more cock-eyed the better," Brulov notes. The images of staring eyes suggest Ballantine's alienation from other people, who are presented as faceless, unloving stares. Later the faceless proprietor echoes these images. The eyes also symbolize the guilt that psychoanalysis stirs up in him; the cutting of the eyes in half expresses his desire to be free of Constance's probing. The "kissing bug," which is Constance, suggests how he wants her love together with the oblivion of amnesia—a return to infantile oneness with the mother.

The fact that the dream takes place in a gambling house further suggests irrationality of chance and luck—further showing Ballantine's wish to escape the world of logic and guilt. But even in the dream he can't escape his guilt. Gambling also suggests adversarial relations with others. Ballantine's is a world of competition, not friendship, where others are turning out the lights, keeping people in cells, denying him the peaceful oblivion of his guilt complex. The middle sequence of the dream, wherein the bearded man falls as the proprietor is seen hiding behind a chimney and dropping a wheel, point to Ballantine's great secret—the falling death of his brother. These images of falling are further evoked in the last sequence as Ballantine runs down the hill while being chased by a pair of wings. While Brulov interprets the wings as Angel Constance, in fact they are Ballantine's guilt complex as harpy wings running from the guilt that plagues him.

The dream spurs his longest fugue, apparently from Rochester to Gabriel Valley, and a tentative ending of the inexplicable journey. Skiing down the mountain, reminiscent of running down the roof in his dream, Ballantine is shocked out of his trance and out of his amnesia as he remembers how he slid down the banister, pushing his brother lethally onto fence spikes. During this sequence, Hitchcock perfectly divides point of view between Ballantine and Constance, both responding to the situation independently while together. The painted backdrop of mountains, linking the scene further to his dream, surrealistically represent Ballantine's mind at the border between reality and dream. When Ballantine and Constance fall together in joyous embrace, the Eurekan fragments seem to collapse into one, the dream of diffusion apparently over. However, as in "Pit," *North by Northwest*, and "Ulalume," the protagonists are re-

duced to helplessness one last time after seemingly finding wholeness. Ballantine's arrest shocks him back into a psychic twilight,
leaving the true climax of the film for Constance to encounter. As
Ballantine's rights are read, the camera closes in on Constance. The
nightmare now becomes more fully hers, leading directly into the
surrealistic trial sequence of suggestive shadows. *She* has now entered
her own dreamland of guilt and anxiety. Murchison's slip becomes
another surrealistic moment when his words echo in her mind, this
time waking her from her nightmare. This enables her to become the
heroine, the LaSalle who pulls Ballantine out of the pit. At this
point, the film has one final significant point of view shift, as we see
the gun following Constance from Murchison's perspective. Again,
Hitchcock uses surrealism to express a troubled mind. We now see
Murchison's paranoid dreamworld replacing Ballantine's, and he becomes the "obvious suicide" once prophesied by Fleurot.

The film concludes with the couple together at last, free of dark
dreams, their love creating meaning and order in the universe. As in
North by Northwest, love becomes the key to light, overcoming the
repulsive electricity alienating people and reason. As in the later
film, the happy couple in *Spellbound* once again travel by train in a
happy reversal of the film's nightmare journey. Hitchcock's happy
endings brings the diffused fragments back together from their unnatural state of many to their natural state of unity. Unlike
"Ulalume," Ballantine does not return to a dream state. Hitchcock's
world, like Poe's, is a world of fragile emotions and delicate mental
balance where characters are capable of dizzying reversals and
changes. To audiences, Ballantine's deep-seated, lifelong guilt could
seem suspiciously healthy, based on ninety minutes of viewing his
psychic roller-coaster ride. Audiences would seem naive to leave expecting a fairy-tale ending. But this is in keeping with *Eureka*'s ambivalent hints that once reunited, the unified particle, still composed
of attractive and repulsive elements, may again fragment and diffuse.
This kind of ambiguous resolution hovers at the end of *Rebecca, Foreign Correspondent, Suspicion, Shadow of a Doubt, Saboteur,* and *Lifeboat*. None of these films leaves viewers feeling that all is now well.
This period in Hitchcock's work is remarkably unable to bring the
characters to complete wholeness and satisfaction.

Notes

1. Edmund Burke, *A Philosophical Enquiry into the Origin of Our Ideas of the Sublime and Beautiful* (London: Kegan Paul, 1958), 86. Originally published in 1757.

2. Burke's sublime has been used to examine "The Pit and the Pendulum," though not in relation to *Eureka*, in Kent Ljundquist, "Burke's Enquiry and the Aesthetics of the Pit and the Pendulum;" *Poe Studies*, December 1978, 26–29. He focuses on how the sublime helps define inexpressible ultimates in the tale.

3. Poe and Jung make a good pair themselves. Both like to speculate beyond the limits of empiricism, both explore marginal states of consciousness, and both conceive of the mind and its development in terms of opposites.

4. Marie Bonaparte, *The Life and Works of Edgar Allan Poe: A Psycho-Analytic Interpretation* (London: Imago, 1949), 575–93.

5. See James Lundquist, "The Moral of Averted Descent: The Failure of Sanity in 'The Pit and the Pendulum,'" *Poe Newsletter*, April 1969, 25–26. He also traces a pattern of stages, but in religious terms.

6. C. G. Jung, *The Development of Personality*, in *The Collected Works of C. G. Jung*, trans. R. F. C. Hull (New York: Pantheon, 1954), 17:53.

7. Jung tentatively agrees here with Poe's protagonist: "Maybe, too, there is no unconscious psychism which is not at the same time conscious" (*Structure and Dynamics of the Psyche*, in Bollingen Series 20, trans. R. F. C. Hull (New York: Pantheon, 1960), 188.

8. Jung states the case for the importance of the unconscious for the development of the conscious mind: "We can . . . say that the unconscious actually creates new contents. Everything that the human mind has ever created sprang from contents which, in the last analysis, existed once as unconscious seeds" (*Structure and Dynamics*, 364).

9. C. G. Jung, *Word and Image*, Bollingen Series 97:2, ed. Aniela Jaffé (Princeton: Princeton University Press, 1979), 107.

10. See Peter Wollen, "*North by Northwest*: A Morphological Analysis," in *Readings and Writings: Semiotic Counter-Strategies* (London: Verso Editions/NLB, 1982). Wollen uses a Propp's folktale study to chart Thornhill's progress in terms of magic.

11. Cary Grant, whose role in the film has often been commented on, proves to be the most perfect casting imaginable. Grant was nearing the end of his career and only made a few films after this. He faced the challenge of making himself once again a convincing romantic lead. His situation in some ways parallels Thornhill's, both having made a career out of charm and creating false impressions. Like Thornhill, Grant failed at marriage multiple times and never

had children (to that time). His immortal good looks finally deserted him and he retired a few years later, finally giving in to the inevitable.

12. See Josef Goldbrunner, *Individuation: A Study of the Depth Psychology of Carl Gustav Jung* (New York: Pantheon, 1956), 121–22.

13. Brill best covers this as part of the film in *The Hitchcock Romance*.

14. Thomas Ollive Mabbott, ed., *Collected Works of Edgar Allan Poe: Poems*, vol. 1 (Cambridge: Harvard University Press, 1969). "Ulalume" is found on pages 415–19 of this edition.

15. Glen A. Omans, Poe's 'Ulalume': Drama of the Solipsistic Self," in *Papers on Poe*, ed. Richard P. Veler (Springfield, Ohio: Chantry Music Press, 1972), 62–72, interprets the dreamland as the solipsistic imagination of the artist's annihilating reality.

16. See *The Portable Jung*, ed. Joseph Campbell (New York: Penguin, 1972), 150.

17. See James E. Mulqueen, "The Meaning of Poe's 'Ulalume,'" *American Transcendental Quarterly* 1 (1969): 27–30. Using *Eureka* to analyze the poem, he agrees that Astarte suggests an ideal rather than physical love.

~

CHAPTER FIVE

Doubles:
A Universe of Others

The motif of the doppelgänger, or double, is among the stock elements in the narrative repertoires of Poe and Hitchcock. A quick glance over their works suggests an obsessive insistence whose roots must go deeper than mere convention. This obsession is revealed in pairs of doubles in tales such as "The Fall of the House of Usher," "The Man of the Crowd," "Ligeia," "Morella," and "The Black Cat," and in films such as *Shadow of a Doubt, Notorious, Rope, Rear Window, To Catch a Thief, Vertigo,* and *North by Northwest* (to name a few). The example of the mutuality of their approach can be observed by comparing "The Raven" and *Shadow of a Doubt* (1943). This will lead into the more complex use Poe and Hitchcock make of the double motif.

The struggle between a pair of doubles is a common narrative approach to the doppelgänger theme in Poe and Hitchcock that interlinks several of their works. Just as the narrator of "The Black Cat" becomes embroiled in a psychological struggle that is embodied in the figure of the cat, so Father Logan and Otto become antagonists in *I Confess* (1952). In both, the repeated appearance of the dark one perpetually disturbs as one half of the doubles pair has the other psychologically trapped. *The Family Plot* (1976), like "William Wilson," uses the unique approach of documenting the dark character's concern over the perceived "persecution" of the good pair. As in "Wilson," *Family*

Plot leads to the inevitable life-and-death struggle in the end, though in this case good triumphs. "The Black Cat," another story told from the perspective of the bad character, like one of Hitchcock's more famous doubles films, *Shadow of a Doubt*, features a narrative curve in which the doubles pair gets along at first. But over time antagonism develops, and finally the weaker, positive character gets the upper hand after the negative character attempts to do away with the positive.

The clearest parallels of both plot and theme can be drawn, surprisingly perhaps, between "The Raven" and *Shadow of a Doubt*. In terms of plot, both begin with the suffering protagonist. In "Raven" the narrator is sorrowing over the loss of his lover, Lenore, seeking "surcease of sorrow" through his study of old books. In *Shadow*, young Charlie is suffering from boredom with the routines of small town family life. She feels she is in a "terrible rut" and awaits a "miracle" to save her and her family from bourgeois mediocrity. This initial moment is followed in both by the diverting and pleasant arrival of the double, which in both cases functions as an extension of the protagonist by literalizing latent qualities. The raven makes its appearance "with many a flirt and flutter," promising the narrator a delightful escape from his grieving: "this ebony bird beguiling my sad fancy into smiling." Like the raven, Uncle Charlie seems to arrive from the "Night's Plutonian shore" as his train fills the sky with foul black smoke. He too promises "surcease of sorrow" as Charlie's admiration for her double grows into hero worship. In addition, she is delighted by the telepathic bond she and Uncle Charlie have, a novelty parallel to the narrator's delight at the raven's ability to speak.

Initially, the raven's "nevermore" is taken by the narrator as merely a comic enigma: "much I marvelled this ungainly fowl to hear discourse so plainly." Similarly, early dark signs from Uncle Charlie, such as violently grabbing Charlie's wrists to get his newspaper back and embarrassing Joe at the bank, are taken by Charlie as evidence that "his ideas are not ordinary," as she tells the reporter/detectives. In both cases, the true darkness of the doubles becomes terrifyingly evident. As the narrator begins "linking fancy unto fancy" and becomes "engaged in guessing," he begins to ask questions about reuniting with Lenore that bring him to a fever pitch of anguished rage: "Get thee back into the tempest and the Night's Plutonian shore!/ Leave no black plume as a token of that lie thy soul hath spoken!" Correspondingly, young Charlie's curiosity is kindled by the accusations of Jack Graham, leading her to discover the black truth about Uncle Charlie. She too becomes furious: "I don't want you here. Go away or I'll kill you myself. See—that's the way I feel about you." At this point in both narratives it becomes a life-and-death struggle: for the poem's narrator it is a psychological and emotional battle to overcome his grief; for Charlie it's physical as her uncle booby-traps the backstairs and locks her in the carbon monoxide-filled garage. In the end, of course, Charlie overcomes her uncle during their final struggle on the train. But like "The Raven," where the narrator's soul will be lifted from the raven's shadow "nevermore," Charlie's innocence has been destroyed and she is left in the shadow of Uncle Charlie's dark vision of the world. As Jack affirms, "Sometimes it needs a lot of watching. Seems to go crazy now and then."

The two narratives are also linked thematically. In both the appearance of the double signals a major change in the lives of the protagonists. In the poem, the young narrator, who has just lost his lover, is facing his future with new soberness. The hopeful idealism of his springtime youth has become a "bleak December" note of the soul. Similarly, young Charlie is on the verge of growing up. Her complaints to Joe about boredom with the rhythms of family life suggest that she is ready to leave home, get married, and be independent—all of which lie just ahead by the end of the film. Uncle Charlie's funeral represents the burial of Charlie's innocent illusions about life. Thus both stories are situated on the cusp of dramatic changes for young people who must experience the hard realities of life.

In many of the doubles stories of Poe and Hitchcock the doubles proliferate as if the characters inhabited a house of mirrors.[1] In "Usher," for example, Roderick is doubled by his twin sister, his friend/narrator, and the house—including the "haunted palace" of the interpolated poem. In addition, the house is split in half, doubling itself, and its image is further reflected in the tarn. Late in the tale the events of "The Mad Tryst" are doubled by the apparent movements of Madeline Usher as she rises from the dead. Hitchcock's *Shadow of a Doubt* similarly multiplies the double motif. In addition to the two Charlies, Herb and Joe virtually mirror each other, as do the merry widows whom Uncle Charlie lumps together as "fat wheezing animals." The citizens of "ordinary little" Santa Rosa who lionize the visiting serial killer as a hero are all equally gullible and naive. Further, Hitchcock reflects this emphasis on doubling in such details as two detectives, two criminals sought, two Santa Rosa girls with glasses, and numberless other doublings of characters and situations (aptly summarized by Donald Spoto).[2] In this chapter I will explore the background of this tendency to multiply doubles in two stories that are doubles of each other: Poe's "William Wilson" and Hitchcock's *Strangers on a Train* (1951).

The concept of the double in Poe is easily inferred from *Eureka* as the essence of the postapocalyptic diffusion of the fragmented universe. Since the original primordial particle was one, unique and individual, designed by God to constitute the universe via fragmentation and diffusion, its fragments represent a virtual infinity of doubles. As Poe describes it, the fragments differ from one another in form, size, and distance. Further, each fragment is characterized simultaneously by the contradictory impulses of attraction and repulsion. The tendency to reunite is the attractive principle, while the repulsive force keeps the fragments separated until the diffusive "epoch" has spent itself in fulfillment of the "Divine purposes" (*Eureka*, 32). Given Poe's universal physical laws, the nearer two particles come to each other, the more "electricity" (his physical metaphor for the repulsive power) is generated.

> That no two bodies are absolutely alike, is a simple corollary from all that has been here said. Electricity, therefore, existing always, is *developed* whenever *any* bodies, but *manifested* only when bodies of appreciable difference, are brought into approximation. (*Eureka*, 34)

Therefore, very similar particles can pass near each other without generating appreciable electric friction. Only dissimilar particles particularly generate friction to a degree that generates considerable repulsive responses. Paradoxically, if we apply these laws to characters in the stories of Poe and Hitchcock, true doubles, as antagonistic halves of one self, become those "characters" between which there is the greatest dissimilarity, thus generating the most friction. In "William Wilson" and *Strangers on a Train* the closer the principal doubles come to each other the more friction, and therefore repulsive electricity, is generated, mounting toward an inevitable and fatal confrontation that ends their association.

What distinguishes these "twins" from each other to the degree that antagonism is particularly present? An obvious corollary to Poe's univer-

sal laws, in evidence in most of his tales, is that the diffused particles—
or characters—are distinguished by various ratios of positive (attractive)
and negative (repulsive) energy. Sometimes, inexplicably, those ratios
change within a character. The narrator of "The Black Cat," for example, seems to begin life loving his wife and animals but eventually, via
the imp of the perverse, becoming a monster of irrational and obsessive
hatred. In his case, two halves of his inner self, represented by the animal lover (attractive) and imp of the perverse (repulsive shadow self),
are in a war that the repulsive energy wins.[3] Poe's tales of doubles are
merely the two halves of one psychomachic personality split into two,
each struggling for dominance. Hence, when a character with a strong
positive charge comes into proximity with one having a strong negative
charge, friction naturally develops. In such cases, doubles become opposites that definitely don't attract. So by analogy, in Poe and Hitchcock,
character doubles are those who are generally opposite in orientation,
progressively becoming repulsed by the other's difference—or opposi-
tion. Jung's analysis of the mind helps describe in human terms, on a psychological level, how these opposite charges function within individuals.
The shadow can be equated with the repulsive force, the repressed negative impulses in the personal unconscious. It is the "inferior," lower side
of the self that lacks self-control and moral judgment; as a passive victim
of emotion, it behaves like a primitive. One moral problem associated
with the shadow is the difficulty in recognizing it. The conscious self
tends to project its shadow onto others.[4] This dynamic is evident in the
characters discussed in this chapter. For example, in "William Wilson"
the narrator fails to recognize that his double is part of him. Likewise, in
Strangers on a Train Guy does not see Bruno's role as agent of his darkest
desires to murder his wife ("I could strangle her!").[5] The ratio within the
individual of positive to negative forces correlates with the power of the
unconscious shadow self to escape the watchful eye of the conscious
mind. In "Wilson," the repulsive power is so strong that eventually it
squelches the voice of the positive altogether. Poe's is the story of the
unconscious shadow actually becoming the conscious mind. In *Strangers*,
based on the symmetry of shots and near equality of screen time for
Bruno and Guy, the struggle between the conscious and unconscious
selves is nearly an even matchup. Guy's own negative side gives Bruno
ascendant power through much of the film.

However, the relationship between "Wilson" and *Strangers* goes far beyond thematic or theoretical connections. In addition to both stories centering on a "pair of doubles," they crisscross each other in multiple areas. Like the two Wilsons, Guy and Bruno are look-alikes: same height, medium build, and dark, wavy hair. In both stories, one half of the double's pair has the other feeling trapped within an insoluble predicament. In both stories the doubles grow in mutual animosity during the course of the narrative, one harassing the other in the form of a guilty conscience (not recognized by the characters as such) through a series of encounters that eventually lead to a climactic life-and-death struggle. Like the doubles in the Poe tale, Guy and Bruno continually quarrel. As in the Poe story, in which Wilson Two seems only to exist in the narrator's mind and is therefore unrecognized by others, Guy and Bruno seemingly inhabit a world of their own that others don't recognize (until late in the film when Anne suspects Bruno of being Guy's agent: "How did you get him to do it?"). Just as Wilson daily feels challenged by his double, though no one else notices, Guy sees Bruno challenging him everywhere from the Jefferson Memorial to his tennis practice—though entirely unnoticed by others. Further, like the two Wilsons, Guy and Bruno have a climactic midnight encounter in a bedroom that leads to a surprising and horrifying revelation and becomes an important turning point in the tale.

An additional set of correspondences between "Wilson" and *Strangers* is found in the affinities between Wilson One and Bruno Anthony. While Wilson inherits the "family character" of being imaginative, excitable, self-willed, and full of "wild caprices," Bruno inherits his mental instability and wild imagination from his mother (she paints insane-looking abstract art). Like Wilson, Bruno is the victim of "ungovernable passions" and "evil propensities" ("William Wilson," 427). Just as Wilson One takes psychological control over the family at a young age, so, except for his father's trepidations, Bruno rules over his mother and has free rein to pursue his wild fancies. Bruno's authoritative but ineffectual father is echoed in Poe's tale by Dr. Bransby, the schoolmaster-pastor perceived as a harsh and hypocritical obstacle by Wilson. Both feel imprisoned by their circumstances: Wilson by the school and Bruno by his father, whom he determines to kill in order to free himself of his interference. Both Wilson and Bruno are cynosures who eventually become feared and detested because of their antisocial behavior. The major change by Hitchcock functions as an intertextual crisscross, reversing Poe's story focusing on an evil central character by having the more positively charged Guy as the central identifying figure.

Beyond these narrative affinities, there are the biographical ones—Poe and Hitchcock approaching the material with similar self-projections, in effect doubling themselves in their stories. Poe, for instance, gives Wilson his own birthdate, January 19, the same schoolmaster, Dr. Bransby, whom Poe had known, and a history of gambling and school expulsions similar to his own.[6] For his part, Hitchcock gives Bruno his own iconoclastic black humor in social situations. Just as Bruno says outrageous things that embarrassed or silenced his auditors ("I'm already developing my faculty for seeing millions of miles," he confides to a perplexed Senator Morton), Hitchcock liked to shock people. He once told Hume Cronyn during the filming of *Shadow of a Doubt* that when the day's work was done he went with others into the area vineyards to "squeeze the grapes through our hair" (*Dark Side of Genius*, 271). And just as Bruno discusses ways to commit murder by strangulation at the Mortons' party ("You don't mind if I borrow your neck, do you?"), Hitchcock had a famous penchant for demonstrating strangling techniques at parties (often photographically documented)—particularly how to strangle a woman with one hand.[7] Whether consciously or unconsciously, both Poe and Hitchcock project, or exorcize, their shadow selves on their characters, a process that marks the personal, obsessive investment in the concept of the double. Like the god of *Eureka*, Poe and Hitchcock endlessly create doubles of themselves in their works.

"William Wilson"

Reflecting the fact that the doubles tale partakes of the inexplicability of the fragmentation and diffusion stage of the *Eureka* cycle, Wilson One, the narrator of his own story, is perplexed by his experience. He longs for some sympathetic understanding from the reader that he is unable to bring to the details of his biography: "I would wish them to seek out for me, in the details I am about to give, some little oasis of fatality amid a wilderness of error" (427). He further seeks "relief" in recalling the "rambling details" of his childhood, hoping to find, though so far unable, some "adventitious" pattern in details that for him are "utterly trivial, and even ridiculous in themselves" (428). The center of the mysterious inexplicability of his experience seems to center in his extreme reaction to Dr. Bransby, the principal and pastor of the school. He views Bransby in the chapel with "wonder and perplexity," his "demurely benign" countenance one he knew to normally be a "sour visage"(428–29). In noting the presence of both piety and "Draconian" authority in Bransby, Wilson can only throw up his hands in despair: "Oh, gigantic paradox, too utterly monstrous for solution!" (429). Taking Wilson's cue for help in solving the meaning of his experience in the details of his life at the school, scholars have proposed numberless patterns to explain the meaning of Wilson's experience. Among the more convincing interpretations is that of Valentine C. Hubbs, who also finds the source of Wilson's dilemma in the example of Dr. Bransby:

> the paradoxical behavior of Dr. Bransby has revealed a flaw in his own character which will inexorably cause his downfall. He simply cannot comprehend how two contrary personalities can function harmoniously within one human being, or that it is the nature of an individual to incorporate into his complex personality many inconsistencies and ambiguities which, when considered separately, seem incompatible, even mutually exclusive. To Wilson One this inconsistent and paradoxical reality is monstrous, and he feels compelled to struggle against all opposites within his own developing personality.[8]

Hubb's insightful recognition of the importance of Bransby in Wilson's dilemma effectively answers Wilson's plea for a sympathetic, amoral explanation showing some psychological causality that would relieve him of some of the guilt his behavior suggests. I'm not convinced Poe is looking for liberal sympathy for his creation, though I too believe the key to explaining Wilson's behavior is found in Bransby.

To understand Bransby's significance we must go back to Wilson's childhood. He describes the traits of imagination, excitability, wild caprices, and "ungovernable passions" that he inherited from his family. Unable to control his "evil propensities," Wilson's parents give up. Wilson is "left to the guidance of my own will, and became, in all but name, the master of my own actions" (427). Because he never knew authority in his life, as he himself notes, his evil and ungovernable side, his shadow self, takes over. In essence, the unconscious shadow actually becomes his conscious self; his better instincts are submerged into his unconscious. Thus his personality becomes shaped around the fulfillment of his primitive instincts for "unqualified despotism" and "arbitrary dictation" (431). With such a background, Bransby and his school become a problem, forcing this shadow being to deal with authority and law for the first time. Bransby, with his "Draconion" rule, becomes a double of Wilson's own reign over fellow students. However, Bransby's pious side poses an inexplicable paradox for Wilson, introducing the complexity of religion and appearances to one's public self. The powerful result on Wilson's psyche seems to (1) fire Wilson's imagination (and contemporary memory) to project, or double, Bransby's paradox onto all he experiences and (2) cause his repressed unconscious and undeveloped better side to assert itself as an imaginary double that competes for dominance of the self. All that Wilson repressed, and apparently triumphed over, surrounds him through his "ungovernable" imagination. As Jung notes of the shadow, its projections are invisible to the one projecting it. What is projected here, however, is not the shadow but the paradox of unconscious goodness that can only reveal itself as inexplicable to a psychic primitive. Hence, Poe's tale itself, in creating a protagonist out of a man's shadow self, becomes a "gigantic paradox" of the endless battle between attractive and repulsive forces in a postapocalyptic psychic universe in diffusing fragments.

That Wilson sees Bransby in all, including himself, is first evident in his descriptions of the school. His likening his experience to "living in a dream" perfectly captures the irrational basis of his existence. If one's unconscious shadow self becomes consciousness itself, life inevitably becomes a perpetual dream state. Like Bransby, who is an insoluble paradox and irregular in his hypocrisy, the school grounds, particularly the main house, are so seen by Wilson. The "extensive enclosure was irregular," but the house itself was a "veritable . . . palace of enchantment." Its subdivisions (like the subdivided character of Bransby) are "incomprehensible" and its "lateral branches were innumerable—inconceivable." Gigantic paradox indeed: "during the five years of my residence here, I was never able to ascertain with precision, in what remote locality lay the little sleeping apartment assigned to myself and some eighteen or twenty other scholars" (429). The "deep awe" with which Wilson beholds the school's ponderous gate echoes the "wonder and perplexity" with which he views Bransby himself. Like the schoolmaster, whose flowing clerical robes are "so rigid and so vast," the grounds are "extensive" and the wall enclosing the schoolyard is "ponderous" (428). Like the iron rule of Bransby, the school seems "prisonlike" (428). The emphasis on vast size and power ("iron bolts" and "jagged iron spikes") is an expressionistic picture of the sublime difficulty faced by the young Wilson encountering the "gigantic paradox" of his own subdivided mind and imprisoned consciousness.

The most loaded of the projections from his "mental sorcery (431)," of course, is his double—Wilson Two (W2). Wilson One (W1) perceives his double in terms of resistance and competition, a rival to be bested and overcome (432). Just as he does for Bransby, he feels "wonder" for W2 because, though he doesn't acknowledge it, W2 represents his own hypocrisy within—a gigantic paradox. By resisting the better promptings and "affectionateness" of his double, W1 tries to deny his better, but largely unconscious, side (432). In his reverse dreamland state, as a conscious shadow self, W1 feels only friction and repulsion for all things positive that W2 represents. He receives W2's affectionate manner as insulting and vulgar (432). He also finds W2's attempts to counsel him a "disgusting air of patronage" and "officious interference" (435). As dissimilar fragments generate electricity, W1's irrational responses to his double are the sparks created by these very unlike sides of the mind coming into proximity. W1's confusing combination of responses to W2 reveal the double charge within:

> It is difficult, indeed, to define, or even to describe, my real feelings toward him. They formed a motley and heterogeneous admixture;—some petulant animosity, which was not yet hatred, some esteem, more respect, much fear, with a world of uneasy curiosity. (433)

In denying his double, W1 finds himself inexplicable. Everything about W2 is a mystery to W1: how he feels publicly to win the "palm of victory," but his double privately makes him "feel that it was he who had deserved it" (433); how W2 has the same name as W1 and contrives to dress like him (though no one else notices); how W2 has the same birthdate and leaves school on the same day as he; and later how he had no "heel of Achilles" that W1 could exploit in their rivalry (433). In short, in W1's dream state, W2 is a complete and inexplicable mystery: "But who and what was this Wilson?—and whence came he—and what were his purposes?" (439).

During his midnight venturing into W2's apartment the mystery of the double comes to a head. After seeing W2 sleeping and finding himself breathing heavily and his knees tottering, he feels "abjectless yet intolerable horror" (437). "What was there about [his lineaments] to confound me in this manner?" (437). Here he sees in W2 more clearly what he has been seeing all along—a perfect imitation of himself. But what he had assumed before was a mere sarcastic imitation, he now suspects is something else—a deeper mystery than he had before realized. Perhaps he suspects momentarily that W2 is the product of his own "mental sorcery," the embodiment of a part of himself he has suppressed. Just as he felt "wonder and perplexity" upon seeing the hypocrisy of Bransby, he feels "awestricken, and . . . a creeping shudder" (437). Perhaps he sees the suppressed goodness in himself, highlighting his own hypocrisy. Whatever he perceived when looking at W2 in bed, he flees in terror. As a student at Eton he works at repressing W2 until he can "effect a material change in the nature the feelings with which I remembered" the events at Bransby's school (438). He succeeds to the degree that he only conjures W2 on occasions of great wrongdoing as an imp of the perverse that causes him to confess his sins. In his attempt to fill his life with "soulless dissipation," he only creates an opposite and equal reaction from his suppressed unconscious.

What for him is the inexplicable mystery of his experience is W1's attempt to suppress all authority, originally suppressed when he triumphs over his parents' rule. In essence, he cannot interpret his own dream because his shadow self is an irrational primitive who can't reason self-consciously or introspectively. In finally overcoming his better rival self, he finds himself in "a cloud, dense, dismal, and limitless" (426). W1 is a near perfect embodiment of the alienation of a fragment in the diffusing universe. Inverted into largely negative energy, he is horrified by inexplicability and attraction above all things. His description of the school's main house almost seems a representation of the postapocalyptic universe, with its "incomprehensible subdivisions" and innumerable "lateral branches" that resist all attempts at rational comprehension: "our most exact ideas in regard to the whole mansion were not very far different from those with which we pondered upon infinity" (429). The various parts of the building seem to be "returning in upon themselves" (429), perfectly describing W1's experience of seeing himself in everything—Dr. Bransby, the house, and his double. The inexplicable dream of existence is Poe's theme, where we live in an infinity of doubles projected psychically as fragments from the original particle diffusive near infinitely.

Strangers on a Train

As Rohmer and Chabrol note in their pioneering study of Hitchcock, doubling is part of a parallel vision of reality in which "the *same* principle on which the foundation of the world is based is simultaneously the principle that can preside at its destruction." Recognizing the positive (creative) and negative (destructive) charges infusing everything in Hitchcock's world, they make the inevitable association with Poe: "We are literally caught up in the maelstrom of universal gravitation. Edgar Allan Poe, the author of *Eureka* has not been invoked in vain."[9] Part of Hitchcock's use of the double, important to understanding his vision in relation to Poe's, also goes back to the director's system of transfers and substitutions. Going beyond the usual view of this concept, Poe's example leads us to see a meta-level of transfers and substitutions outside of the character perspectives on the screen. *Strangers on a Train*, like so many other Hitchcock films, presents the viewer with a double or multiple experience that challenges a stable point of view. Of course, this complexity in experiencing Hitchcock's films accounts for much of their pleasure, and probably their persistent popularity. *Strangers* is doubled at least twice, providing three distinct perspectives by which to view it: (1) Guy's perspective, a nightmare journey of the innocent into Bruno's underworld, (2) Bruno's perspective, which compromises Guy's, and (3) the director/audience experience of doubled images and themes that are invisible to the characters themselves but complicate and discomfort the film. The viewer's position is thus slippery, constantly changeable, and trying. Such slipperiness involves the viewer as a meta-character, experiencing the images of the film in a way analogous to the psychological and emotional experience of Wilson 1 or Guy. In short, living through the film's various changeable dimensions is like dreaming. When the film is approached on all three levels, and particularly the often overlooked third, Poe's Eurekan infinity of doubles, fully realized in "William Wilson," can emerge.

Perhaps the most evident level on which the story operates for the casual viewer is Guy's ordeal. Popular audiences only viscerally sense the darker implications of Guy's relationship to Bruno as a dark double. However, Guy as the innocent victim-hero is rarely, if ever, discussed by interpreters, who mainly see him unsympathetically by focusing on the dark imagery that surrounds him. As a result of a random encounter with a psychopath, a basically innocent man is suspected by the police of murdering his unfaithful wife. While Guy becomes angry at one point, even expressing a desire to "strangle her," this is easily dismissed (especially in the 1950s) as the result of normal feelings of frustration any man would feel toward a scheming and adulterous wife. Also encouraging the audience to identify and sympathize with Guy are his embarrassed, indignant responses to Bruno on the train, reflecting the audience's distaste for Bruno's prying and impolite forwardness. Guy's boyish charm and good looks further elicit our assumptions of his basic innocence. The problem in this picture, of course, is that Guy is not telling what he knows about his wife's murder to the police. But again, the film shows Guy trapped by circumstantial evidence and an unparalleled, difficult, and morally ambiguous predicament that is not easily solved. Guy's not telling the police is presented more as a hesitation about what would be right and a desire to avoid involving Senator Morton's family in a scandal. As the film is set up, Guy seems to have little time to decide what to do after his alibi (the drunken math professor) vanishes. With his alibi in place, we assume he will tell the police everything he knows. Importantly, the audience is somewhat distracted from Guy's moral obligations by our sympathy for his situation. Following his wife's murder, he is caught up in a nightmare world of doubt, anxiety, and paranoia created by Bruno's sick imagination. As in "William Wilson," Guy is beset by his double everywhere: tennis matches, Washington landmarks such as the National Gallery and the Jefferson Memorial, and social gatherings. Furthermore, he is plagued by phone calls and notes encouraging him to kill Bruno's father, a plea that is an obvious crisscrossing of the idea of justice and fair play between the two men. Bruno seems ubiquitous, like a nightmare fixation that won't go away, making Guy a confused victim of a psychopathic killer. In Guy's defense, at no point is he seen to relish in his wife's murder, or in any way to seem callous to the implications of his situation. His is a situation of life and death one doesn't quickly or glibly confess. We agree with him that to go to the police would destroy his chances for happiness as well as elicit punishment for someone else's crime ("How did you get him to do it?"). Whether we buy this view of Guy or not, we are aware that the film continues to present him in this light as a possible interpretation of his character.

Shifting the balance a bit in Bruno's direction, lending some credence to his remarks and the implications of his presence in the film, reveals the darker side of Guy. On the one hand Bruno is simply insane, and his wild schemes, murder of Miriam, and irrational hostility toward Guy justify dismissing him.[10] On the other hand, viewing Guy through Bruno's eyes distorts the image of an innocent protagonist into a suspiciously ambitious overreacher who seems to have things to hide. In their initial conversation on the train Bruno, like a clever and aggressive reporter, uses insinuation and shocking frankness to open Guy up for us:

> Bruno: From A to G. I'll bet I can guess who A is.
> Guy: Yeah?
> Bruno: Ann Morton. You see sometimes I turn the sports page and I see the society section . . . and the pictures. She's very beautiful. Senator Morton's daughter.
> Guy: Your quite a reader, Mr. Anthony.
> Bruno: Yes I am. Ask me anything—I know the answers. Even news about people I don't know. Like who would like to marry whom when his wife gets her divorce.
> Guy: Perhaps you read too much.
> Bruno: Uh, when's the wedding?
> Guy: What?
> Bruno: The wedding—you and Ann Morton? It was in the papers.
> Guy: It shouldn't have been, unless they've legalized bigamy overnight.
> Bruno: Oh, I get it. A little chat with your wife about the divorce.
> Guy: Close enough.

Like one harassed by a reporter, Guy is put at a disadvantage by Bruno's "news about people I don't know." Such revelations make Guy feel uncomfortable and seem guilty: "I'd rather not discuss it." Bruno begins to put a story together: "Marrying the boss's daughter . . . that makes a nice shortcut to a career, doesn't it?" Guy angrily refutes Bruno's conclusions: "Marrying the senator's daughter has nothing to do with it. Can't a fellow look beyond a tennis net without being out for something?"

Bruno's interview brings out Guy's darker side, and links him with Bruno, becoming the key to their crisscrossing fate. By being able to extract information from Guy about his problems, Bruno is activated as Guy's double and agent. Bruno's quick read of Guy is not flattering, with its assumptions that Guy would go along with his crisscross murder scheme. From this perspective, Bruno is clearly Guy's dark double, the only one who can intuit Guy's deepest unstated desires and willing to act them out as agent. Since Guy first bumped Bruno's foot, establishing communication with his shadow self and later leaving his lighter behind as contractual symbol, Guy creates and activates Bruno. This makes Guy's later doubt, nervousness, and especially anger at seeing Bruno everywhere look more like justifiable guilt. Reinforcing this perspective on the film is the unstable, nightmarish carnival atmosphere associated with Bruno—which is not too far removed from the entertaining tennis world Guy's conscious self inhabits. Bruno becomes the moral creditor of Guy's murder, the demander of payment for services rendered. In addition to everything else, Guy thus reneges on the deal tacitly made with Bruno on the train. From these perspectives, Guy's embarrassed patronizing of Bruno is no longer mere boyish charm but a conscious denial of his darker feelings. Interestingly, seeing Guy through Bruno as shadow self, Bruno's wild caprices and big ideas become related to Guy's political ambitions and his desire to do something important.

The third important perspective allows discriminating audiences to see events in the film from another perspective, which is somewhat removed from that of the characters. While Guy is surrounded by doubles—he and Bruno, Babs and Miriam, Morton and Mr. Anthony—he sees none of it. From the audience perspective, partly that of Hitchcock's camera, the actors and the characters are cattle. They blindly deal with situations, without any knowledge of the deeper meaning. They are there to provide the audience with its own experience, which in the case of Hitchcock's films often does not center around audience identification with characters. Great directors, like great writers, seek to elevate an audience to their level, seeing irony, intertextual references, and image patterns that add layers of additional meaning. From this perspective, Hitchcock and his audience, more than Guy or Bruno, see an infinity of doubles. Hitchcock, doubling as Poe, puts us in Wilson One's position of seeing the world as a dream.

This dreamworld of doubles has been well documented, which includes crosscutting between Guy and Bruno to establish their true relation. The first example, of course, is tracing the pairs of legs and feet moving from opposite directions toward the inevitable encounter. Initially, the differences are emphasized: one emerges from the taxi in a dark tunnel wearing gaudy light and dark wingtips and striped slacks (such flamboyance is a Hitchcockian sign of evil—reminding us of Uncle Charlie in *Shadow of a Doubt*); the other emerges into the light wearing sensible plain oxfords and slacks. These initial visual impressions of Guy's superior nature are continually at odds with later camera doublings that continue to blur the initial impressions of difference between him and Bruno. On one level we are encouraged to view the film from Guy's perspective, but several visual disconnects darken our impressions. For example, on returning to his apartment, Guy is summoned by Bruno out of the shadows. Shown together as Guy expresses shock and confusion over Miriam's murder, at first they are on opposite sides of the barred gate. As the police approach Guy's apartment to question him, however, Guy and Bruno become one in the shadows behind the barred gate. The effect of this move is stunningly shifty: Guy becomes at once a trapped victim cut off from the establishment and a guilty double inextricably linked to Bruno. Later the cut from Bruno's to Guy's watches again links them. In fact, the major camera strategy of the film is to link them, having the effect of sharing guilt between them. Even the long crosscut sequence, in which Guy anxiously plays tennis and Bruno struggles to recover the dropped lighter, links them in equally self-interested purposes. We realize that the real struggle is the one each is involved in with the other. Several other visual commentaries on the narrative are recognized only by the audience—the stripes on Guy's tie and at the Forest Lawn tennis tournament, both linking him to the carnival world of Bruno. Even more effective are the columns in the National Gallery, where Bruno emerges, reminding us of the poles on the carousel later. Along these lines (pun intended), Bruno's standing at the circular Jefferson Memorial foreshadows the carousel encounter later, particularly as the camera circles the monument and gives the impression of carousel movement. This sequence also links for us the parallel journeys of Bruno's carnival murder and Guy's political ambitions.

Why Hitchcock goes to this trouble, beyond the unconscious emotional power such connections create in the viewers, has to do with Poe as the source of why he makes thriller/suspense films of this type. It also answers why audiences are so taken by Hitchcock. He tries to give himself, and the audience, the kind of experience he remembers from first reading Poe: the intense pleasure of feeling terror when you know you are safe. Intensifying the onscreen narrative with the meta-narrative details he's famous for, he lets the audience in on the film experience in a unique way. Unlike Poe's stories in which the characters directly experience terrifying predicaments, Hitchcock reserves a share of the terror for himself and his audience. While Guy doesn't see the doubles surrounding him, we do and our experience is distanced from his on one level and made closer on another.

In some ways the camera thus plays practical jokes on Guy. Even in the end, while on one level he is legally exonerated, the audience does not leave the theater with an entirely positive view of him. Many commentators have noted in this regard Guy's and Ann's guilty escape from a conversation with the minister who recognizes Guy. Maybe, like Bruno, he could see through Guy. But here is the Hitchcockian rub—neither does the audience feel entirely great about themselves, at least to the degree we identify with Guy. The effect of this film's strategy is to make the audience realize more clearly their own shadow self as seen from a perspective beyond the immediate—feeling more condemned by their own dark thoughts. Yet even this strategy is slippery, since audiences find pleasure in temporarily, and safely, examining their darker sides. This is how Hitchcock, in film after film, recreates his initial sublime sense of delight and terror in reading Poe.[11] Hitchcock becomes the god of *Eureka*, fragmenting and diffusing his characters into nightmares of disorientation and terror, while we sit back on the sublime level and enjoy the ride. Like the Professor in *North by Northwest*, he places his characters in predicaments, gleefully watches them struggle, then saves them at the last moment. Hitchcock projects and explores, as does Poe, his shadow self onto characters like Bruno and Guy, vicariously—and safely—living out dark fantasies that he wouldn't dare try in real life. Like Bruno delighting the two older women at the senator's party with his talk of murdering their husbands, Hitchcock enjoys shocking, embarrassing, and humiliating us—though all in fun. Thus Hitchcock is always the star of the show; the cameo is merely the tip of the iceberg. He is the principal experiencer of the dilemmas presented on-screen—and we look over his shoulder.

Notes

1. In both Poe and Hitchcock doubles can have seemingly supernatural connections. Poe, for example, often treats the theme of transferring a soul into another body. Morella seems to possess the body of her daughter; the second black cat, with its missing eye and gallows mark, seems to be the first cat as it takes its revenge. Other examples of supernatural links between souls include "Metzengerstein," "Ligeia," and "Fall of the House of Usher." In Hitchcock's *Shadow of a Doubt* there is a telepathic link between Charlie and her uncle. She is inspired to telegraph him to come even as he sends a telegram announcing his arrival. In addition, she claims to know when something is up with him, and they both seem to know each other very well although apparently they are not together much. In *Spellbound* Dr. Constance Peterson has a long argument with her mentor, Dr. Brulov, over the special or magical insight her love for John Ballantine gives her. Their link goes beyond the limits of the scientific rationalism that would dictate calling the police. Finally, in *The Wrong Man*, Manny's prayer, which seems to invoke his double in an impressive superimposition, functions like a magical link between the bass player and the thief.

2. See *The Art of Alfred Hitchcock: Fifty Years of his Motion Pictures*, 2d ed. (New York: Anchor, 1992), 120.

3. D. H. Lawrence made a statement concerning Poe that can also apply to Hitchcock: "He is absolutely concerned with the disintegration-processes of his own psyche. As we have said, the rhythm of American art-activity is dual. (1) A disintegrating and sloughing of the old consciousness. (2) The forming of a new consciousness underneath." See *Studies in Classic American Literature* (New York: Penguin, 1978), 70.

4. See *Portable Jung*, 145–47.

5. Donald Spoto notes that Bruno is Guy's "'shadow,' activating what Granger [Guy] wants, bringing out the dark underside of Granger's potentially murderous desires." *The Dark Side of Genius: The Life of Alfred Hitchcock* (New York: Ballantine, 1983), 328.

6. Kenneth Silverman points out this pattern of biographical projection in his tales, showing that Poe had his own past in mind during this time. "In the dialect sketch 'Why the Little Frenchman Wears His Hand in a Sling,' written at around this time [When "Wilson" was written, 1839–1840], he settled his narrator at '39 Southhampton Row, Russell Square,' the Allans' actual address in London." *Edgar A. Poe: Mournful and Never-ending Remembrance* (New York: Harper Perennial, 1991), 151. As J. Gerald Kennedy has stated, "The Raven" was written as a dress rehearsal for how he might respond to Virginia's impending death (statement made on *Biography* television documentary, *Edgar Allan Poe*). Poe, like his mourning student, obsessively and perversely wallows in his sorrows and losses. With "Ulalume" and "Annabel Lee," and a host of tales from "Eleonora" to "Ligeia," Poe, like other writers, translates and explores his life through the distance of art. Many of these characters are morbid, obsessed otherworldly dreamers whose hold on reality is tenuous. On the other side of the divided self, Poe created Auguste Dupin, the man of analysis and logical rationalism. A romanticized version of the Poe who hoaxed readers with his cryptographic challenges, Dupin used his superior genius to solve crimes the pedestrian police force were unable to cope with.

7. Hitchcock often divided himself into various characters on the screen. *North by Northwest*, a film that doubles several characters, including Vandamm/Professor and Thornhill/Kaplan, presents different aspects of Hitchcock—some of which may be wishful thinking. On the one hand he is the mother henpecked Thornhill who drinks too much and is fascinated with cool blondes. We know that Hitchcock was often infatuated with his actresses and would love to have been as appealing to them as they were to him. On the other he is the cool and unfeeling "Professor," who directs his intelligence agency like a Hitchcockian director, moving people around like cattle. Even Vandamm is forced to ask, "What little drama are we in for today?" The Hitchcock who can terrorize Tippi Hedren for a week while shooting the bird attack on her at the end of that film is also the Professor who can send Eve to bed with Vandamm and Thornhill to his death in the cornfield. L. B. Jeffries, the convalescing photographer of *Rear Window*, has often been noted as a stand-in for Hitchcock. With his telephoto lens carefully scrutinizing the people who live in his apartment's back courtyard, Jeff, like Hitchcock, creates little stories for each one as if planning a script. In fact, his brainstorming

sessions with Lisa and his policeman friend are not far from what he did daily in collaboratively preparing his film treatments.

Among Hitchcock's most famous, if embarrassingly confessional, explorations of himself through a character occurs in *Vertigo*. The scenes in which he carefully and obsessively transforms brunette Judy back into blonde Madeleine mirrors his own behavior in developing "properties" like Vera Miles and Tippi Hedren. In addition to dictating wardrobe, hair, and makeup, he told them who they could and couldn't see socially—or at least he tried. Scottie even showcased both sides of Hitchcock—the analytic detective/lawyer and the wandering, obsessive romantic. The film echoed what Hitchcock must have felt as his ultimately unsatisfiable longings. *Vertigo* even highlights his relationship with his mother through the character of Midge. Hitchcock, who was dominated as a young man by his mother, often depicted controlling mothers and weak sons (*Notorious*, *North by Northwest*, *Psycho*, and *The Birds*). His wife, Alma, seems to have become the indispensable mother figure in his life. Like Midge, she couldn't understand his equally indispensable romantic obsessions over Vera Miles, Joan Harrison, Tippi Hedren, and others. The Scottie figure of romantic and helpless longing also appears in Devlin from *Notorious* and Keane from *The Paradine Case*.

8. See "The Struggle of the Wills in Poe's 'William Wilson,'" *Studies in American Fiction*, Spring 1983, 73–74.

9. Rohmer and Chabrol, 112 n.

10. Thomas Leitch makes a good case for Bruno's own "childlike charm" in *Find the Director*, 155.

11. Another level of Hitchcockian touch makes *Strangers* his *High Anxiety* homage to Poe. Robert Walker as Bruno actually looks like Poe and, like him, the character has been kicked out of colleges and is a victim of the imp of the perverse. Like the narrator in "The Tell-Tale Heart," Bruno wants to kill his father and has wild ideas about seeing long distances (as the TTH character thinks he hears voices in hell). Two other elements relate to TTH: first, the nighttime sneaking into a father's room, and, second, Bab's story of an ax murderer (also related to "The Black Cat"). Bruno is like a conscience, as is Wilson 2, and the carousel image is reminiscent of the maelstrom in Poe's story.

A wiser Jeff (James Stewart) now practices his voyeurism closer to home in *Rear Window.*

On the set of *Frenzy*, Hitchcock plays with one of his favorite motifs, the double.

Hitchcock as the master of suspense and mystery.

In this climactic moment in *Rope*, Farley Granger (left) and John Dall (right) display both fear and a perverse desire to be caught.

A sample of Hitchcock's visual humor from *The 39 Steps.*

Hitchcock publicizing *The Birds* and perhaps his acknowledged debt to Edgar Allan Poe.

CHAPTER SIX

~

Imps of the Perverse:
The Diffusion from the Self

Poe defines the "imp of the perverse" primarily in two tales, "The Black
Cat" and "The Imp of the Perverse," but manifestations of it are pervasive throughout his work. Hitchcock too created self-destructive characters. In "The Tell-Tale Heart" and *Rope* (1948), Poe and Hitchcock
explore the two opposing dimensions of the imp: (1) the arbitrary per-
petration of a crime, followed by (2) the obsessive need to confess it.
Beyond the parallel modus operandi of their "protagonists," Poe and
Hitchcock create stories implicitly about the creation process itself,
which here involves the doubling of themselves as their imp-possessed
characters. Behind his narrator in "The Tell-Tale Heart," Poe's voice
speaks in a parallel, subtextual narrative exalting in the ingenious
structure of the tale. As in "The Philosophy of Composition" (or the
Dupin tales, for that matter), Poe confesses the greatness of his narrative conceptions. Just as in *Rope*, when Brandon creates his party to cel-
ebrate and possibly share the secret of his brilliant murder with an ad-
miring Rupert, Hitchcock murders traditional montage, hoping
audiences and critics will notice his brilliant innovations. Hence Poe
and Hitchcock themselves are under the sway of the imp of the perverse, committing artistic heresies (turning murder into high art) and
showing it off, an almost predictable strategy by two artists who loved

to explain ideas and methods. In essence, Hitchcock uses his camera in ways that reflect Poe's mad narrator. In creating characters influenced by the imp of the perverse and presenting their narratives through their eyes, both artists recreate the world in distorted, surrealistic ways that echo their themes.

The narrator of "The Black Cat" is the first of Poe's imp victims, blaming his "final and irrevocable overthrow" to "the spirit of PER-VERSENESS." He describes "perverseness" as "one of the primitive impulses of the human heart—one of the indivisible primary faculties, or sentiments, which gives direction to the character of Man." He goes on to define this sentiment as an "unfathomable longing of the soul to *vex itself*—to offer violence to its own nature—to do wrong for the wrong's sake only." The narrator is thus compelled to cruelly murder his cat by an irresistible desire to place his immortal soul "even beyond the reach of the infinite mercy of the Most Merciful and Most Terrible God."[1] This first explanation of the principle emphasizes the self-destructive aspects of the imp of the perverse as well as the arbitrariness of these impulses: he hung the cat "*because* I knew that it had loved me, and *because* I felt it had given me no reason of offence" (852).

In "The Imp of the Perverse," written two years later in 1845, Poe defines the further operations of the impulse that were only suggested in the earlier tale. While in "The Black Cat," the narrator reveals his murder by arousing the walled-up cat, his action isn't consciously self-destructive. In "Imp of the Perverse," however, the narrator's confession of murder is quite conscious: "And now my casual self-suggestion that I might possibly be fool enough to confess the murder . . . confronted me, as if the very ghost of him whom I had murdered—beckoned me on to death" (1225). The linkage between his impulse to confess and the ghost of the man he had murdered make an obsessive and irresistible conscience an important dimension of the imp of the perverse. In both tales, as well as in "The Tell-Tale Heart," the imp lures its victim to commit an evil act and then to confess it. The imp of the perverse itself seems perverse, an impulse divided against itself. While this structure suggests a guilty conscience working overtime, guilt is never explicitly an issue except in "The Black Cat," though it is ineffectual even there. Poe's narrator says of the imp that "we might, indeed, deem this perverseness a direct instigation of the Arch-fiend, were it not occasionally known to operate in furtherance of good" (1223). This two-part aspect of the imp, which involves an orderly—even moral—rectifying justice following criminal chaos, makes the imp a foreshadowing of the cyclic rhythms of *Eureka*.

As noted earlier, *Eureka*'s universe, like the psychology of Poe's characters, exhibits a dual nature. The "Divine Will" both willed "into being the primordial Particle" and forced "the original and therefore normally *One* into the abnormal condition of *Many*" (27–28). The diffused fragments of the original particle are torn between attractive and repulsive forces—compelled both to reunite with other fragments (gravity) and to stay separate (electricity). Why this is so even Poe can't explain. Like the imp of the perverse, which will not "admit of analysis" (2:1221), some aspects of God's will in the creation can only be understood as "an intuition altogether irresistible" (*Eureka*, 26).[2] Whatever the explanation for God's creating unity and then fragmenting it, "multiplicity" is the object of that fragmentation. Like the imp, which fragments the mind, causing its sane unity to fragment into an insane self-destructiveness, the universe has self-destructed into seeming madness. In fact, as Poe notes, "matter *exists* only as Attraction and Repulsion" (*Eureka*, 34). Hence the universe, in each of its numberless elements, is divided against itself with opposing impulses. And like the conscience function of the imp of the perverse, the fragmenting of the universe will finally reunite itself. But even after this winding-up scene, Poe hints at cyclical fragmenting and reuniting: "On the Universal agglomeration and dissolution, we can readily conceive that a new and perhaps totally different series of conditions may ensue; another creation and radiation, returning into itself; another action and reaction of the Divine Will" (133–34). "Action and reaction" capture the essence of the imp, causing a person to do one thing and then its opposite.

The characters in Poe and Hitchcock's imp texts are as divided and unpredictable as the Poe-esque universe they inhabit. Many of the similarities between "Tell-Tale Heart" and *Rope* center on their perverse central figures. In both stories the protagonists murder close acquaintances for perverse, eccentric reasons. In "Tell-Tale Heart" the narrator actually loves the old man he kills: "Object there was none. Passion there was none. I loved the old man. He had never wronged me. He had never given me insult" (792). The narrator's motive is inexplicable, and he arrives at it with the least certainty of anything he claims in the text:

> I think it was his eye! Yes, it was this! He had the eye of a vulture—pale blue eye, with a film over it. Whenever it fell upon me, my blood ran cold; and so by degrees—very gradually—I made up my mind to take the life of the old man, and thus rid myself of the eye forever. (792)

Brandon and Philip similarly kill without rational motive: "We've killed for the sake of danger and for the sake of killing." Theirs is an experimental murder based on theories of the superiority of an elite few that they learned in school. Brandon makes it clear following the murder that the success of their murder is the result of "the difference between us and the ordinary man." While Philip is visibly upset by what they've done, Brandon makes jokes about their victim: "Of course, he was a Harvard undergraduate. That might make it justifiable homicide." Poe's narrator too acts as if he were above moral law.

A further similarity between Poe's narrator in "The Tell-Tale Heart" and Brandon in *Rope* is their extreme, exultant pride in the technique of their crimes, as well as in the result. "But you should have seen *me*. You should have seen how wisely I proceeded—with what caution—with what foresight—with what dissimulation I went to work," Poe's narrator brags (792). Concerning the eighth night of his death watch of the old man, he glories that "never before that night had I *felt* the extent of my own powers—of my sagacity. I could scarcely contain my feelings of triumph" (792). Brandon takes to celebrating his brilliance with even more enthusiasm: "You know I'd never do anything unless I did it perfectly," he notes to Philip. Speaking of murder as an art, he punctuates his triumph: "Not a single, infinitesimal thing has gone wrong. It was perfect—an immaculate murder." Finally, about to toast his victim, Brandon goes over the top in his hubris: "Even champagne isn't equal to us or the occasion." Related to such exultation, the murderers in both stories share feelings of almost superhuman superiority. Poe's narrator, for example, explains his superior sense of hearing, that he could hear "all things in the heaven and in the earth. I heard many things in hell" (792). For his part, Brandon reminds Philip that "the lives of inferior beings are unimportant" and that "moral concepts of good and evil and right and wrong don't hold for the intellectually superior." He goes on to explain the new morality: "We agreed that there was only one crime either of us could commit, the crime of making a mistake."

Such visions of superiority lead to a sense of invulnerability that tempts both protagonists to live dangerously by placing their corpses in the main room of the house precariously under the noses of visitors. Here, the imp of the perverse indirectly prompts confession, at first disguised as a mere whimsical caprice. Poe's narrator brings the inspecting police officers into the room under which the corpse is buried, "while I myself, in the wild audacity of my perfect triumph, placed my own seat upon the very spot beneath which reposed the corpse of the victim" (796). Brandon startles Philip when he places the candelabra on the chest in which David resides to make "our work of art a masterpiece." Rather than keep people away from the chest, Brandon thinks "it would be nice to have supper in here." Adding to Philip's consternation, Brandon informs him that he intends to tempt fate further by inviting their former schoolmaster, Rupert Cadell, to the party. While Philip knows that Rupert is the one man who "is most likely to suspect" their crime, imp-inspired Brandon relishes the increased danger and the potential boost to his insatiable ego: "He's the one man who might appreciate this from our angle, the artistic one. That's what's exciting." As is evident from the above exchange, Hitchcock embodies both aspects of Poe's narrator, as well as the imp of the perverse, in Brandon and Philip. Brandon's is the will to commit murder haughtily while Philip's is the urge to break down and confess. In fact, Philip confesses in front of Rupert near the end of the film: "He knows!"

The physical and metaphorical mutilation of the corpse becomes another point of striking affinity between "The Tell-Tale Heart" and *Rope*, linking them in terms of revulsion and humor. Poe's narrator recounts how he "dismembered the corpse" carefully to create "no bloodspot whatever" (796). The literalness of his details strikes us as comic in just the way Stella's statements in *Rear Window* make us laugh about Thorwald's mutilation of his wife's body: "Hmm. Must have splattered a lot." Brandon and Philip, of course, don't physically mutilate David's corpse, though Brandon festively alludes to the chest as a "ceremonial altar" on which they can "heap the foods for [their] sacrificial feast," suggesting cannibalism. Such black humor is pervasive and further links Poe's and Hitchcock's tales of the imp of the perverse. In "Tell-Tale Heart" the humor is in the ironic insanity of a man desperately trying to convince his auditor that he is sane. He constantly repeats words ("very," "cautiously," "closed," "all in vain") and phrase structures ("you should have seen," "with what—," "—there was none"), and he incorrectly attempts to predict our reaction to his competence ("you would have laughed"). In *Rope*, the humor is both physical (Brandon's dropping the rope into a drawer with a flourish between swings of the kitchen door) and verbal. When Kenneth asks if he is attending a birthday party, Brandon comes back with a dark inside quip: "it's really almost the opposite." In addition, innocent characters in *Rope* voice dark ironies, such as when David's aunt predicts for Philip that "these hands will bring you great fame." Such black humor is itself perverse, paralleling the effect of Poe's mad narrator and Hitchcock's experimental camera, and creating an unsettling atmosphere for readers and audiences of the stories. When Brandon drops the rope between door swings, we smile as much at Hitchcock's cleverness as at Brandon's.

Although there are numerous minor affinities between Poe's "Tell-Tale Heart" and Hitchcock's *Rope*, the settings and parallel functions between the old man and Rupert seem most relevant. Both stories have minimal, claustrophobic settings that at first reflect the maniacally narrow focus of the characters. Second, these confined spaces represent the tension within the characters and increasingly suggest a sense of their psychological entrapment. This feeling of entrapment links the roles of the old man and Rupert. Like the old man, Rupert is "loved" by his former students, Brandon and Philip, though Rupert's insistent prying at the party soon unnerves Philip in a way analogous to the effect of the old man's vulture eye on Poe's narrator: "Whenever it fell upon me, my blood ran cold." Philip becomes increasingly unsettled by Rupert until sheer panic grips him at Rupert's phone request to return after the party in order to retrieve a cigarette case. With Philip's panic comes a desire to murder not only Rupert but also Brandon, his alter ego: "I'd just as soon kill you as kill him." Philip's breakdown echoes Poe's narrator's breakdown in the face of what he perceives as police knowledge of his crime: "I could bear those hypocritical smiles no longer! I felt that I must scream or die!" (797).

In addition to the many remarkable affinities between the stories, the imp of the perverse in both Poe and Hitchcock is as much a matter of technique and style as theme. In the rest of this chapter I will examine "The Tell-Tale Heart" and *Rope* in terms of their methods of subjective narration. Among Hitchcock's major lessons from Poe was the need to produce an "effect" on his audience. In *Rope*, Hitchcock finds ways to use the camera to recreate the mad voice and dreamscape vision of Poe's narrator, sharing with his audience—as did Poe—the terror and delight of their vicarious experience.

"The Tell-Tale Heart"

I basically agree with James W. Gargano's conclusion that "though [the narrator] does not understand his own character or actions, unconsciously [he] provides all the clues necessary to a comprehension of them."[3] Despite numerous contradictory interpretations of the tale, however, virtually all interpretations agree that (1) the narrator is mad and unreliable and (2) the narrator actually killed an old man because of his evil eye. Thus the narrator's unreliability is found in his assumptions of sanity and in some of the details of the tale. In keeping with this scenario, readers assume that he is telling his story to a priest or other counselor, probably just before he is hanged. I argue for the plausible but mostly overlooked possibility that his experience never happened at all. The implausibility of the narration's details suggests a dream narrative more than evidence of the narrator's obvious madness. This is an obvious deduction given the interchangeability of madness and dream states in Poe's work. Looking at "The Tell-Tale Heart" from this perspective reveals additional insight on issues such as the narrator's paranoid concern with his auditor's opinion of his sanity, the identity of his auditor, the mysterious significance of the evil eye, and several anomalous events in his narrative.

While I contend that the narrator's tale is his description of a dream, he himself seems unaware of the fact—a twist on the unreliability theme.[4] And since he is clearly mad, is it too much to assume that he inhabits an insane asylum and may be telling his dream tale to his doctor, a man who knows him to be insane? Thus the narrator's obsessive need to convince the doctor of his sanity becomes understandable.

John A. Dern notes that "the narrator . . . quite obviously, has been called 'mad' by his now silent interlocutor."[5] The narrator's relationship to the doctor is crucial to the dream's content. Freud recognized a resistance on the part of most patients to discuss painful memories. The adversarial relationship between doctor and patient is created as the doctor attempts to force revelations from the resistant patient: "psychoanalysis consists in an examination of these 'resistances' and the 'transferences' that accompany them, and of little else."[6] Here Freud is describing what in some form took place also in Poe's time. The transference Freud refers to concerns transferring feelings about others, particularly parental figures, onto the doctor, charging that relationship even further and potentially leading to greater resistance. From such a perspective, the old man, usually seen as a father figure, becomes an emblem of the prying doctor with his peering eye, trying to see into the soul of the paranoid patient. "Whenever it fell upon me, my blood ran cold" (792). Like the peering "vulture" eyes in Poe's "Sonnet—To Science," the doctor's powerful and analytical gaze in "The Tell-Tale Heart" upsets the narrator violently. Significantly, psychiatrists are usually perceived as parental figures. Further linking the old man and the narrator's doctor is the fact that the old man's eye is described as vulture-like, echoing the scientific connection to his terrifying gaze. His dream of killing the old man becomes his desire to kill his unyielding and tormenting doctor, thereby denying his insanity. Dreams and insanity were often linked by psychologists in Poe's day; these findings explain the behavior of the narrator with remarkable accuracy. Freud quotes Hohnbaum's 1830 findings that "delusional insanity often originates in an anxious or terrifying dream."[7] At times, according to de Sanctis, "significant dreams were followed by mild hysterical attacks" (*Interpretation of Dreams*, 120). Tissie notes that dreams can cause insanity: "conduct based on delusional premises and obsessive impulses were derived from dreams" (*Interpretation of Dreams*, 121).

What we learn of the narrator in "The Tell-Tale Heart" through his twisted tale certainly conforms to descriptions of madness extant in the first half of the nineteenth century. From this perspective, the narrator's attempt to separate nervousness and insanity is the crux of Poe's irony: "True!—nervous—very, very dreadfully nervous I had been and am; but why *will* you say that I am mad?" (792). In fact, the accepted psychological wisdom at the time was that "a disorder of the nerves may be, and frequently is, the immediate cause of insanity."[8] Furthermore, excess mental excitement, which is the distinguishing characteristic of the narrator, "is a very frequent predisposing cause of every form of nervous disease and insanity itself."[9] Radestock is quoted by Freud to the effect that the insane, in both waking and dreaming states, can overevaluate their "mental achievements" (*Interpretation of Dreams*, 123). Violent passions and intense emotions, evident in the narrator, were also thought to lead to insanity. "Who can tell . . . the murders . . . which violent passions have predisposed multitudes to suffer or to commit" (*Eleven Chapters*, 42–43). The narrator's violent passions are paralleled by his enthusiasm for his murderous plans: "enthusiasm and insanity bear such close affinity, that the shades are often too indistinct to define which is one and which is the other" (*Commentaries*, 41). Nineteenth-century science may also explain another of the narrator's symptoms—his imagined hearing of the old man's beating heart. Some interpreters have reasonably assumed he was hearing his own heartbeat. This would also correspond to early explanations of insanity, which blamed a "determination of blood to the head" as the cause of nervous or mental disease, as well as insanity itself (*Eleven Chapters*, 46). In Poe's day, mental patients were bled as commonly as other patients. Clearly the combination of nervous excitement and a surplus of blood might explain the narrator's hearing his own heartbeat.

Like Roderick Usher, the narrator's nervous condition in "The "Tell-Tale Heart" leads to an extreme sensitivity: "The disease had sharpened my senses—not destroyed—not dulled them. Above all was the sense of hearing acute" (792). As quoted from Schubert, "dreams are a liberation of the spirit from the power of external nature, a freeing of the soul from the bonds of the senses" (*Interpretation of Dreams*, 96). In addition to extreme sensitivity, such patients exhibited a need to "shrink within themselves, [to] live in a circle of their own construction" (*Eleven Chapters*, 43). Thus the tale's narrator lives in a world of his own that seems little adapted to outsiders. He unwittingly describes himself as a textbook case of what early-nineteenth-century scientists considered insane. As the narrator attempts to convince the doctor of his sanity, he tries to reassure the doctor, before whom he had likely been hysterical in the past, of his ability to be reasonable: "Hearken! And observe how healthily—how calmly I can tell you the whole story" (792). Here again he inadvertently admits to other symptoms of insanity: "excess excitement" (*Eleven Chapters*, 44) and "cunning."[10]

Beyond the contextual evidence placing the narrator in an asylum, whether his tale is a dream depends on the dreamlike details of the tale. E. Arthur Robinson refers to Poe's device of reduplication as a means of providing the tale with structural power.[11] Reduplication is also a major characteristic of dream narratives that typically double back on themselves and, in addition to reduplicating characters, obsess on certain images and situations. The narrator's subjectivity manifests itself in several forms. First is the narrator's uncertainty about his own motives for murdering the old man: "I think it was his eye! Yes, it was this" (792). Such uncertainty and vagueness about details are principal signs of dreams, though not necessarily a sign of insanity. The sparseness of setting and character detail is also typical of a dream. We learn nothing substantial about the old man, who is obviously a stand-in for someone or something else. Additionally, we learn no real details about where they live, why they live together, nor the nature of their relationship. As one critic perceptively pointed out, we don't even know for sure that the narrator is a male.[12] Additionally, certain impossibilities, or at least implausibilities, cast doubt on the reality of the narrator's experience, including the impossibly long night vigils at the old man's doorway: "It took me an hour to place my whole head within the opening so far that I could see him as he lay upon his bed" (445). "According to Lemoine (1855), the 'incoherence' of dream-images is the one essential characteristic of dreams" (*Interpretation of Dreams*, 87). Further, we didn't need Freud to tell us that "in dreams *anything* is possible" (*Interpretation of Dreams*, 95).

Incoherence also characterizes the identity of the old man. Gargano, along with others, notes that "because of their 'common' emotions, the murderer and the old man appear to be not only related, but identical" (380). Here the story gets as complicated as a dream, since the old man has a double identification—with the narrator and the doctor. However, identity confusion and personality splitting is typical of dreams. That the narrator and the old man share thoughts and feelings equates them as doubles—the part of the old man that the narrator "loved." The hated eye equates with the doctor, on whom no love is lost.[13] Again quoting Radestock, Freud notes that in dreams the personality may be split—when, for instance, the dreamer's own knowledge is divided between two persons and when, in the dream, the extraneous ego corrects the actual one. This is precisely on a par with the splitting of the personality that is familiar to us in hallucinatory paranoia. (*Interpretation of Dreams*, 123)

In addition to these dream implausibilities are the narrator's quick dismemberment and silent entombment of the body before the police arrive hours after they would have ordinarily been expected. The narrator describes how "the night waned" as he cleans up the crime scene. But as Poe describes in "Dream-land," dreams exist "Out of Space—out of Time" (l.8), causing the police investigation to invoke other dream-like characteristics of the tale. Robinson notes Poe's "psychological handling of time" (372), meaning the subjective way time is used to mirror the narrator's state of mind. This is shown as the narrator claims he is foaming and raving while the police chat pleasantly, not noticing his behavior. Here time is divided into parallel planes, a typical dream situation in which people fail to act or react according to ordinary standards. The lack of distinguishing details about the policemen, as with the old man, further characterizes the narrator's experience as a dream, in which people often appear as "shrouded forms" that the dreamer "dare not openly view."[14] Further, sitting and chatting pleasantly at four in the morning is clearly not standard police procedure.

Finally, the overall narrow scope of the tale, taking place at night, in the dark, and in bed, along with the prolonged silences, suggests a recognizable type of monochromatic and repetitious dream. In these dreams the mind seems to endlessly circle around a place or an idea, the setting monotonously static throughout. In "Dream-land," Poe links the dream and the dreamer in ways that are relevant here:

> But the traveller, travelling through it,
> May not—dare not openly view it;
> Never its mysteries are exposed
> To the weak human eye unclosed;
> So will its King, who hath forbid
> The uplifting of the fringed lid;
> And thus the sad Soul that here passes
> Beholds it but through darkened glasses. (ll.43–50)

In this description, conditions of the dream depend on the fact that the dreamer is asleep with eyes closed. Similarly, "The Tell-Tale Heart" parallels the reality of a sleeping dreamer who is in bed in a dark room at night. The dreamer's dream is subject to alteration according to "external sensory excitement": "The sensory stimuli that reach us during sleep may very well become sources of dreams" (*Interpretation of Dreams*, 56–57). What better opportunity to be aware of one's own groans and heartbeat than as displaced elements in a dream? The fact that he kills the old man in his bed, knocking him out of bed and pulling the mattress on top of him, might be credibly explained by the narrator's actually falling out of bed during this climactic moment of his dream. Freud refers to a dream by Hoffbauer, who "dreamt when he was a young man of falling down from a high wall, and when he woke up found that his bedstead had collapsed and that he had really fallen on to the floor" (*Interpretation of Dreams*, 58). Such sensory stimuli also explain the clicking of the death watches as sounds that enter the ear of the dreamer and become part of the dream narrative. Finally, the plain setting of the dream, with no distinguishing features, suggests the monotony of the asylum itself—rooms, beds, doors, and little else. As Hildebrandt notes, dreams "derive their material . . . from what has already found a place somewhere in the course of our waking thoughts—in other words from what we have already experienced either externally or internally" (*Interpretation of Dreams*, 44).

While Poe's tale successfully forestalls any conclusive reading by the vulture eyes of his critics ("observe how healthily [and impenetrably]. . . I can tell you the whole story" perhaps implies the voice of Poe himself), attention to the tale's allusions to his own dreamland mythology suggests reasonable answers to questions that have been perpetually raised. "The Tell-Tale Heart" is a madman's dream of, and ironically, defense of his imagined sanity.

Rope

If Hitchcock learned from Poe that it is fun to be scared when you know you are safe, he also learned that it is fun to be crazy when you know you are sane. From these insights came Hitchcock's obsession with micromanaging the audience experience of his films. In

Rope, the subtext is the creation process—specifically the audience's relationship with the director as it is sometimes humorously aligned with the issues in the story itself. In order to put his audience in, as well as through, his film, Hitchcock recreates Brandon's (and at times Philip's) mind with his experimental camera. Hitchcock's infamous long-take camera in *Rope* shares the same perverse tension between sanity and madness that is at the heart of the narration of "The Tell-Tale Heart." Hitchcock's original explanation for using the long takes, rather than standard editing, stems from his continuous fascination with drama. While he plays with theater imagery in *Murder!* (1930) and later in *Stage Fright* (1950), in *Rope*, he wanted to do a film in "actual time." "The only way to achieve that, I found, would be to handle the shooting in the same continuous action, with no break in the telling of a story that begins at seven-thirty and ends at nine-fifteen. And I got this crazy [read: perverse] idea to do it in a single shot."[15] While he admits, nearly twenty years later, that the idea was crazy, he still feels compelled to defend its merits:

> When I look back, I realize that it was quite nonsensical because I was breaking with my own theories on the importance of cutting and montage for the visual narration of a story. On the other hand, this film was, in a sense, precut. The mobility of the camera and the movement of the players closely followed my usual cutting practice. In other words, I maintained the rule of varying the size of the image in relation to its emotional importance within a given episode. (*Hitchcock*, 131)

Despite his reservations since filming *Rope*, it is clear from this statement that he maintains an enthusiasm for his technique that, in its muted way, echoes Poe's narrator's glee—as well as Brandon's pride—in his artful murder. Hitchcock repeatedly brings up problems—the noise in moving the furniture, the lighting, the actors doing long takes, the reloading of the camera, and so on. For all these problems he carefully creates his clever solutions. After detailing the meticulous preparation, the role of the dollyman in getting the camera in position, the moving of walls, and rolling of furniture, Hitchcock triumphs: "It was an amazing thing to see a shot taken" (134). Hitchcock glories in his cinematic sin! Hume Cronyn, who worked on the screenplay early on, noted

Hitchcock's enthusiasm: he "became so fascinated with the images that sometimes the direct line of the story got lost."[16] Yet Hitchcock's other side admits in the end that "no doubt about it; films must be cut" (134). Hitchcock knew his "pure cinema" of linking bits of film by cutting and editing was his native language, but he couldn't resist a technical challenge. Like Brandon, Hitchcock sometimes felt cinematic convention and old rules "don't hold for the intellectually superior."

Analogous to Poe's own split focus between reason and chaos in his tales, reflecting positive and negative forces within, Hitchcock's account of filming *Rope* demonstrates his tension between wanting to be an artist who experiments in radical ways and wanting to rely on tried-and-true methods. The fact that his radical side triumphed in this case is his imp of the perverse. However, Hitchcock's Rupert-like critics at the time paid little attention to his technique, though Howard Barnes noted that "one wishes that he had taken greater advantage of the motion picture form."[17] Many critics have continued to disparage it. Donald Spoto, for example, forcefully asserts the received wisdom of many that *Rope* is an "intriguing failure."[18] Raymond Durgnat traces the failure of Hitchcock's camera experiment to its inadequate recreation of traditional camera setups and montage.[19] Others have found method in the master's madness, seeing ways that the camera effectively reinforces the tension at the party over the missing David and the increasing feeling of entrapment and suspicion as the party winds down.[20] In the remainder of this chapter I will explore how the camera reflects Brandon's mind, behaving perversely and creating a dreamlike relationship between the audience and the film.

Like the ostentatious Brandon, Hitchcock's camera moves with a sense of visible superiority, swaggering about the film, calling attention to its own wit and brilliance. It is this visibility that made Hitchcock's experiment so controversial. Among the benefits of montage is its unobtrusiveness—an effectively cut sequence can move an audience as subtly as an effective film score. This is why Hitchcock, who prided himself on the subtlety of his touch, later disparaged the obvious camera work in *Rope*. Like Brandon, who knows the great secret of the party ("Let the fun begin"), the camera too knows its secrets and anticipates where characters will be and what will happen. Brandon manipulates relationships at the party ("I have a feeling that you have a

better chance with the girl than you think"), provides hints to his guilt
("I'm a creature of whim"), and plays ironic jokes on others like tying
Mr. Kentley's books with the rope that was used to murder his son.
Hitchcock similarly indulges in a joke at the buffet where Mrs. Atwa-
ter and Janet are discussing movies they've seen lately, one of which
stars Cary Grant and Ingrid Bergman and is called "just plain something," obviously *Notorious*, released two years earlier.

Hitchcock's camera, also like an omniscient god, anticipates movements of characters such as tracking back just in time to reveal Rupert's
arrival in the room and staying with the housekeeper as she prepares to
place the books back in the chest while everyone else is offscreen. Only
at the last minute do we realize that Brandon has also had his eye on
her, aligning him with Hitchcock's camera. Another such alignment
demonstrates parallel whimsy when Brandon plops the rope in the
drawer between swings of the kitchen door, making the maneuver simultaneously his and Hitchcock's humorous flourish.

Finally, Brandon and Hitchcock's camera have a similar secret sense of
black humor, for example, explaining to the housekeeper that they intend
to have the buffet in the living room on the chest. Brandon declares festively that the chest is a ceremonial altar on which "you can heap the
foods for our sacrificial feast." This sort of tone, meant for Philip and us,
is consistently echoed by the camera throughout the film. Hitchcock, like
Brandon, has his own in-jokes—such as the subtext of getting his revenge
on David O. Selznick for his aesthetic interference in making Hitchcock
reshoot a long-take sequence in *The Paradine Case* (1947). From this perspective, the beefy, wavy-haired David Kently becomes a stand-in for
David Selznick, while Brandon stands in for Hitchcock. With the insuf-
ferable and inferior David safely stowed away in a chest, Hitchcock
blithely makes an entire film out of long takes.[21] Another black joke is the
suggestion of sensual satisfaction exuded by Brandon and Philip as they
smoke and drink champagne immediately after the murder, discussing
how they felt "doing it." Their breathless speech and the tight two-shot
strongly reinforce this impression. Other veiled in-jokes by Hitchcock include the references to Poe, including the Poe-esque "Mistletoe Bow" tale
and "The Tell-Tale Heart" beating of the metronome that so unnerves
Philip. Like Brandon, who loves to shock others verbally, Hitchcock's
camera loves to shock audiences with imagery, as when Rupert is about

to come back to retrieve his lost cigarette case. The camera is focused on the door when suddenly we see Brandon's hand enter the screen with a gun, checking to make sure it's loaded. At just that moment, the doorbell rings. Like Brandon, Hitchcock's camera delights in both shocking and withholding, teasing and then changing directions. For example, as Rupert speculates on how to "get rid of David," the camera documents Rupert's description of David's coming in the door, walking inside, and sitting down. Without cuts, without inserted film, Hitchcock uses his camera to create a flashback in the audience's mind. We "see" that part of the film that had been kept back, even though it never actually appears on the screen.

The credits also suggest one thing and then give another, keeping us off balance. The opening credit sequence begins over a quiet, orderly upper-class neighborhood, showing a woman pushing a perambulator down the sidewalk, accompanied by soft introductory lines of strings and flute music, building steadily toward a lush arrangement of Poulenc's simple *Perpetual Motion*. This reassuring opener is quickly undercut by the blazing, ragged title *ROPE*, deliberately meant to contrast with the peaceful scene behind it. The lovely music maintains a sense of incongruity, the audience expecting music more like the tense thudding title music of *Saboteur* (1942). This pattern of contrasts continues following the credits when the camera presents a man escorting children safely across the street. The camera then pans up to a curtained window, a moment shattered suddenly by a scream that cuts us directly into the room where a man is being strangled by a rope. Like young Charlie in *Shadow of a Doubt* (1943), we are shown that appearances lie, that all is not as peaceful and serene as it looks. This has a powerful effect on the rest of *Rope*, turning the impressive New York skyline into Uncle Charlie's "sty," where we imagine the many other murders that may be taking place on this particular day. Foreshadowing the shocking shower murder in *Psycho* (1960), which colors every other scene in the film, *Rope*'s graphic strangulation, and the knowledge of the corpse's presence in the room throughout the party, taints every other image before us (who's drinking out of the glass from which David had his last drink?). The continually moving camera, which first brought us into the strangulation scene, has itself become a subliminally disturbing presence.

Finally, the camera's black humor, in-jokes, and shocking contrasts effectively making Brandon the film's narrator, immerse *Rope* in perverseness just like Poe's "Tell-Tale Heart." Sudden directional shifts are the very madness of the imp of the perverse, and like a dream in which the same situation is repeatedly played out, reality becomes skewed. Foreshadowing the alternately flashing red and green lights in *Vertigo* (1958) that begin Jeff's mad nightmare, the flashing red and green near the end of *Rope* affirm that this story, like "The Tell-Tale Heart," simulates a dream. The experimental camera, surrealistically gliding among the characters and defying the realistic setting, creates a new reality all its own, much like the peculiar landscape the narrator describes at the beginning of "Fall of the House of Usher." And like the narrator of "Tell-Tale Heart," Hitchcock's camera madly defies the rules of grammar and film etiquette as much as Poe's narrator subverts ordinary discourse. As Hitchcock himself said of pure cinema, "films must be cut." His violation of his own basic narrative logic perfectly embodies the subtle chaos on the screen.

Notes

1. "The Black Cat," in Thomas Ollive Mabbott, ed., *Edgar Allan Poe: Tales and Sketches*, vol. 2 (Urbana: University of Illinois Press, 1978), 852.

2. This idea of irresistibility of ideas and intuition, like the prompting of the imp, comes up throughout Poe's writing, including his essays. In "The Philosophy of Composition," for example, the impossibility of overlooking the word "nevermore" is an instance of Poe's manner of combining logical and intuitive thought.

3. See James W. Gargano, "The Theme of Time in 'The Tell-Tale Heart,'" *Studies in Short Fiction* 5 (1968): 379.

4. While it doesn't matter to the reader whether he knows he is dreaming, cases of patients believing in what hasn't actually happened are plentiful. From guilt complexes to hysterical symptoms, the imaginative creation of reality out of actual reality is common.

5. John A. Dern, "Poe's Public Speakers: Rhetorical Strategies in 'The Tell-Tale Heart' and 'The Cask of Amontillado,'" *Edgar Allan Poe Review*, Fall 2001, 53, notes too that "the narrator . . . quite obviously, has been called 'mad' by his now silent interlocutor."

6. Quoted in Ernest Jones, *The Life and Work of Sigmund Freud* (New York: Anchor, 1963), 302.

7. Quoted in Freud, *The Interpretation of Dreams*, trans. James Strachey (New York: Avon, 1965), 120.

8. George Man Burrows, *Commentaries on Insanity* (London: Underwood, 1828), excerpted in *Madness and Morals: Ideas on Insanity in the Nineteenth Century*, ed. Vieda Skultans (London: Routledge & Kegan Paul, 1975), 35.

9. William Willis Moseley, *Eleven Chapters on Nervous and Mental Complaints* (London: Simpkin, Marshall, 1838), excerpted in *Madness and Morals*, 43–44.

10. Henry Maudsley, Body and Mind (London: Macmillan, 1873), excerpted in *Madness and Morals*, 249.

11. E. Arthur Robinson, "Poe's 'The Tell-Tale Heart,'" *Nineteenth-Century Fiction* 19 (1965): 371.

12. Gita Rajan, "A Feminist Rereading of Poe's 'The Tell-Tale Heart,'" *Papers on Language and Literature* 24, no. 3 (1988): 283–300.

13. See Christopher Benfey, "Poe and the Unreadable: 'The Black Cat' and 'The Tell-Tale Heart,'" in *New Essays on Poe's Major Tales*, ed. Kenneth Silverman (Cambridge: Cambridge University Press, 1993), 28. Benfey discusses the issue of knowing other people as a Poe puzzle.

14. Thomas Ollive Mabbott, ed., *Collected Works of Edgar Allan Poe: Poems*, vol. 1 (Cambridge: Harvard University Press, 1969). "Dream-land" is found on pages 343–45 of this edition.

15. Hitchcock quoted in Francois Truffaut, *Hitchcock* (New York: Touchstone, 1967), 130–31.

16. Quoted in E. W. Smith, "Thereby Hangs a Tale: Rope in the Hands of Plautus, Porter, and Hitchcock," *Arachne* 5, no. 1 (1998): 73.

17. See Howard Barnes's *New York Herald Tribune* review, quoted in Robert A. Harris and Michael S. Lasky, *The Films of Alfred Hitchcock* (Secaucus, N.J.: Citadel, 1980), 143.

18. Donald Spoto, *The Art of Alfred Hitchcock: Fifty Years of His Motion Pictures*, 2d ed. (New York: Anchor, 1992), 167.

19. Raymond Durgnat, *The Strange Case of Alfred Hitchcock: Or The Plain Man's Hitchcock* (London: Faber & Faber, 1974), 208.

20. See Thomas Leitch, *Find the Director, and Other Hitchcock Games* (Athens: University of Georgia Press, 1991) in which he notes how the camera heightens the claustrophobia inherent in the story (139); William Rothman finds the camera a "palpable presence" that echoes Brandon's murderous hubris (*Hitchcock: The Murderous Gaze* [Cambridge: Harvard University Press, 1982], 247). Gene Phillips claims that the camera makes us feel as if we are in the picture as one of the guests. *Alfred Hitchcock* (Boston: Twayne, 1984), 110.

21. See Dennis Perry, "The Selznick Case: The Revenge of Alfred Hitchcock," *Film and History CD-ROM Annual*, 1999.

~

CHAPTER SEVEN

Voyeurism:
Eyes of the Perverse

Poe and Hitchcock express a deep fascination with the many dark facets of seeing and being seen. For both of them, voyeurism is a double-edged sword. In his article on Hitchcock's vision Peter Wollen suggests one dimension of this theme, linking "watching and hunting, voyeurism and sadism" in the films.[1] These voyeuristic themes can easily be documented in *Notorious* (1946), *Vertigo* (1958), *North by Northwest* (1959), *Psycho* (1960), *Marnie* (1964), and many others about the negative—often cruel—aspects of voyeurism or gazing. Even in a film like *Rebecca* (1940), in which voyeurism is not usually noted as among its main themes, Mrs. Danvers's gaze at the new Mrs. DeWinter is sadistic and even homicidal. Poe too was peculiarly concerned with the many dark sides of the gaze. The gaze kills, for example, in "The Oval Portrait," when the artist-husband coldly saps the life from his bride. In "Ligeia" as well, the narrator's endless contemplation of his wife's fascinating facial features, which he fragments into constituent parts, seems to sap her life.[2] In Poe's "Man of the Crowd" gazing and hunting are clearly linked as the narrator stalks the man of the crowd for twenty-four hours. But this aggressive aspect of gazing is only one facet of the Poe and Hitchcock prism of voyeurism. Other facets include fear of being seen and the more complex self-destructive impulse to be seen.

Both Poe and Hitchcock explore the terror of being seen. These uncanny psychological moments are examined in several of the texts and films. As we have seen, Poe's narrators can show absolute horror at the gaze. The narrator of "The Tell-Tale Heart" is so horrified by the gaze of the old man's vulture eye that he resorts to murder to permanently shut it. In "The Black Cat," the narrator removes a cat's eye and finally hangs it. Hitchcock also depicts the horror of being seen. In *Notorious* Alicia feels this terror when she realizes that she is being poisoned, indicating that her cover has been blown and that she is known for the spy she is. At that moment her own vision fails, expressing a psychological as well as a physical breakdown. There is a chilling moment in *Strangers on a Train* when Guy realizes he is being seen by Bruno, whose head is the only one in the crowd of tennis fans not swinging back and forth. The theme of the terrorizing gaze is emphasized in scenes that horrify the audience. The pecked-out eyes of Dan Fawcett in *The Birds*, the slashed eye curtains in *Spellbound*, and the blinding of Thorwald with flashbulbs in *Rear Window*, together with cutting out the pet's eye in "The Black Cat," the dislodged eyeballs in "A Predicament," and the eternally closed eyes in "Dreamland" all suggest deeply disturbing aspects of the gaze, particularly a fear of being seen.

But that is only half of the story. Perhaps more disturbing is the simultaneous opposite impulse to be seen. In *Vertigo*, Judy/Madeleine fears being seen, or caught, while also wishing to be seen and loved for herself. On one hand, she resists being recreated as Madeleine because Scottie's look of recognition could ultimately kill her. On the other hand, she dons the Carlotta necklace to win the full measure of the love Scottie has for her as the first Madeleine. This double desire has its roots in the imp of the perverse with its twin need to commit a crime and confess it. Other Hitchcock examples include Norman's desire to both hide his mother and expose her at the window in *Psycho*, Brandon's desire to both hide and show off his murder in *Rope*, and, in an ironic reduction of these graver tensions, Melanie's desire to both hide and be caught when delivering Cathy's lovebirds in *The Birds*. Poe's examples include the need of the narrators in "The Tell-Tale Heart" and "Imp of the Perverse" to confess in the end, Minister D—'s double impulse to hide and expose his purloined letter, and the narrator of "Man of the

Crowd" who confronts the old man who ultimately refuses to see him. This double movement mirrors the need of both Poe and Hitchcock to be invisible and yet to expose themselves in their art. Both are well-known as self-reflexive artists who find ways to explore their personal obsessions and guilty desires through their characters. Poe thinly disguises his own situation in "The Raven" and "Annabel Lee," and he uses personal biographical facts in "William Wilson."[3] Hitchcock, through his cameos and character stand-ins like Jeff in *Rear Window*, Devlin in *Notorious*, and Brandon in *Rope*, both hides and exposes himself.

Poe and Hitchcock demonstrate their narcissism in their endless fascination in displacing their own ego on page and screen. John Fawell claims that Hitchcock

> recognized that the darkest aspect of voyeurism, and the part that cinema caters to, is our desire for awful things to happen to people, even people we know and care about, for our own personal amusement, to jazz up our otherwise slow lives, to make ourselves feel better, to relieve ourselves of the burden of examining our own lives.[4]

While Fawell's point is well taken, voyeurism is ultimately an indirect attempt at self-examination. The voyeurism in Poe's and Hitchcock's work shows the gazer, like the artist, to be a lonely romantic who isolates himself from others in order to ponder the spectacle of human beings as both other and reflections of the self. The self-centered artist looks out at the world with a predatory gaze—or what Emerson called the "tyrannous eye"—seeking images to transform into art. As Emerson stated regarding the role of the ego in creative expression, artists see that "the Universe is the externalisation of the soul" (1148). This reflects the universal and microcosmic psychomachia described in *Eureka*, where God has diffused himself as an act of creation and perhaps curiosity. Voyeurism can thus be a narcissistic activity analogous to the tensions inherent in the imp of the perverse: the creative process becoming self-destructive in the process of isolating the self from others, mirroring the irreconcilable opposites of the Eurekan universe. Narcissism, then, cuts two ways with its desire to look at the self and to have others also see and admire the beloved self, and with its repressed self-loathing resulting from feelings of social, sexual, or creative inadequacy.

A crucial element of the gaze in Poe and Hitchcock is the idealization of women as visual icons, employing narcissism, self-destruction, cruelty, and the contradictory desires to both see and be seen—all of the facets of voyeurism discussed so far. Narcissism manifests itself in idealization of itself, which processes the woman's image as a reflection of the self. Clearly, for example, Poe's Ligeia, Morella, Eleanora, and Berenice, as well as Hitchcock's Melanie, Marnie, and Madeleine, exist above and beyond the earthly. The problem arises when the ideal threatens to become real. Since the ideal is based on a narcissistic projection of the protagonist's self, the resulting destruction of the ideal becomes self-destruction at the same time. As will be examined below, examples of this process are evident in the deterioration of the narrator in "Ligeia" and of Scottie in *Vertigo*. Cruelty to the female object of the gaze is a by-product of self-destruction. The women react with contradictory impulses to hide and to be seen, as in "The Oval Portrait," *Notorious*, and *Rear Window*.

Poe-esque fetishism sets a pattern for Hitchcock's obsession with the cool female as much as did the Hollywood manner of framing its female superstars.[5] Poe's "To Helen" (1831) is an early example in which a real woman is associated with the mythic Helen of Troy. The poet sees in his lover "Naiad airs" that translate him from the mundane present "to the glory that was Greece, /And the grandeur that was Rome."[6] Further removing her from any sense of present reality, she becomes objectified into something "statue-like," and finally into his own soul—"Psyche." Following the narcissistic pattern, such romantic idealizations of women ultimately transform them into reflections of an intellectual ideal. The woman thus enables the lover's imagination to take wing in sensations of beauty, leaving all that is not beautiful and earthly behind. In a sense, the real woman is sacrificed on the altar of an idea that she represents, as if cast in a theatrical role. In Poe's "Morella" and "Ligeia" the idealizing male performs a metaphysical sacrifice of the female object by willing her destruction. Here the male seems to find romantic satisfaction only in the complete physical annihilation of his lover, death enabling the ultimate idealization. Following Ligeia's death, the narrator creates a dream bower designed to facilitate the drug-induced idealization of Ligeia's memory. Here the furnishings are described in eclectic terms similar to the allusions used to describe

Ligeia earlier. Thus, for some of Poe's characters, the longing for the impossible is the only possible female ideal. After all, in "The Philosophy of Composition" Poe declares emphatically that the most beautiful and poetic sentiment can be found only in the death of a beautiful woman. In this statement of literary criticism, narcissism, creativity, and idealization come together.

Hitchcock, who idealized a number of his female stars in his personal life, specialized in idealizing and objectifying female icons with his camera. *Rebecca* (1940), his first American film, invokes a beautiful woman who dies before the film begins. Rebecca's handmaid idealizes her memory, fetishizes her belongings, and eventually goes insane in her attempt to protect Rebecca's memory from worldly tarnishing. Her room, like the Ligeian dream bower, seems to make her presence palpable. The key here, as well as in *The Paradine Case* (1947) and *Vertigo*, is that the idealized woman is not what she seems to the obsessed lover, a twist on Poe, whose women are merely blank screens for the male imagination to write on. In *The Paradine Case* a woman of apparently immaculate dignity turns out to be in love with a stablehand; in *Vertigo* Madeleine is an actress pretending to be someone she isn't. Hitchcock problematizes, even while indulging in Poe's romantic idealization of women. Often these women are punished or must die for not being what they seem—or, perhaps, for merely being a remote ideal: in *Vertigo* she dies, in *The Birds* she is attacked by birds, and in *Marnie* she is raped. At times the males idealize these women because they are exotic—the women in *Paradine Case*, *The Birds*, and *Marnie*, for example, are all criminals. Hitchcock comes very close to Poe in *Vertigo*, his ultimate expression of longing for the absent female ideal. Poe's fetishism over a woman's eyes (Ligeia's) or teeth (Berenice's) is echoed in Scottie's fetishism over Madeleine's high heels, gray suit, and blonde maelstrom of a hairdo.

The other side of voyeurism, and another concept linking Poe and Hitchcock, is that it is a disease which infects the object/victim of the gaze. In Poe's "The Oval Portrait," and in Hitchcock's *Notorious* and *Rear Window*, the two artists explore the dangers of idealizing women, both from the perspective of the men and the women. In these stories women who are both seen and not seen become conflicted in their own desires (like the narrator of "Ligeia," they are both "delighted and appalled" by the gaze). These women both submit to and resist the male gaze, which leads to self-destructive behavior. This pattern echoes the diffusive phase in *Eureka*, in which positive and negative charges keep individual fragments divided against themselves as well as each other. The obvious attraction between the sexes in these stories, despite the obstacles forestalling romantic fulfillment, suggests progress in the Eurekan cycle. The diffusive power seemingly weakens, enabling some contact between particles, if only through the gaze itself. However, the diffusion has only dissipated enough to enable the counterfeit romantic oneness of fetishism and idealism, a partial and distorted version of the final collapse into oneness and unity that ends the *Eureka* cycle. In this narrative framework, men become women's "spirit of perverseness," an electricity that seriously challenges the women's natural attraction and longing for oneness. In this chapter I will begin with a comparative analysis of "Oval Portrait" and *Notorious*, reading them as the women's stories, and then bring in added dimensions of these themes from "The Man of the Crowd" and *Rear Window*.

"The Oval Portrait," *Notorious*

Both "The Oval Portrait" and *Notorious* are tales are set in Latin countries (Spain and Brazil), and the major action takes place in luxurious palaces. Poe's setting is a gothic castle in the Apennines, much like the castles in "Mrs. Radcliffe" (662). The castle is furnished "sumptuously" with "rich" though "tattered" decorations. Like the gothic novels, this is the setting for a virtual entrapment for the young bride of the artist who owns the castle. *Notorious* likewise takes place in a large, richly decorated Brazilian mansion that becomes a terrifying gothic prison for Alicia, who, like the heroine of "Oval Portrait," is slowly dying. The male protagonists in both "Oval Portrait" and *Notorious* face personal stress and crisis. Poe's narrator is "desperately wounded" and can do little besides read and sleep as he holes up in a ruined castle. (The original version of this tale reveals that his wounds come from an attack by banditti.) Devlin, as an American intelligence agent in *Notorious*, is wounded in another sense. He has been hardened and made cynical by his role as a spy. Having seen human corruption and duplicity, he is cynical, making him unable to trust his own powerful instinct to love

Alicia Huberman, playgirl daughter of a convicted Nazi agent. He can see her fast living but is insensitive to what motivates her. The wounds of these protagonists remove them from direct action, making them intellectual gazers who live only within themselves.

Poe's narrator sets himself up in bed so that "[he] might resign [himself], if not to sleep, at least alternately to the contemplation of these pictures." G. R. Thompson notes clues to the fact that once he closes his eyes, "the narrator is indeed dreaming the rest of the tale."[7] Such an idea, of course, heightens the idealization of his gaze. This is borne out when he fixates on a portrait of a young girl; his first glance so excites him that he must close his eyes to "calm and subdue my fancy." Here the link between idealizing and the creative process is implied. Thereafter, he looks "fixedly at the painting," which serves as witness of the self-centered artist-husband who painted this portrait of his bride. Seeing her as mere fodder for his art, the artist is coldly insensitive to her human needs, his neglect directly causing her death. His gaze is simultaneously sensitive and blind. For the wounded gazer, there is similarly no note of anything but a fetish in his obsession with the enchanting portrait. Hitchcock's Devlin, whom we first meet from behind as an anonymous silhouette closely following Alicia's movements at a party, is also a cold watcher (like the reporters who insensitively trail Alicia in the opening scene). A wounded voyeur like the gazer in "The Oval Portrait," Devlin is "confounded, subdued, and appalled" by what he sees. The result for Alicia is that he similarly fails to detect her human needs, therefore compounding and encouraging a situation that becomes life or death for her. Like the artist in "Oval Portrait," Devlin can only see Alicia with blinded eyes, making love a test she can only fail.

The parallel double structure of male gazers in "Oval Portrait" and *Notorious* is striking. In Poe's tale the artist-husband owns the gaze that drains his bride's life. But he is doubled by the wounded aristocrat who spends the night in his castle. Like the artist, the aristocrat appreciates fine art and can contemplate it for hours. And like the artist himself, he is struck by the quality of the portrait, its uncanny lifelike character. *Notorious* also has two male figures who double each other. Alex, like the artist, is the one responsible for Alicia's slow dying. And like the wounded man in Poe's tale, Devlin is the passive gazer who can only view the process (until the end of the film). Like Poe's wounded man,

Devlin closes his eyes to Alicia's self-destruction actions, only able to perceive her as the product of his hurt and cynical imagination.

The heroines in "Oval Portrait" and *Notorious* are also quite alike. The maiden in Poe's tale is "of rarest beauty, and not more lovely than full of glee" (664), a description used twice. In addition, she is described as "all light and smiles, and frolicsome as the young fawn." She is also "humble and obedient," submitting to endless hours of posing for her husband's brush, though she hates the art that obsesses her husband. Alicia, as played by Ingrid Bergman, is also quite beautiful and has a naturally ebullient personality. She likes to tease Devlin with her witty and lighthearted play, giving Devlin nicknames ("Mr. D") and generally playing off of his straight-man persona. The wholesome expression of her high spirits has been distorted temporarily because of her father's treasonous scandal, causing her to force some of the "glee" in partying (the only side of her that Devlin can perceive). Like Poe's heroine, she meekly accepts her spy assignment because of her love for the protagonist, for whose pleasure, or displeasure, she is willing to sacrifice herself. Their few happy days together provide glimpses of a healthy Alicia that Devlin's love could bring back. Thus Devlin's gaze can either heal or destroy. The heroines in both "The Oval Portrait" and *Notorious* occupy the same central position in their stories. Because the flawed male figures objectify these heroines, Hitchcock and Poe focus our sympathy on the women rather than the men.

Importantly, each woman responds to her lover's blindness by self-destructive behavior. In "The Oval Portrait" the artist's wife is jealous of the art that stands between her and her husband, but she submits obediently to her fate by sitting for him weeks on end in a "dark, high turret-chamber" which "withered [her] health and . . . spirits" (665). If she can be nothing else to him, she is willing to be his art object and "smile on and still on" as she slowly dies. The fact that she dies just at the moment he finishes the portrait affirms the power of the male gaze to kill. As the artist wills his wife's life onto his painted canvas, he leaves her body dead. Joan Dayan explains that "the last-line revelation of this tale forms the sacramental exchange, the resurrection of a second, more sacred reproduction—a more spiritual body—on the ruins of the natural."[8] The artist's self-destruction is at least psychically implied as he grows "tremulous and very pallid, and aghast" when he completes the portrait. Since he idealized her in art ("This is indeed *Life* itself!"), his guilty doom is sealed.

In *Notorious*, Alicia also hates Devlin's art—spying. At first she hates him for spying on her: "Why you double-crossing buzzard—you're a cop!" She recognizes herself as the hunted and Devlin as the hunter (her zebra-patterned blouse is worth noting here). Her failure to maintain his temporary expression of love becomes the catalyst to a round of emotional self-destruction. Under Devlin's withering gaze, she seems to find her self-image, "Why won't you let me be happy, Dev?" Without his love, she no longer cares what happens to her and perversely tries to both punish him and resecure his attention by throwing herself at Alex. Like Poe's heroine, Alicia submits to the art she hates and nearly succumbs to emotional and physical death after Alex begins poisoning her.

Alicia continually self-destructs in response to Devlin's vision of her: drinking in his presence when he fails to believe in her, and denying that she is sick in order to fulfill Devlin's assumptions that she is drinking excessively with the Sebastians. One of her most telling statements to Devlin along these lines comes early on at the racetrack: "You can add Alex Sebastian to my list of playmates." When Devlin comments that it didn't take her very long, she counters angrily: "That's what you wanted, wasn't it?" As clearly as anything she says, this question demonstrates that she takes her self-destructive cues from Devlin, his gaze becoming her script.

In "The Oval Portrait" and *Notorious*, then, the self-destructive behavior of the women is directly attributable to the abusive male gaze, the gaze functioning like a mirror transferring the interior image of the gazer onto the objectified female. She literally creates herself in the gazer's image, suggesting a version of Poe's metempsychosis, the theme of the transmigration of souls. The artist in "The Oval Portrait" lives entirely in his head; "passionate, studious, austere," he transforms all of reality into the art that is his interior vision. At one point, while painting his wife, the artist leaves the real world entirely behind, turning "his eyes from canvas rarely, even to regard the countenance of his wife" (665). The monomania becomes hers as she turns all of her attention to pleasing her husband, eschewing her previous life of exterior glee. As already observed, the remote turret becomes the expression of the painter's mind in which he has entrapped his wife. In a distorted and counterfeit way, the couple has become one as she too leaves the world; but in her case it is physical as well as intellectual. Declaring "this is indeed *Life* itself!" (666) when the painting is finished, he un-knowingly but accurately measures the ironic dimensions of his be-trayal of life as his once "frolicsome" bride is now dead.

In *Notorious* Devlin and Alicia have a "hunter" and "hunted" rela-tionship in a familiar Hitchcock formula. After "begging" Alicia to per-form a spy mission, Devlin, like Vandamm in *North by Northwest*, mis-takes Alicia's true identity. She becomes, therefore, the "wrong woman," a twist on the "wrong man" theme. Like Thornhill, she is per-petually mistaken as someone else, the amoral party girl enjoying her degrading mission. As one of the intelligence people comments, "A woman of that sort. I don't think any of us have any illusions about her character." Since this is the person Devlin sees, she becomes that char-acter—as if he had painted a portrait of her without looking any more than Poe's artist. In another way, Devlin creates Alicia in his image by making her a spy. Her involving herself in his "art" provides her with a gaze of her own. The fact that her gaze is often shown to be distorted completes the migration of Devlin's soul to Alicia's through the power of his gaze; her distorted gaze becomes a reflection of Devlin's.

Hitchcock's camera emphasizes Alicia's distorted gaze more theatri-cally than it does Devlin's, the camera becoming the character's gaze, as in *Spellbound*. When we first see Alicia at her party, she is flirting with Devlin's silhouette. Even though we can't see Devlin from her per-spective, he is as much a mystery to her as the silhouette is to us. Later, when we see her driving from her point of view with hair blowing across the camera, she comments that "this fog gets me," foreshadow-ing the fog that envelops her relationship with Devlin for most of the film. (This scene also foreshadows Thornhill's drunken drive in *North by Northwest*, which is also characterized by visual distortions.) Waking from her hangover the next morning, she sees Devlin leaning in the doorway and then sees him rotating as he enters the room toward her. This humorous circling shot, reminiscent of the spiraling imagery in *Vertigo*, foreshadows not only Devlin's unstable view of Alicia, alter-nating between desire and cynical despair, but also her own continuous distortions. Like Scottie Ferguson in *Vertigo*, Devlin is dizzily in love, but we see it through Alicia's reflecting gaze. Finally, as Alicia fears that something is wrong at "home," and then quickly realizes that she is being poisoned, the subjective camera becomes surrealistically distorted, suggesting her darkening fears of death in the shadowy images before her. But these images, framed by shots of an increasingly troubled Devlin, echo his movement from growing suspicion to outright fear. A most important dimension of Devlin's mind is its conflict, which makes Alicia conflicted as well. She both loves and hates Devlin, as well as herself. Like him, she doesn't really know her own mind.

In an ironic revision of the male gaze, then, Alicia's gaze vicariously and indirectly displays her own as well as Devlin's distorted picture of her and the world in general. She cannot see that Devlin really loves her but can't let himself admit it any more than she can. That her distorted gaze reflects the self-destructive influence Devlin has on her means that she is, in effect, entrapped as much in Alex's mind as in his house. Devlin's mind is the gothic castle, his confusion and pain the poison that is really killing her. Like many gothic housemasters, Devlin is dark and troubled. Finally, Alicia's twisted vision not only reflects her and Devlin's blindness, but that of the other major gazers in the film. Alex's sharp-eyed mother speaks for many in the film when she admits following the revelation that Alicia is an American agent: "I knew but I didn't see." Alex, of course, doesn't see past Alicia's love, Prescott only sees Alicia as a playgirl, and in the end the Nazi group cannot see the truth as Devlin brings Alicia down the stairs. Virtually everyone in the film is involved in what Prescott calls "a little theatrical plan," making everyone part of an audience that gets deceived. Alex's comment that Nazi hit man Eric "likes to go to the movies to cry—he's very sentimental" applies to all of the characters at one point or another in the film, as well as the film's audience. Hitchcock's theatrical plan is nicely laid out by Susan Smith, who describes the main phases of suspense episodes that keep audiences mystified and engaged, particularly concerning little things (like keeping the stolen key in her hand hidden from Alex).[9] Hitchcock, as well as his characters, manipulates the gullibility of others to accomplish certain theatrical effects, whether to entertain or spy. As an audience, we "know" that Alicia and Devlin will somehow get together in the end, but we are unable to "see" how this will happen.

Despite the many affinities between "The Oval Portrait" and *Notorious*, the differences are also salient. Among the most significant changes Hitchcock makes to the Poe formula is centering the story on the woman/victim. The woman becomes elevated beyond object to subject, her gaze most closely aligned with the camera. We are asked to identify with her and feel her pain of being looked at but not seen. Neither Devlin's conflicted gaze, nor Captain Prescott's aloof and unfeeling gaze, nor Alex's murderous gaze is admirable. While it is true that the patriarchal government institution has the more powerful gaze, Alicia's gaze elicits our sympathy. In addition to this subjective view of the female, Hitchcock has out-Poe'd Poe by tying more aspects of the story into the gaze motif, centering it around spying. This complicates the story line, as well as its effect, as each relationship has multiple ironic subtexts. For example, the "villain" Alex is often more sympathetic than the hero, and the kiss staged between Devlin and Alicia in the cellar for Alex's sake involves real passion, making Alex's conclusions about their clandestine relationship affair simultaneously right and wrong. This complicated network of gazing, longing, and repression redefines the Eurekan fragmentation and diffusion phase in new ways, giving ironic psychological depth to attraction and repulsion within and between characters.

"The Man of the Crowd," "The Oval Portrait," and *Rear Window*

Rear Window is Hitchcock's most celebrated and discussed film about voyeurism, particularly because of its self-reflexive function as an examination of the cinematic experience. In fact, it is among the indispensable films in any discussion of cinematic voyeurism.[10] While critics vary in their interpretations of how the gaze functions in *Rear Window*, virtually all agree that the meaning and evolution of Jeff's voyeurism is the focus of the film.[11] When placed in the context of Poe's major tales concerning the gaze, however, *Rear Window* reveals itself to be two different films. When looked at beside "The Man of the Crowd" *Rear Window* is clearly Jeff's story about becoming obsessed with looking at and penetrating the activities of a suspicious man. This reading allows for interpretations centering on the saga of Jeff's voyeurism and how that self-reflexively explores aspects of the cinema. On the other hand, placed beside "Oval Portrait," *Rear Window* becomes equally Lisa's story, about the burdens of being the idealized object of the male gaze. These two strands of the film butt heads with each other in an attraction-repulsion structure that mimics the diffusion phase of the Eurekan cycle, creating an energy that, as in *Notorious*, places the genders and their gazes at odds. Jeff's story concerns the dark side of the gaze in three ways. First, Jeff and Lars Thorwald are doubles, linked in their inability to enjoy a happy relationship with a woman. Second, Jeff's voyeurism verges on criminal behavior, as often hinted in the film. Third, Jeff's perspective draws in the audience's own guilty voyeurism. On the other hand, Lisa's story is the more heroic struggle against the constructed image she inherits from society (embodied in Jeff's idealizing and stereotyping gaze) and her quest to maintain her integrity despite feeling compelled to satisfy Jeff's vision.

The narrator of "Man of the Crowd" and Jeff are both presented at the beginning of their stories as convalescents confined in their activity, leading to what becomes a delightful obsession with looking at and analyzing others. Poe's narrator describes finding himself "in one of those happy moods which are so precisely the converse of *ennui*— moods of the keenest appetency" (507). Looking out the window of the London coffeehouse he patronizes, he finds that "the tumultuous sea of human heads filled [him] . . . with a delicious novelty of emotion. [He] gave up, at length, all care of things within the hotel, and became absorbed in contemplation of the scene without" (507). In a leg cast, the usually active Jeff has become bored with his apartment confinement and has turned his attention to the life of his neighbors in the Greenwich Village courtyard of wide-open rear windows. Our first glimpse of Jeff awake comes as he talks with his boss on the phone while surveying his neighbors. The sequence centers around a shot/reverse shot pattern showing him voyeuristically enjoying the scantily dressed ballerina in the window across the way while she eats and dances. The sequence includes five shots of the ballerina that total over thirty seconds. Though he claims to be bored after six weeks in his cast, he is obviously riveted by the view. Clearly, by beginning the study of Jeff's voyeurism with the lengthy and titillating ballerina sequence, Hitchcock simultaneously arouses and implicates audience voyeurism. Moving his glance around to other windows, Jeff is doing what he does daily, monitoring his exposed neighbors, including the argumentative Thorwalds.

Like Jeff, Poe's narrator in "The Man of the Crowd" "descended to details" in regarding the people outside his coffeehouse window during the course of the day, studying "with minute interest the innumerable varieties of figure, dress, air, gait, visage, and expression of countenance" (507). He prides himself on a Dupin-like ability to read the classes and types of people according to their manner of dress and expression. Jeff too regards his motley collection of neighbors with a clear sense of superiority. Like Poe's narrator, he delights in recognizing the stereotypes around him, the frustrated composer, the ill and nagging wife, the lonely old maid ("Miss Lonelyhearts"), the bohemian sculptress, and the honeymoon couple behind the shaded window. Jeff's knowing grin as these characters live up to type suggests his comfortable vision of the world, with everyone in his or her place. Reading others is an important value in the film, even with the nurse Jeff's insurance company supplied. She predicted the stock market crash as she nursed the president of General Motors: "Kidney ailment they said; nerves I said. Then I asked myself, 'What does General Motors got to be nervous about?' 'Over production,' I said. 'Collapse.' When General Motors has to go to the bathroom ten times a day, the whole country's ready to let go."

While Jeff is cynical about her linking kidney ailments and economic theory, she proves prophetic when she "smells trouble" in his apartment: "You get to lookin' out the window, [you'll] see things you shouldn't see—trouble." Voyeurism in the film is an active agent in a chain of cause and effect.

As in Poe's tale, the protagonists begin to find things really interesting, as well as disturbing, at night: "as the night deepened, so deepened to me the interest of the scene" (510). The protagonists in both "The Man of the Crowd" and *Rear Window* notice figures who do not fit the stereotypes they have neatly put into personal taxonomies. Poe's narrator finds a man with an "absolute idiosyncrasy of . . . expression," causing him to feel "singularly aroused, startled, fascinated" (510). As the narrator determines to crack the mystery of this strange man, he begins following him in the rain and becomes increasingly puzzled by his odd behavior of seeking crowds (curiously, the narrator never suggests that he might be a pickpocket, who certainly would seek crowds). Jeff also becomes fascinated by Thorwald, who begins behaving in a strange way one rainy evening, performing a series of errands while his wife seems to have disappeared. Like Poe's narrator, Jeff becomes absorbed by Thorwald's mysterious behavior and asks questions. But rather than follow Thorwald around, Jeff is forced to watch him from his window. Neither the old man in Poe's tale nor Thorwald are apparently aware of being watched (though there are clues that perhaps the old man figures it out).

Poe's narrator and Jeff also share a common obsession with forbidden knowledge—knowing what is outside the pale of their stereotypes—and this fascination with strange behavior links them both to those they watch with voyeuristic obsession. The emotional distance from people suggested by the cool analysis of Poe's narrator links him with the old man whose behavior paradoxically takes him physically close to crowds of people while keeping him emotionally distant from them. Likewise, Jeff's typing of his neighbors and his poor relationship with Lisa link him with Thorwald and his bad marriage. Thorwald shows early on, before he is suspected of murdering his wife, that he is an unpleasant neighbor (telling his friendly sculptress neighbor to "shut up"). The double aspects of character development in these stories suggest the dark side of looking into the self, the difficulty in seeing one's self for what one is.[12] In "Man of the Crowd" and *Rear Window* both Poe and Hitchcock explore the "type and genius of deep crime" that is in each of us but is difficult to detect. Our "self" is ultimately the text that Poe notes "does not permit itself to be read" (506). (Importantly, applying this dark paradoxical project to ourselves is the reader's and viewer's task.) In both the tale and the film there is a face-off at the end between the doubles, but little of depth is revealed. When the voyeuristic mystery game is over for Jeff, he never really sees Thorwald as his double. His development centers on his increased understanding and appreciation of Lisa.

To understand Lisa better, as well as her role in this drama of the gaze, we can refer to Mulvey's classic essay, "Visual Pleasure and Narrative Cinema." As a passing example, Mulvey notes that in *Rear Window* Jeff discovers Lisa erotically only when she goes to Thorwald's apartment, becoming an object of desire for Jeff's gaze.[13] Robert J. Corber finds this a misinterpretation, claiming instead that "Jeff's . . . looking at Lisa through his telephoto lens as she searches for the incriminating ring is important not so much because it allows him to master her but because . . . [it] returns [his gaze] to the private sphere. His interest in his neighbors' activities is no longer 'diseased' but personal."[14] Both readings, though disagreeing on interpretive details, assume that Lisa is the passive object and Jeff the active gazer whose self-assertive responses to Lisa turn the plot.[15] In reality, far from a passive object of the gaze, Lisa is controlling and deconstructing Jeff's gaze. While Stam and Pearson don't assert this view, they indirectly support it by calling into question the long-standing assumption underlying the idea that the film restricts itself to Jeff's perspective: "it is manifestly not true that we see only what he sees."[16] They go on to demonstrate, using Thorwald's, Lisa's, Doyle's, Stella's, and the camera's point of view, that there is a "gestural autonomy of the camera and [an] independence from any particular vision." This perspective is further supported throughout the film's "progressive shattering of Jeffries's illusion of voyeuristic separation from life" ("A Loneliness," 142). Together these ideas invite us to see ways in which Lisa shares the story.

This process can begin as we place *Rear Window* next to "The Oval Portrait" and examine the different story that emerges. As in Poe's tale, Hitchcock's protagonist becomes the female character who is victimized by the male gaze. Just as the narrator of "The Oval Portrait" is surrounded by framed paintings to contemplate, so Jeff is confronted by a series of framed windows with moving pictures. Like the artist's bride in "The Oval Portrait," Lisa is full of life and fun. In her first appearance in the film, she kisses Jeff awake and introduces herself with theatrical aplomb, speaking each of her three names as she turns on the three lights in Jeff's dark apartment. She further seeks to please, surprise, and entertain the convalescent by bringing him a catered meal from the 21 Club. But just as the artist-husband's monomania wears down his wife's "glee" in "The Oval Portrait," so Jeff's determined anti-high style stance, along with unappreciative comments ("It's all perfect," he sarcastically sighs), slowly wears Lisa down. She knows she exists only as a phantom of Jeff's dream life. We first view Jeff as he sleeps, and he is asleep when Lisa makes her appearance (presented in dreamy slow motion). This suggests that Jeff, like the narrator in "Oval Portrait," is dreaming.[17] Even the idea of a rear window itself suggests the unconsciousness of a dream (just as the front window suggests conscious reality). In essence, the film moves from unconsciousness to consciousness, a private sleeping life to a more public waking life, based largely on what Lisa does.

Meanwhile, like Alicia Huberman in *Notorious*, Lisa struggles to survive under the withering gaze of a cold male. Like the artist-husband in "The Oval Portrait," who fails to see his bride's real feelings and terminal condition, Jeff also fails to see Lisa's real potential as something more than a mere clotheshorse. Jeff's immature gaze can only see the cultured, worldly playgirl whom he assumes couldn't possibly have the grit to handle the physical dangers and privations attached to his profession. Despite her arguments to the contrary that "it is ridiculous to say that it can only be done by a special private little group of anointed people," Jeff superficially perceives Lisa as "a queen bee with her pick of the drones." By evening's end, the once playful Lisa Carol Fremont leaves depressed. For the moment at least, Jeff, like Thorwald, becomes a murderer, succeeding in killing Lisa's spirit. At the same time, Hitchcock depresses his audience with the sad spectacle of loneliness visible in Jeff's rear window: "We view that suffering from a distant perspective, with a context that can seem both cruel and sadly sympathetic" ("A Loneliness," 116). This emotional convergence of Lisa's and the audience's temperament reflects the importance of her position in the film. Like the other characters, whose rear windows resemble "a number of cages at a pet store" ("A Loneliness," 113), Lisa, like Alicia, is trapped by the loneliness of Jeff's gaze. As an audience, we rarely sympathize with voyeuristic Jeff, agreeing with Stella's commentary that he should see himself.

Even before their argument we have already sided with Lisa, since her understanding of the neighbors seems more sympathetically humane. (Like the narrator in "The Man of the Crowd," Jeff is unreliable ["Art, Ambiguity," 25].) If the casting of James Stewart in *Rope* is questionable, it is unassailable in *Rear Window*. As the archetypal stubborn American male he is flawless, always a step behind the more knowing and intuitive women at every turn. His only insight into Thorwald is based on what he can see, plus a few obvious deductions. It requires Lisa's special insider knowledge and application of women's behavior to affirm suspicions about the Thorwalds. Despite her obvious superiority, Lisa is trapped in Jeff's dream assumptions about her, and her inability to make him see by argument makes their relationship as fragile as the Thorwalds'. To Jeff she is temperamentally an invalid, like Mrs. Thorwald who must live within the severe limits of New York's high society. And like Thorwald, Jeff is getting tired of arguing the point ("shut up," he finally says, echoing Thorwald's dismissal of his friendly neighbor). Further like Thorwald and Poe's artist-husband, Jeff is blind to the results of his mistreatment of his female companion.

Although Mrs. Thorwald refuses to submit to Thorwald's philandering, resisting with self-destructive nagging, Lisa responds in a complicated way, ultimately winning the day. While on the surface she seems like the artist's wife, trying to please her man by fulfilling his vision of her, she wisely adopts an indirect strategy in their ongoing argument, eventually demonstrating her courage and competence. In bringing her compact overnight case to prove how well she could travel to foreign parts, she becomes both humorous and seductive—"previews of coming attractions," she says as she holds up her negligee. She also becomes more assertive and dictates Jeff's gaze: "Show's over for the night." She further asserts herself by linking herself linguistically with Jeff. "We think Thorwald's guilty," she remarks to Detective Doyle. She realizes, however, that such a strategy will not be enough in the long run, that she must actually put herself on the line. As she and Stella are digging in Thorwald's garden, she impulsively climbs into Thorwald's apartment to seek solid evidence of the wife's murder. This accomplishes at least three things: first, it forces Jeff to recognize the depth of his feelings for Lisa in his fear for her life; second, it demonstrates to him that she is resourceful, daring, courageous, and supremely capable (even of breaking the law—a clear sign that her commitment to civilization is at least as tentative as Jeff's); and third, it shows her commitment to Jeff's cause. Ironically, though very Hitchcockian, Lisa and Jeff are brought together by murder and mystery.

Lisa's self-imposed oneness with Jeff also seems to transfer some of his self-destructive tendencies to her (a talent in his profession). Jeff's self-destructive side is shown by the souvenirs he has in his apartment: a smashed camera and a photograph he took of an atom bomb. In addition, as he explains the hardships of his profession to Lisa, the audience gets the distinct impression that the more dangerous and "repulsive," as she puts it, the better for Jeff. As the radio blares a rhetorical commercial question, "Are you tired, rundown?" we realize that Jeff was literally run down by a race car as we see in a photograph tellingly near the smashed camera. His self-destructiveness is most clearly displayed psychologically in his perverse rejection of a mature and permanent love relationship with Lisa. To Jeff, she is "too perfect." He initially has no more interest in her than an eight-year-old would have in his pretty babysitter. He'd much rather romp with the other boys in the mud and rain of the extended scout camp of his profession than stay home and play house with Lisa with her talk of Paris fashions and Park Avenue gossip.

Like a disease, voyeurism infects the object as well as the subject of the gaze. From the highly civilized woman, Lisa becomes self-destructive, responding to impulses that are at once admirable and disturbing. The fact that she can enter a murderer's apartment as if she were playing a college prank suggests how far she will go to satisfy Jeff's gaze. Like her double in the film, the suicidal Miss Lonelyhearts, Lisa is desperate (note that Lisa's theme song is playing as Miss Lonelyhearts takes an overdose of pills). However, Lisa fights fire with fire, taking risks to compel and control Jeff's gaze and finally deconstructing it. She accomplishes this by changing her own role in the film, and subsequently the film itself, from glamorous object of the gaze in a mystery film to adventuress in Hitchcock's version of *The Perils of Pauline*. Lisa's exhibitionism actually forces Jeff to look away repeatedly when Thorwald arrives and begins to manhandle her. Here, Lisa has taken control of the gaze, and the "coming attractions" she'd spoken of earlier turn out to be of *Psycho* (which also begins from the perspective of voyeuristically looking inside an urban window). Jeff is no longer the cool, superior voyeur we meet at the beginning of the film. As Stella warned him, he now sees something he wishes he hadn't. Again, as in *Notorious*, the self-imposed predicament of the heroine melts the cool male gaze and unites the couple. But in this case, Lisa is far from helpless. When the police arrive after she was nearly killed by Thorwald, she does some fast talking and manages to show off Mrs. Thorwald's ring to Jeff. The fact that Thorwald looks up at Jeff at that precise moment links her deconstruction of Jeff's gaze with his unveiling. Jeff's voyeur's license is at that moment revoked as Lisa ironically pulls him into the thick of real action. Jeff himself had become the passive one of the couple, despite his contrary arguments to Lisa, and she indeed wins their war of words with action. Finally, as Jeff sleeps in his wheelchair, Lisa proves her independence once and for all—maintaining both of her true selves. As she shifts from adventure to fashion reading, she controls not only the gaze but her identity as well.

The structure of the film reflects this power shift. In the beginning we think this is going to be Jeff's film about a voyeur who stumbles onto a murder mystery while Lisa's role seems merely the typical Hollywood "token" romantic distraction. However, our allegiance soon shifts from Jeff to Lisa, just as the film's attention does. Lisa wins over not only Jeff but the cinema audience as well. Yet it happens before our eyes. The film stays with Jeff's gaze, but the meaning and character of that gaze changes radically. In fact, all of the individual "resolutions" in the various window screens in the courtyard are withheld from Jeff in the end. He becomes the subject of Lisa's and our gaze. Reversing "Oval Portrait's" shocking ending, when the artist realizes that his bride is dead, Jeff is the one who most resembles death, upended by his own gaze. Just as he was originally injured by gazing too closely at a race car, resulting in his broken leg, so gazing at Thorwald is self-destructive and has led to another broken leg. We get the feeling that Jeff may soon be settling into a nice portrait studio—perhaps the symbol indicated by Lisa's reading *Bazaar* magazine in the final shot. Since Lisa now controls the gaze, Jeff's will potentially seems as passive as his body.

While Poe and Hitchcock explore several facets of voyeurism, their focus on the response of the female object of the gaze creates and defines the significance of their narratives. For both, voyeurism can be a communicable disease, infecting both the voyeur and the subject of his gaze. In addition, it is first passed on by the artists themselves to their characters, making them vehicles for exploring their own obsessions. Robert Mollinger's insightful reading of "Oval Portrait" as a meta-fiction nicely fits both *Notorious* and *Rear Window*. In "Portrait," the various characters are psychologically fused so that they all double each other—and all double Poe himself. Hitchcock doubles himself in *Notorious* as both the cold watcher Devlin and the pathetic, undesired Alex. In *Rear Window*, Hitchcock is at once both Jeff, passively peering through his camera, and Lisa, the catalyst for the film's action. These structures bring us back to the idea of artistic narcissism as a basis for voyeurism, with its attendant self-destructiveness, idealization, cruelty, and contradictory impulses to hide and be seen. Such a deep fascination with gazing inevitably has roots in the personal experiences of Poe and Hitchcock, and is reflected in their personal and philosophical perspectives. As artists they are naturally careful observers, and they have observed how separate people are despite their proximity to one another. Voyeurism reflects the complex network of transference and exchanges between motivations and blind whims. Like the imp of the perverse, it is "an innate and primitive principle of human action, a paradoxical something" ("Imp of the Perverse," 638) that characterizes everything.

Notes

1. Peter Wollen, "Hitchcock's Vision," *Cinema* 3 (1969): 4.

2. See Daniel Hoffman, *Poe, Poe, Poe, Poe, Poe, Poe, Poe* (New York: Avon, 1978), 246–47, where he discusses the impotent narrator's need to wish Ligeia dead in order to protect himself as a prey from her tumultuous "vultures of stern passion."

3. Poe works himself into his tales in infinite ways. In "The Oval Portrait," for example, he doubles himself in both the artist and the narrator, their obsession with the portrait reflecting his own obsession with his mother and his one portrait of her. Robert N. Mollinger, "Edgar Allan Poe's 'The Oval Portrait': Fusion of Multiple Personalities," *American Imago* 36 (1979): 147–53.

4. In John Fawell, "A Loneliness amidst a Populace: Hitchcock's *Rear Window*," *North Dakota Quarterly* 68, no. 1 (2001): 112.

5. Most films in the Hollywood tradition present female stars as either wholesome (June Allison, Donna Reed, Deborah Kerr) or ambiguous (Joan Crawford, Bette Davis, Susan Hayward)—but rarely as mysterious mythic presences. Two obvious exceptions are anomalies such as Garbo, whose stardom was based on her exotic but subdued sexuality, and Hedy Lamarr in such films as *Algiers* and *White Cargo*.

6. Thomas Ollive Mabbott, ed., *Collected Works of Edgar Allan Poe: Poems*, vol. 1 (Cambridge: Harvard University Press, 1969). "To Helen" is found on pages 165–66 of this edition.

7. G. R. Thompson, *Poe's Fiction: Romantic Irony in the Gothic Tales* (Madison: University of Wisconsin Press, 1973), 135.

8. Joan Dayan, *Fables of Mind: An Inquiry into Poe's Fiction* (New York: Oxford University Press, 1987), 201.

9. See Susan Smith, *Hitchcock: Suspense, Humor, and Tone* (London: BFI, 2000), 27–29.

10. For a discussion of the way Poe's "Man of the Crowd" is self-reflexive, see Ray Mazurek, "Art, Ambiguity, and the Artist in Poe's 'The Man of the Crowd,'" *Poe Studies*, December 1979, 25.

11. The focus on Jeff's experience in the film, and particularly in terms of his role as a stand-in for the camera, began with Jean Douchet, "Hitch et son public," *Cahiers du Cinema*, November 1960, 7–15. Critics since then have for the most part merely fleshed out that theme.

12. Mazurek, "Art," 25.

13. In Laura Mulvey, *Screen* 16 (1975): 15–16.

14. Robert J. Corber, "Resisting History: *Rear Window* and the Limits of the Postwar Settlement," *Boundary*, Spring 1992, 141.

15. Sander H. Lee also views Jeff as master of his own development: "Jeffries' suspicions of Thorwald lead him to act in ways which eventually engage him in his own life." "Escape and Commitment in Hitchcock's *Rear Window*," *Post Script*, Winter 1988, 24.

16. Robert Stam and Roberta Pearson, "Hitchcock's *Rear Window*: Reflexivity and the Critique of Voyeurism," *Enclitic*, Spring 1983, 142.

17. Several critics note the suggestion that Jeff is dreaming, including Stam and Pearson (138).

~

CHAPTER EIGHT

Romantic Obsession: Return to Transcendence

We have seen how Poe and Hitchcock explore various theaters in the psychological war between attraction and repulsion: apocalypse, inexplicability, doubles, imp of the perverse, and voyeurism. These local battles represent the human psyche struggling through the various stations of the Eurekan cycle. The ultimate station, or expression of this psychomachia, is obsession, particularly romantic obsession. Like the Russian *matroishka* dolls, in which increasingly smaller dolls fit inside one another, the mystery of romantic obsession is, so to speak, the largest doll, or obsession, in which the others fit. Poe's famous critical dictum that the death of a beautiful woman is the most poetic subject matter is an important theme in his poems and tales. No other subject fascinated him so deeply nor so continually. Hitchcock is no less famous for his obsession with immaculate blondes whose sexuality seethes under their cool surface. These women are made mysterious, enigmatic, and imaginatively compelling by Hitchcock's seductive camera. For both artists love is traumatic and elusive, playing devil with one's imagination and sanity. This coincidence between Poe and Hitchcock tempts us into psychological and biographical speculation as a context for understanding how romantic obsession functions in their works. While the double, the imp of the perverse, and voyeurism dramatize the protagonists' inner battles, with the theme of romantic obsession

Poe and Hitchcock explore how these sublime psychological conflicts create the paradoxical desire and fear for one of the most powerful of human impulses—romantic union.

At the heart of romantic obsession in Poe and Hitchcock is romanticism itself. The romantic mind, which we encounter in Poe and Hitchcock, ever strives toward the ideal, making the love most desired the love that can never be; romantic obsession becomes an obsession for what is forbidden. It is an old story. Mature, grown-up love, from an idealized standpoint, soon becomes ordinary and mundane, a sentiment echoing Emily Dickinson's words: "I cannot live with You—/ It would be Life—" (no. 640). Dickinson, like Poe and Hitchcock, finds real "life" the death of the creative imagination. If creativity is the thrill of the hunt, what happens after the capture is merely dull routine. Emerson put it well in these lines from "Each and All":

> The lover watched his graceful maid,
> As 'mid the virgin train she strayed,
> Nor knew her beauty's best attire
> Was woven still by the snow-white choir.
> At last she came to his hermitage,
> Like the bird from the woodlands to the cage;—
> The gay enchantment was undone,
> A gentle wife, but fairy none.

Consummated love, whether with the unexciting Rowenas and Midges of the world or with the mysterious Morellas and Madeleines, awakens from an enchanted dream. Why this is so goes back to the mother, with whom the infant lives an enchanted dream of complete love and contentment until awakening into the dull routine of consciousness (what Freud would call falling from the pleasure principle into the reality principle).

Poe and Jung

As evidenced in chapter 4, Poe and Jung are both interested in the processes of development and degeneration. Thus *Eureka* and Jung's theories of human development tell similar stories in different languages. What follows is an attempt to translate Poe and Jung into each other's languages, with the intent of shedding light on the maternal role in potential development, stagnation, and degeneration in the romantic imaginations of Poe and Hitchcock.

As with the voyeuristic phase of *Eureka*, tales of romantic obsession microcosmically enact the galactic quest toward the ideal, matter's attempt to accumulate and return to the state of original unity. However, romantic obsession takes matters a step further than voyeurism, as characters pass through the proscenium arch separating the hidden male gaze from the theatrical female spectacle. So too Eurekan atoms analogously close the gap between themselves in an aborted attempt to merge. Poe's grand conception of the sublime unity of the movement of atoms toward a common center suggests the movement from what is (reality) to what could be (ideality)—the purely spiritual. That is, when matter collapses again into one united particle, "it will sink at once into that Nothingness which, to all finite perception, Unity must be" (*Eureka*, 133). Poe explains further that "the re-gathering of this diffused Matter and Spirit will be but the re-constitution of the *purely Spiritual* and Individual God" (*Eureka*, 136).

Significantly for the theme of obsession, Poe describes the quest of the Eurekan universe for lost unity in the language of parenthood. Concerning the attractive impulses among atoms, he asks, "Does not a sympathy so omniprevalent, so ineradicable, and so thoroughly irrespective, suggest a common paternity as its source?" (*Eureka*, 40). Later he describes the common center toward which the atoms tend as the ultimate unity: "*This* is their lost parent. *This* they seek always—immediately—in all directions—wherever it is even partially to be found" (*Eureka*, 41). This seeking of the lost parent, more particularly the lost mother, is the heart of Poe's, and subsequently Hitchcock's, tales of romantic obsession. In this quest the female, unconsciously idealized into the figure of the mother by the male, becomes the imaginative key back to divine unity. But under these conditions, the encounter between male and female inevitably ends in failure, since it is only the woman who represents the forces of attraction. The romantic male, unlike the female, is not seeking earthly unity of the flesh, but imaginative and ideal unity of mind and spirit—an impossible and "forbidden" relationship untainted by earthly attachments. Such works have in common a dreamlike ambiance that expressionistically reflects the idealism of the male protagonists.

This obsession with the mother takes us back to Jung and his description of the process of infant development, the separation of its identity from the mother's known as differentiation. As noted in chapter 4 in relation to "The Pit and the Pendulum" and *North by Northwest*, this process can be difficult, and some never complete it. Males in particular may have a midlife crisis as they unconsciously attempt to complete the process of individuation.

Jung's theory of development helps uncover the invisible center of Poe's *Eureka*. In Eurekan terms, Jung's description of how the infant's discontinuous consciousness grows in awareness through separation from the mother and the attendant frustrations, reacting to situations and people around it, parallels the process of separation from the original unified particle. For Jung this is a process of learning to separate opposites in a fragmented life in which perfect unity and happiness are impossible. Just as Poe describes the diffusion through space, Jung describes how the ego identity continues to develop as if on a journey, exploring and learning methods of adapting to the environment as well as to the behavior of others. Mirroring the final stages of the *Eureka* cycle in which fragments unite and collapse back into a single particle, Jung's movement toward individuation (full, independent maturity) eventually enables one to fall in love and marry. These later aspects of ego development, Jung argues, happen twice: once as we grow to adulthood and again between thirty-five and fifty, creating the midlife crisis. He describes this process as a time of introverted, personal explorations, again trying to shed youthful illusions about the self. It is here that we face our dark side, experiencing what literary critics have called the "night sea journey," a narrative search for self that is often pervaded with images of death and rebirth. In the works of Poe and Hitchcock, which abound in such imagery, this process often becomes a tragic revelation of the impotent attempt to complete individuation and achieve stable happiness.

In many Poe and Hitchcock stories, attraction to the opposite sex is psychologically forbidden because it threatens the ideal relationship of imagined oneness with the mother. This is the deep structure of romantic obsession. Within this framework, even wives and lovers can only become objects to voyeuristically admire and idealize into myths, dreams, and goddesses, thus kept at a safe psychic distance. In essence, the romantic obsession of Poe's protagonists becomes an attempt to shortcut or transcend the journey, to cut prematurely to the point of collapse and return to safe, all-consuming oneness with the mother. In terms of the premature completion of the *Eureka* cycle, the dominance of the negative charge separating atoms/characters is still in force. In Jungian terms, the psychologically unhealthy protagonist is unable to find fulfillment apart from the mother, making him ambivalent about the idealized female over which he is obsessed. He both desires and is repulsed by her, seeking—even to the point of her death—to maintain her as an ideal only.

Before we consider how these patterns function in the romantic obsession stories of Poe and Hitchcock, I will explain two contexts necessary to framing the discussion. First, I will clarify my use of Jung and his theories about maternal influence; second, I will supply some biographical background on our artists that both links their attitudes and offers perspective on their interest in this subject.

First, the "mother" principle is the rationally inexplicable hunger for transcendence that certain females engender in certain males. Such fulfilling enchantment activates the imagination, bringing an overarching purpose and coloring to life that becomes a form of salvation. In Poe and Hitchcock this hunger is for an ideal and has nothing to do with sexual excitement; as in "Berenice," the passion is for "des idées." The process is one of trying to recapture an intangible wisp of memory or feeling, reaching for a star. For me, Jung's explanation for such behavior is more plausible than Freud's Oedipal construction—as interesting as it is. Jung's theory allows for the mother figure to be a nonsexualized archetype or myth—an idea that enters the collective unconsciousness through everyone's common experience. As such, the mother is the temporary peace, security, and happiness of earliest consciousness, the loss of which becomes what Poe calls a "mournful and never-ending remembrance."

While Poe expressed this more explicitly and more often than Hitchcock, the presence of rarified female icons in Hitchcock's films are witness of his obsession with the female ideal (more explicitly and personally explored in *Vertigo*). In most of his films, it isn't so much the characters who idealize these women as it is Hitchcock's camera. In *Rear Window*, for example, the camera's and Jeff's views of Lisa couldn't be more at odds. The camera is infatuated with and sympathizes with her, while the rugged and immature Jeff is contemptuous of everything the camera loves—her elegance, high style, and grace. Appropriately, while Jeff sleeps, the camera indulges in a slow-motion close-up of Lisa approaching him. The same is true in *Notorious*, where Devlin sees a corrupt party girl while the camera sees a vital but unhappy woman. Later, while Devlin sees her as Alex's prostitute, the camera shows a dignified and glorious creature worthy of love and affection. In these films Hitchcock seems to be the silent rival of his leading men, creating a fascinating tension that somewhat echoes reality. The key difference, then, between reading a Poe tale of romantic obsession and seeing a Hitchcock film is that in Poe the character becomes obsessed, while in Hitchcock, it is the audience that follows the camera's obsessive lead. This pattern goes a long way to explain Hitchcock's concern for getting the right female starts, and for his disappointment with Kim Novak. While his camera enchanted the audience (and Truffaut) with Novak, he himself was never moved. Being moved himself, imaginatively and emotionally, makes creating films a fulfilling substitute for letting himself fall into a dangerously real romantic obsession.

The second context of Poe's and Hitchcock's interest in romantic obsession is the biographical. Kenneth Silverman found the title and theme for his study, "Mournful and Never-Ending Remembrance," in Poe's comments on "The Raven" (*Edgar A. Poe*, 240). He explains that Poe's mother, Eliza, died when he was too young to complete a healthy bereavement, and consequently he magnified her in his mind instead of diminishing her. Children often find it hard to accept death and often expect the loved one to return. Hence many of Poe's tales and poems are focused on the loss and possible return of the beloved.[1] Poe typically idealizes the women he portrays as angels and goddesses, impossibly beautiful, good, and/or intelligent. In his personal life, his many worshipful or self-destructive relationships with women, and his marriage to his thirteen-year-old cousin, Virginia, have caused many to question his sexual potency. Biographers Marie Bonaparte, Hervey Allen, and Joseph Wood Krutch have suggested that he was impotent. This is sometimes blamed on opium, but more commonly on a mother fixation. Buranelli responds that the facts are obscure and that there is no warrant to suggest positively that Poe's relationship with Virginia was not normal. Silverman notes, however, that Poe's statement that he didn't "assume the position of husband" for two years is so ambiguous and secondhand that it is "uncertain whether he had sexual relations with his wife even after the two years."[2] Such unconsummated love would have enabled him to find a perfect compromise between the ideal and the real. Although we can't know, Poe's behavior left him open to suspicions about psychosexual abnormalities that perhaps are enacted and explored in his work.

Poe's complex expression of romantic love can be summed up in the mutually exclusive terms of the sublime that Ligeia's husband uses to describe his response to her eyes: they "at once so delighted and appalled me" (315). The ideal itself stirs within the narrator contradictory emotions, while later in the tale Rowena (representing the real) creates feelings of pure disgust. Poe's narrators are typically torn between opposite feelings, becoming another reflection of the universal principle of the imp of the perverse, which diffuses the original unity and continues within each human fragment. Their reaction to their lovers includes both delight and horror, a sublime experience that alienates them from their lovers. Poe hints at his obsession with these contradictory feelings in "The Lake" when he states that "terror was not a fright,/ But a tremulous delight."[3] In "The Raven," for example, the young narrator mourns the lost Lenore on the one hand, and seeks actively to blot out her memory through reading the quaint volumes of "forgotten lore" on the other. He desires to torture himself with the knowledge that he can never see her again. Lenore's memory, supposedly a good thing, becomes a painful, tormenting, and maddening experience reflecting his delightful and appalling feelings about her. "Ulalume" too enacts a seasonal torture cycle of hopeful amnesia and painful remembrance. In fact, the entire poem is poised on oppositions, in a "misty mid region" between a "volcanic" heart and the "boreal pole," between crisp, sere, and dead October and the fertility of Spring's Astarte (415–19). In "Morella" as well, the narrator's feelings for her turn from "joy . . . into horror"—and the "most beautiful became the most hideous" (230). Love cannot be allowed to come too physically close, only in "his heart . . . Her image deeply lies—" ("To the River," 134–35). As he asks in "The Valley of Unrest," "All things lovely—are not they/ Far away—far away" (191–93), perhaps as distant as where Helen resides in the "glory that was Greece,/ And the grandeur that was Rome" (165–66). In the fragmented, diffuse world of Poe, real love is not possible; it must be relocated to dreamland and kept alive through the constant psychomachic battle staged by the imp of the perverse between delight and repulsion, love and hate, hope and despair.

After his mother and several other idealized women died, Poe possibly sought escape from the physical aspects of married life by marrying his thirteen-year-old cousin as a sexless companion. Continuing the avoidance trend later in life, he had a string of infatuations, proposals, and rejections that reflect the ambivalence in his stories. Through his drinking and eccentric behavior he managed to subvert the very relationships he seemed to need so desperately. Feelings of both delight and dismay found expression repeatedly. For Poe romantic love was a two-edged sword, a paradoxical and psychological minefield. His "Holy-Land" of ideal love can never be any more than a painful memory or a dream. In "To Helen," for example, love is merely a springboard for the ideal imagination ("To the glory that was Greece") while Helen herself becomes "statue-like" framed in a "window-niche." Love and mourning since his mother's death are, like Roderick and Madeleine Usher, twins who cannot be separated for long. The real world can bring only pain to Poe and his characters, pointing inevitably to the "route obscure and lonely" where the pains of the world can be temporarily overcome in dreamland. In "The Assignation" only death can appropriately enable the couple to pursue perfect happiness.

Hitchcock's life and work raise similar questions about his mother. He was brought up in semi-isolation and, according to available information, his mother was central to his young life and to some extent dominated him. Emma Hitchcock was a regal woman who, from her bed, daily interrogated her son concerning his activities in what he called "evening confessions." This ritual continued into his young adulthood. As Donald Spoto seems justified in concluding, mother figures in Hitchcock's American films become "personal repositories of his anger, guilt, resentments, and a sad yearning."[4] In some ways his long marriage to Alma Reville, happy but largely celibate, was like a mother–son relationship.[5] Excessively shy and fearful of confrontations, Alma treated him like the boy he partially was, often handling much of the business end of production.

Robin Wood once noted that Hitchcock's "preoccupation with the darker side of motherhood may be a consequence of Hitchcock's experience of America rather than of personal psychology."[6] While we can't be sure of what Wood meant, surely Hitchcock didn't make films to express intellectual opinions of American motherhood. More likely we can find hints in his age when he came to America, his marital situation, his profession, and his relationship to his mother. He turned forty the year he arrived in Hollywood, finding himself suddenly thrust into the intimate company of vivacious and beautiful women. They were goddesses for whom he felt both attraction and terror. Understandably, this boy/man with romantic vertigo fell into a string of obsessive infatuations, beginning with his first star, Joan Fontaine, leading him through the years to Ingrid Bergman, Grace Kelly, Vera Miles, and Tippi Hedren. At times his eye even veered toward his collaborators, such as Joan Harrison. He depended on Alma's practical opinions and aesthetic judgments, and she served as a comfortable, motherly companion. But something inside him was reaching out for more. Alma was to Hitchcock what Midge is to Scottie, real and vital—but a bit mundane to his romantic imagination. Alma was important and stable, but neither as exciting nor as exotic as the ideal women with which he surrounded himself, literally and imaginatively.

Hitchcock often cultivated his relationship with his leading ladies and demanded their attention far beyond professional necessity, particularly with Miles and Hedren. To them he constantly sent gifts, took proprietary interest over every aspect of their lives, and called daily, private rehearsal sessions, in many ways, of course, repeating his mother's controlling behavior. Like Poe, the romantic Hitchcock thrived creatively on these fantasies. Yet Hitchcock, like Poe, had mixed emotions about women. Spoto suggests that he was hurt when, unlike Chaplin, Selznick, and other filmmakers, he was unable to attract the romantic interest of the beautiful stars with whom he worked. On the other hand, it seems more plausible that his inability to break away from the maternal sphere of his mother, wife, and Catholic upbringing made such ideas unthinkable. His films powerfully express these paradoxes and contradictions. These unresolved feelings seem to be the basis for exploring his fantasy of escaping into an ideal love relationship in the five films about the role of mother in romantic obsession: *Notorious*

(1946), *Vertigo* (1958), *North by Northwest* (1959), *Psycho* (1960), and *The Birds* (1963). Unlike Poe, Hitchcock lived in a post-Freudian world. Psychoanalysis had been the subject of *Spellbound* (1945). Consequently, while his personal life may have been influenced to some extent by the personal but subconscious image of his mother, his films are certainly more explicitly aware of Freudian patterns associated with the mother. The five films mentioned above witness a knowing and often campy awareness of Freud and, self-reflexively, Hitchcock's own hang-ups.

In the five maternal films we see, as subtextual plots, five middle-aged men struggling to transition into adulthood. The release dates for these films include 1946, 1958, 1959, 1960, and 1963. Obviously Hitchcock's interest in the subject of breaking away from the gravity of the anima became increasingly important in his American films. The first two films question the possibility of breaking out of mother's orbit. In *Notorious*, Alex Sebastian discovers that his wife is a spy and he must return, frightened and broken, to the safety and supervision of mother. *Vertigo* also depicts a man who "wanders" from his safely maternal girl-friend Midge to chase the more exciting, if illusory Madeleine that in turn leads him to the very depths of psychological humiliation. *North by Northwest* is a comic interlude sandwiched between the more serious meditations on these issues. Here bad boy Roger escapes mother from the elevator at a dead run, finding redemption and mature love at last in Eve Kendall. *Psycho* and *The Birds* are both optimistic and pessimistic about growing up sexually and psychologically. In *Psycho* Norman overcomes mother by killing her but then resurrects her internally, becoming his dead mother and figuratively returning to the womb of her home. *The Birds* shows the difficulty of leaving mother, as the bird attacks in part suggest Lydia's fury at Mitch's leaving her for Melanie. In the end, Mitch makes Melanie a member of the family, subduing his mother's hostility and settling the birds down considerably.[7] In each case there is both attraction and repulsion in the protagonists as they strive to escape mother, recreate their identities, and finally grow up. Alex and Norman fail in different ways and Scottie's fate is ambiguous, while Roger and Mitch appear to have succeeded.

Given the troubling maternal backgrounds of Poe and Hitchcock, their conflicted attitudes toward women in their works shouldn't be surprising. While they often idealize female characters as perfection and beauty itself, they are equally obsessed with showing them at their worst. Poe's women become emaciated, lifeless, lusterless, and thin. Their lips become shrunken and their lofty, pale foreheads prominently feature blue veins. Hitchcock, while famous for his perfectly groomed, glamorous blonde icons over whose dress and appearance he obsessed, like Poe showed them at their worst: think of the nasty drunk Ingrid Bergman in *Notorious*, the praying Barbara Leigh-Hunt during her rape in *Frenzy*, the drab Grace Kelly after being jailed in *Dial M*, and the shattered Tippi Hedren at the end of *The Birds*. For both Poe and Hitchcock, the female other stirred the most ambiguous feelings, a double impulse to idealize and destroy, worship and escape.

The pattern of fulfillment followed by loss, common in Poe's tales and used by Hitchcock in *Vertigo*, goes beyond explicit concern with the mother. She is the deep structure of their creative lives—a microcosm of the attraction and repulsion of the universe—a metaphor for the purposes of art itself. She is the unreachable on earth, which cannot and must not be attained. She represents the "forbidden" knowledge that the protagonist/narrator can never face but the (m)other figure seems to understand. She is the invisible center and secret of the universe, around which the vortical energy of these tales madly swirls.[8] What fascinates (and torments) Poe and his protagonists, often represented in their obscure transcendental studies, is the inability to arrive on solid psychological ground. The universe is constructed as a fragmenting or collapsing process that promises eternal repetition of this process. Only in the dream of stability is true, if tentative and temporary, wonder possible ("It is a happiness to wonder. It is a happiness to dream"). In Poe the moment of possession is always the moment of renunciation—as in Emily Dickinson ("To comprehend a nector/ requires sorest need"). This sentiment nicely sums up the unspoken, invisible center of Poe's universe. The dream of creative perfection in "Israfel" is powerful precisely because it is unattainable; great poetry, of course, thrives on oppositions. "Dream-land" is a peaceful "home" because it is only a partial realization of desires with its "sheeted memories," "shrouded forms," and "darkened glasses." Therefore, the (m)other figure who brings the suffering narrator too close to fulfillment must be renounced ("I never spoke of passion nor thought of love") and die, becoming an ideal that enables momentary happiness in memory.

Finally, obsession to possess and then renounce the idealized mother figure is the culminating and most dramatic encounter between attraction and repulsion. It powerfully suggests the potential for realizing the peace and security of unity and wholeness and consequently demands the most drastic response by the protagonist. It is this heightened emotional and psychological moment that Poe describes in "The Philosophy of Composition." Why is the death of a beautiful woman the most poetic subject? Because it is the most melancholy. Beauty in art, as Whitman discovers in "Out of the Cradle Endlessly Rocking," only comes at the price of loss.

The Marriage Group

This chapter focuses on *Vertigo's* relationship to three Poe tales regarding the paradoxes of romantic obsession. The first part of the film draws on the mysteriousness of Madeleine, reflecting "Fall of the House of Usher." In *Vertigo*, Elster is Usher explaining his concern for Madeleine, making Scottie the tale's narrator/friend. Simultaneously Hitchcock borrows from "The Man of the Crowd," as Scottie embarks on an extended, inexplicable surveillance of Madeleine, following her to a number of San Francisco landmarks. After what he thinks is Madeleine's death, Scottie, like the narrator of "Ligeia," becomes obsessed with the dead lover and seeks to bring her back. As we will see, there is playfulness in Hitchcock's homage to these Poe tales as he twists them for his own ironic purposes.

Hitchcock plays with formulas that Poe has established, specifically a formula centering around events and characters whose existence is problematical. For example, even if Madeleine Usher were buried alive, how could she ever escape her tomb and break through the iron door of the crypt? Why does Poe coincidentally converge the storm with the sound effects embellishing the reading of "The Mad Tryst"? Finally, readers must consider Usher's accusation that the narrator is mad, throwing the entire story into doubt. Equally inexplicable is Ligeia's tale, told by a partial amnesiac and opium user. Her alleged superhuman command of all branches of knowledge is clearly impossible, throwing all else into narrative limbo. Hitchcock takes the problem of the reality of Poe's women in these tales a step further in *Vertigo* by making Madeleine Elster, as played by Judy Barton, a nonexistent person. Hitchcock provides another layer of irony when Scottie recreates what he thinks is a simulacrum of Madeleine out of Judy. Ironically, this is the "real" Madeleine—who is really the original fake Madeleine Elster. Thus Hitchcock pumps new life into Poe's narratives by first understanding their inner springs and mechanics and then building in a few more. Hence the focus of Hitchcock's complex, intertextual adaptation is on narrative formulas, which, like Poe's, have the power to mystify audiences and reinforce the transcendent theme of romantic obsession.

The major patterns of romantic obsession can be established in three tales that Daniel Hoffmann calls Poe's "marriage group": "Morella," "Berenice," and "Ligeia."[9] The protagonist in each tale is ambivalent toward his idealized woman in the vacillating impulse to maintain perpetual enchantment through an imaginative and transcendent return to the womb (original unity).

"Morella" establishes the pattern followed in "Ligeia," an intellectual marriage between a subordinate male and a powerful, mysterious female. In these tales the woman dies under mysterious circumstances, leaving the melancholy narrator to await her later return under even stranger circumstances. In "Morella," the narrator marries a woman for whom he feels no romantic love but experiences in his soul "fires it had never before known" (229). Thus he is both attracted and not attracted to her. At the center of this tale is the narrator's obsession with whether one retains identity after death. She divines with her "meaning eyes" the causes of his ambivalence toward her as "fate." At her death, she prophesies that he will "adore" her in death, but that "thy days shall be days of sorrow" (233). As Morella dies giving birth, her infant begins to breathe and in dreamtime grows quickly to resemble Morella. She also dies, but at her tomb, the narrator finds Morella's tomb empty.

From a Eurekan perspective, the narrator's impulse to "abandon" himself entirely to his wife's guidance is the attractive impulse to return to the original unity. His terrified repulsion from her, particularly in light of his intense concern about retaining his identity at death, suggests his fear of losing his individuality here and hereafter. Translated into the parallel Jungian perspective, Morella represents for him the hope of returning to the oneness with mother he once enjoyed as well as an intense fear of it. Like a child, he abandons himself entirely to her, though he does not, contrary to Freud, necessarily feel romantic love for her. And like a child, he inevitably has the contrary impulse to separate from the mother and establish his own identity. Her reference to "fate," which seems to imply the loss of identity (and perhaps his inevitable and childish fear of it), clearly relates here. The "forbidden pages" he pores over with Morella relate to the absorption of the individual into a general soul after death, a thought too horrible for the narrator, leading to his struggle toward differentiation from the "mother" and his somehow willing (or directly causing) her death. Plato's epigraph, "Itself, by itself, solely, one, everlastingly, and single," suggests the ambiguity of the narrator's position. Is oneness found alone or in concert with another? His tale springs from his simultaneous longing for and fear of such oneness.

"Berenice" serves as a gloss on the same issues. It is important in the "marriage group" for revealing more candidly perspectives that clearly underlie some of Poe's less explicit narrators. These candid statements have to do with the narrator's dream life and his feelings for Berenice. The narrator, Egaeus, is one of a "race of visionaries" who lives his life surrounded by art and books in a "palace of imagination." His is a life of uncontrollable and dissipating "revery" in which "the wild ideas of the land of dreams became, in turn, not the material of my every-day existence, but in very deed that existence utterly and solely in itself" (210). His feelings for Berenice are equally explicit: "I had never loved her. In the strange anomaly of my existence, feelings with me, *had never been* of the heart, and my passions *always were* of the mind" (214). Thus he saw her "not as the living and breathing Berenice, but as the Berenice of a dream; not as a being of the earth, earthly, but as the abstraction of such a being; not as a thing to admire, but to analyze" (214). In a trance she enters his study where they stare silently at each other, both in a separate world. He becomes obsessed with her teeth, which for him internally embody Berenice herself—an idea, part of his dreamland "regions of fairy land" (210): "*Des idées!*—ah, here was the idiotic thought that destroyed me! *Des idées!*—ah, *therefore* it was that I coveted them so madly! I felt that their possession could alone ever restore me to peace, in giving me back to reason" (216).

Egaeus's obsession is linked, more explicitly than in other tales, to longing for the mother. Significantly, the library, in which he confines

himself in perpetual dreams, is where he was born and where his
mother died. His inability to leave the library seems related to his loss
of the mother—the place he feels closest to her. Together then, his
dreams, which are intense reveries on objects, and his ties to where his
mother birthed him and died, indicate his desire to return to the infant
state of oneness with the mother and its pleasant, if irrational, dream
state. His obsessive interest in contemplating Berenice, as well as his
desire to marry her, is his attempt to return to the mother. She is *the*
idea of his life, and Berenice's teeth represent for him his mother's loving smile. To his infant eyes her teeth were hugely prominent, connected inseparably with the love, comfort, and security that he has
never stopped missing. Berenice is both an imaginative screen on
which Egaeus inscribes his desires and a physical door into dreamland.
He actually succeeds in leaving the confines of earthly consciousness,
since he is entirely unconscious of his horrible act of removing
Berenice's teeth. However, the final horror of discovering what he did
perfectly contrasts reality with his dream, demonstrating the failure of
permanently leaving the earth and returning to the womb. Removing
Berenice's teeth is perhaps Poe's most violent expression of abstracting
a woman out of her humanity.

   "Ligeia" fleshes out the patterns established in "Morella" and
"Berenice" by emphasizing the dream mind of the narrator. In taking
this dream approach to the tale, I'm well aware that of themselves, such
readings are tired and hackneyed. In terms of our theme of the ambivalent obsession to return to the mother, however, such an approach
becomes key to understanding not only romantic obsession but transcendence itself in Poe. Dream imagery saturates the tale. The key to
this dream tale is how it specifically links the idealization of the mother
with dream itself, by presenting vague memories and descriptions that
become a small child's remembrances filtered through the mind of a lit-
erate, if unstable, adult.[10] The adult narrator is unknowingly describing
his experience as a child with his mother as if it were his experience as
a married man (anticipating Freud with incredible precision). Twice, in
fact, he compares himself to a child, "groping benighted" and with
"child like confidence" resigning himself "to her guidance" (316). In
fact, Poe wrote to Sarah Helen Whitman that "'Ligeia' was . . . suggested by a *dream*."[11] "Dreams," "slumbering," "visions," and "revery"

are words that are named at least eleven times in the tale. Affirming such hints, the narrator notes a couple of times that he "might have dreamed" what he describes (325, 329). What few details he is able to provide at the beginning of the tale suggest the vague memory of a dreamer: an unknown city on the Rhine, its decaying nature, and confusion about motives over why he never knew her family name. Such vagueness of place is typical of dreams, attested to in "Dream-land," with its "forms that no man can discover." On the other hand, his clear memory of Ligeia herself is also typical of dreams, as dreamers usually remember more about the people than the setting. He describes her repeatedly and explicitly in dream terms, moving like a silent "shadow." Her beauty has "the radiance of an opium-*dream*—an airy and spirit-lifting *vision* more wildly divine than the *phantasies* which hovered about the *slumbering* souls of the daughters of Delos" (311, italics mine). In this context, the "ill-omened" nature of this dream marriage he bemoans is that he inevitably wakes up.

The narrator's dream becomes related to maternal memories in the narrator's fixation on Ligeia's features, including the "long hours" pondering them, particularly the eyes, clearly suggesting an infant's perspective. His descriptions of her features as consistently larger than usual denotes a child's point of view: Ligeia is "tall," her forehead "lofty," and her eyes "far larger than the ordinary eyes of our own race" (223). In addition, the "*strangeness* in the proportion" of her features issues from the same extreme close-up perspective that causes her features to appear large (not unlike viewing a film from the first row in a movie theater). Ligeia's chin, another feature particularly prominent from a child's perspective, is likened to "the contour which the god Apollo revealed but in a dream" (312). Finally, the "incomprehensible lightness and elasticity of her footfall," her coming and departing "as a shadow," and her "low sweet voice" (311) all strongly suggest a mother periodically checking on her infant. His detailed meditation on Ligeia's eyes and their mysterious expression suggests the vagueness of a dream ("the beauty of beings either above or apart from the earth"), as well as the half-conscious perspectives of a child unable to articulate concepts like expression ("Ah, word of no meaning!"). The "circle of analogies" he uses to get at the meaning of the eyes obviously suggest movement and metamorphosis (chrysalis, vine, meteor, running water), all of which, in this context, also suggest the dreamlike instability seen in her eyes, hinting that the dreamer must eventually awake. This is also affirmed in his comparing her eyes to distant stars and "divine orbs" (313), acknowledging that she is indeed "apart from the earth." His confession at the end of this lengthy meditation, that ultimately the expression of the eyes "at once so delighted and appalled me" (225), is the crux of his tale. On the one hand, while he is delighted by the love and beauty of her eyes, he is appalled by the potential loss of self—another meaning of the chrysalis, vine, and running water similes. This is the adult dreamer responding to the imagined perspectives of his childhood. The heart of the narrator's conflict lies in loving and rejecting Ligeia, in being delighted and appalled. Such total, childlike dependence on her is a threat to the adult dreamer's individuality.

Ligeia's "immense" learning makes the most sense in light of the child's relation to the mother, whose knowledge of the world so far exceeds his own that she seems virtually omniscient. Translated into the infinite idealization of dreams, she seems acquainted with all human knowledge, especially the "chaotic world" of metaphysical studies. Their joint research project is described as "ethereal" information located down an "all untrodden path" that is "but little sought" by others. (Clearly, his personal dreams are not sought by others and thus untrodden.) Such descriptions easily suggest a mother reading to her son and explaining new concepts. His hope is that eventually he might come to "a wisdom too divinely precious not to be forbidden" (316). Here the adult dreamer translates the magic world of the fairy tales read to him by his mother with mystical mysteries of metaphysical studies. The experience of ethereal beauty can only be vaguely imagined in fleeting insights and impressions—the "route obscure and lonely"— where there is only room for one. What is ultimately forbidden to the child-narrator is continued metaphysical oneness with Ligeia. With her guidance he penetrates the "mysteries of transcendentalism," but as she begins to fail he becomes "as a child groping benighted"—meaning that he is unable to read (316).

As Ligeia dies, their roles are reversed, since she has a "passionate devotion [which] amounted to idolatry" for the narrator. This is best explained in the fact that while she is the goddess—or high priestess— of his dream world, he is the god whose world it is. He soon realizes that the love she has for him, "the principle of her longing" ("all unmerited, all unworthily bestowed"), is really her "vehemence of desire for life—*but* for life" (317–18). That is, he is beginning to awaken, which she knows will spell her death (the "fate" Morella was aware of that baffled the narrator-dreamer). In terms of his maternal dream, this outpouring of love and desperate clinging to life is a dying mother's desire to stay with her son and her fears at leaving him motherless and alone. This is a moving recreation of what may have occurred at Elizabeth Arnold's death.

The emphasis on Glanvill's alleged statements about the power of the human will, which Ligeia quotes with her dying breath, is the dreamer's will to recapture a lost dream. In the second half of the dream, the narrator sets about recapturing his lost unity with the mother by remodeling a ruined abbey in a remote, "wild" part of England. He notes of his dream bower that it "had taken a coloring from my dreams," dreams of one now "a bounden slave to the trammels of opium" (320). Since the descriptive details of this fantastic room are reminiscent of his description of Ligeia earlier in the tale, he is clearly building a simulacrum of the dream that continues to obsess him.[12] A quick list of parallels between Ligeia and the room will suffice to indicate the pattern and its purpose, taking its "coloring from my dreams": the room's high ceiling is Ligeia's lofty forehead (its vines are her hair), the "serpent vitality" of the censor is the worm of her poem, the lack of system in the furnishings is the "strangeness" of her face's proportions, the high walls are Ligeia's height, and the gigantic sarcophagi of Luxor in each corner of the room represent the ill-omened Egyptian goddess that doomed their marriage. Most important, however, are the curtains with their arabesque designs that are made to perpetually move, making them "changeable in aspect." These are the decorative equivalent to the changeable and inexplicable expression of Ligeia's eyes. Further linking them with her in terms of the horrible mutability of dreams, the narrator describes the curtains' effect as "ghastly forms" from the "guilty slumbers of the monk" (322).

An insistent, cyclical parallelism characterizes the resurrection of Ligeia. Rowena, like Ligeia before, is dying, which, like Morella's death, brings about another life. Similarly, the narrator becomes as idolatrous as Ligeia had been in his obsessive creation of a temple to his dead wife's memory. His determination to leave reality and return to his dream of Ligeia is evidenced by his opium use, his repeating Ligeia's name, and especially his use of language associated with dreams: "revery," "waking visions," and twice stating that he "may have dreamed" (325–29). Finally, the description of the violent "whirl of emotions" he felt just before Ligeia appears evokes the archetype of the whirlpool dizziness of falling asleep. Thus the narrator has found a way in his dream to recover Ligeia, by abstracting her first as a room and then as a corpse. This abstraction process makes the story a metaphor for narrative art itself, which in Poe's philosophy is to use a "circle of analogies" by which to recreate an impression: "*All* that we see or seem/ Is but a dream within a dream"("A Dream within a Dream" ll.10–11).

Vertigo and Related Films

Since *Vertigo* is arguably Hitchcock's most important film and his most personal and probing study of obsession, it is significant to this study that it is also among his most Poe-esque.[13] *Vertigo* relates to "Usher," "Man of the Crowd," and "Ligeia" as if they were made up of identically shaped puzzle pieces that Hitchcock assembles randomly to make a single abstract picture. However, the pieces are so mixed up that roles are reversed and situations are displaced in novel ways, much as day residue makes up a dream. Hitchcock self-consciously plays with these narrative fragments, adding further levels of irony and audience involvement. "Ligeia" functions as the fulfillment of themes in "Morella" and "Berenice," and likewise *Vertigo* fleshes out patterns evident in earlier films. *The Paradine Case*, for example, concerns a similar romantic obsession that comes on a once stable and respectable barrister. Keene's obsession, like Scottie's, leads to a breakdown of rational thinking and behavior. The "dreamy," slow-motion kisses in *Spellbound* and *Rear Window* point toward the mood of the climactic 360-degree kiss between Scottie and Judy when she again becomes Madeleine. Finally, Mrs. Danvers's obsession with the memory and intimate belongings of her dead mistress in *Rebecca* introduces the theme of becoming lost in the past. *Vertigo* is Hitchcock's culminating romantic statement, a crescendo of fetishistic and introverted feelings of loss and longing. What makes it a great film is the ironic circumstances of Elster's murder plot, which create and sustain these feelings, making the film at once romantic and modern in sensibility.

"Usher" and *Vertigo* bear a singular resemblance, almost as distorted doubles of each other. In both, the plot is generated when a desperate man desperately summons an old school friend for help. The desperate man in *Vertigo* is Gavin Elster, whose surname sounds suspiciously like Usher. Not unlike the tottering mansion with a mysterious past near a lake in "Usher," Elster's San Francisco is a storied city of dizzying heights poised along the edge of a bay.[14] Like Usher, Elster is surrounded by art and is upset about a woman named Madeleine who is inexplicably ill. These women, who are both subject to trances, are first seen by the protagonist in a captivating but fleeting glimpse, of which they apparently are not aware.[15] Finally, both stories develop around an increasing air of tension that culminates in the death of the women, the madness of the protagonists, and the reappearance of the dead Madeleines.

Despite these and other similarities, the puzzle pieces get mixed up here and there. In many ways, for example, Scottie is more like Usher than Elster is, his vertigo and breakdown paralleling Usher's "nervous agitation" and growing madness. Similarly displaced is the fact that Usher's superstitious certainty about his impending mysterious death more nearly resembles Madeleine Elster's certainty that she is doomed to die by mysterious supernatural circumstances. Like Roderick and Madeleine, Scottie and Madeleine are in many ways doubles, both romantic wanderers and both obsessed with troubling dreams that lead to total mental collapse, but only fakes in her case.[16] Finally, both "Usher" and *Vertigo* are dreamlike. The strange atmosphere surrounding the house of Usher is compared by the narrator to "the after-dream of the reveller upon opium"(397). Later the narrator mentions listening "as if in a dream" to Usher's guitar playing (404). *Vertigo*, unlike its source, *The Living and the Dead* (Boileu and Narcejac), which presents a crowded and realistic Paris, takes place in a series of often empty, almost haunted spaces in and about San Francisco that reflect Scottie's all-consuming and solipsistic obsession with Madeleine. They seem to inhabit a world all their own. In fact, Truffaut calls *Vertigo* a "filmed dream."[17]

Another set of Poe puzzle pieces used in *Vertigo* is from "A Man of the Crowd," whose narrator's obsessive surveillance resembles Scottie's.

Like Poe's narrator, Scottie is convalescing, generally enjoying the chance to laze about. Their common leisure and boredom soon find something to obsess the idle mind, which for Scottie means following Madeleine. Like the old man Poe's narrator follows, Madeleine is an inexplicable mystery. Much of *Vertigo*, like Poe's tale, takes place in an urban setting with the object of the surveillance making seemingly random forays through the city. Just as Poe's narrator thinks he can type-class everyone on the streets, Scottie falsely assumes he can solve Madeleine's mysterious obsession and save her. But he is just as mistaken in his overconfidence as Poe's narrator is. It never occurs to him that Madeleine is not who she claims to be, is not really superstitious, and has been put up to this charade by Elster as a means of murdering his wife. Only in the end does he comprehend the truth, after following Madeleine through the "dark and intricate" passages of his mind for over a year. Like Poe's epigraph to the "Man of the Crowd," referring to the old man, Madeleine is a text that cannot be read by Scottie.[18]

The "Ligeia" pieces of the puzzle come into play when Scottie loses Madeleine the first time—perhaps the most significant Poe-esque element of the film. Just as "Ligeia" is told by a broken man and opium addict who has a spotty memory and is unable to distinguish truth from reality, Scottie is a completely broken man after Madeleine's fall, the death of his identity reflecting her death (particularly in the dream sequence when he falls into an open grave). A virtual catatonic who can't remember who he is, he sits in a trance for a year or so following "Madeleine's" death. After his illness, a shell of what he was, Scottie wanders about helplessly, haunting the places where Madeleine once walked, continually mistaking other women for her (not unlike the grieving student in "The Raven" who jumps at every sound as if his lost Lenore were present). Like Poe's narrator finding Rowena, Scottie finds Judy an inadequate substitute for Madeleine (though ironically she is Madeleine). Judy is too much like Midge, Scottie's mundane mother figure. While Poe's narrator furnishes a room to conjure Ligeia back into his imagination, Scottie refurnishes Judy herself. He completely makes her over, with dresses, shoes, hair, lips, and eyes that match Madeleine's. When the made-over Judy/Madeleine finally enters the room, bathed in a ghostly green light, she, like Ligeia, seems to have returned from the dead. Madeleine seemingly has taken over the body of

Judy, as Carlotta took over the body of Madeleine and Ligeia of Rowena, the dream work of reduplication. Scottie and Judy/Madeleine embrace in the climactic kiss with Hitchcock's camera circling and Scottie's mind reeling in the past memories of their love. This shot is reminiscent of the opium-induced reveries of Poe's narrator leading up to his vision of the reanimated Ligeia. Like Poe's narrator, Scottie brings back his lost love through sheer will.

Beyond the circumstantial plot and character similarities noted above, *Vertigo* resembles "Ligeia" in more basic, thematic ways, particularly in the relationship between dream work and the maternal basis of romantic obsession. *Vertigo* is the closest Hitchcock ever came to filming a dream. Like "Ligeia" *Vertigo* is a dream within a dream in two different ways. First, the basic story of romantic obsession, loss, and return echoes the reduplicative structure of dreams. Second, many of the film's images are fragments of actual dreams we see or hear described. Scottie's pivotal dream echoes images of Madeleine's dreams (of the mission and of an open grave) and other imagery from the film, including the portrait of Carlotta, Elster, Mission Dolores, Madeleine's flowers, and so on. On another level, several camera techniques create a surrealistic feel to the film that is reminiscent of dreams. These include an unusual number of high- and low-angle shots (appropriate to the dizziness motif), blurring and softening of images, and echoing of several shots: blue-lit night shots, profile shots of Madeleine, and crane shots of cars driving. Another reccurring dream motif in the film is Madeleine's disappearing—from the hotel, his apartment, and among the sequoias. The film also shows or mentions three dreams in addition to Madeleine's dreamlike trances and Scottie's catatonia. Of course, the most surrealistic and famous shot in the film is the zoom-dolly shot that surrealistically reveals Scottie's terror of heights to the audience. Such expressionism is the stuff dreams are made of. Finally, as much as anything, the slow and deliberate pace lends an otherworldly atmosphere to the film.

As in "Ligeia," dream is integral to *Vertigo's* theme of maternal obsession. This theme is established in the character of Midge and her inadequate attempt to be a mother substitute to Scottie, or "Johnnyo," her term of endearment for him. As a kind of mother figure, Midge is an important part of Scottie's past because she knows him inside and out. She teases him in motherly terms, saying he's "a big boy now," when he asks about the bra she is drawing. He irritably notes her maternal role as well, telling her at one point not to "be so motherly." When he falls helplessly from the step stool, she is there to catch and comfort him. Much later, following his breakdown, she ineffectually tries to comfort him by saying, "Mother's here." The problem with this arrangement is in the two kinds of roles mothers play. First is the all-consuming lover to the infant; second is the mundane caregiver to the older child and adult. Like Jung's middle-aged man who hasn't completed his individuation, Scottie is only semi-content in the role of mama's boy and is thus primed for a crisis. Trailing Madeleine down the hilly streets of San Francisco represents Scottie's falling into Madeleine's spirographic dream world. Like the city itself, Madeleine is associated with another time. Like the surviving columns from the San Francisco earthquake, she becomes a "portal of the past" for Scottie. She is also linked to the past through Carlotta, the Mission Dolores graveyard, the palace of the Legion of Honor museum, the McKittrick Hotel, and the very distant past through the fallen redwood on which she traces her former life. As in Poe's rubric, the past here is associated with dream—"sheeted memories from the past" populate her "Dreamland." Madeleine describes dreams of Carlotta's death and fragments of a shattered mirror that represent moments in time defying chronological consistency. Scottie's journey into the past, superstition, and dream finds its objective correlative in his vertigo, foreshadowed in the credits. Here we are shown close-up shots of the parts of a woman's face, reminiscent of the close-up descriptions of Ligeia's face—particularly her eyes. As the camera closes in, a swirling spirograph appears in the eye, creating an image of the hypnotic power in the eyes of this generic woman, suggesting how Scottie will fall under the spell of Madeleine, become dizzy and helpless, and finally lose his sense of reality entirely with his breakdown.

This journey is Scottie's return to the womb. In terms of return, this is expressed as Judy emerges from the bathroom as Madeleine and as they kiss. Here Scottie sees actual visions of the past. The kiss perfectly suggests Scottie's return to a blissful oneness in the arms of the eternal mother. In terms of the womb, Madeleine is repeatedly associated with darkness, including the backroom of the floral shop, the low-lit museum, the mission chapel, and her dreams of dark hallways and open graves. Her dream world is associated with darkness and she slowly pulls him down until in his own shattering dream he falls into an open grave. Madeleine is the maternal but tempting threat of total loss of identity associated with the womb—the ultimate fall into the dark past (linked with the dark side of Jung's anima). Having fallen under her spell completely, a vulnerable new Scottie is reborn, one for whom reality has little meaning. No longer the independent, "hard-headed Scott," he is now a helpless child, dependent entirely on the memory of Madeleine. When he discovers Judy, we see a childlike man pathetically seeking a substitute mother. As another Rowena, Judy enables the film, like the dream structure of "Ligeia," to resume the quest for a restoration of the eternal woman. In terms of the ambivalence Poe established in the "marriage group," Scottie both desires and fears losing his identity. While the grave/womb beckons, it also terrifies. The dolly-zoom shot represents not only a fear of heights but also a loss of identity.

In addition to developing his interest in Poe's themes, Hitchcock adapts Poe by playing with these formulas. Hitchcock's displacements prove incredibly similar in external details yet wholly different in meaning. For example, unlike Ligeia's narrator, Scottie is not so much interested in Judy's features (eyes, lips, chin) as in hair color, style, lipstick, and clothing. Therefore, his obsessions are more perverse and fetishistic, fully aware of but unconcerned about the artificiality of his recreation of Madeleine. Similarly, while Ligeia arguably never existed in the form the narrator reimagines her, so Madeleine Elster, as portrayed by Judy Barton, likewise never existed. Yet in a way she does, at least physically. This paradox, revealed in the middle of the film, creates a strange disconnect between the audience and Scottie's dilemma, dividing its sympathy between him and Judy. This revelation of identity, which uncovers the theatricality of everything Scottie has experienced and the artificiality of everything he has felt, abruptly wakes the audience from its dream of a tragic romantic fantasy to suspenseful real-life drama. This sudden complication of shocking narrative information—anticipating the revelation of oneness of Norman Bates and his mother—staggers the audience in a way Poe's more predictable gothicism never attempted. It is also a campy genre leap, not unlike abruptly moving between the second half of *An*

Affair to Remember to *Niagara*. This is an important aspect of Hitchcock's adaptation strategy—to out-manipulate the master manipulator of audiences. He does this by appearing to adapt Poe quite faithfully in many respects, when his actual motives are much more sly as he gives virtually every parallel a wicked twist. Yet, despite the ironies and complexities of Hitchcock's rearranging of Poe's puzzle pieces, he maintains the central core of enchantment—the maternal mystery of the female ideal.

However, her return is as much nightmare as dream come true when he realizes that he has been duped. Then, as in "Morella," "the most beautiful became the most hideous" (152). The 360-degree circular shot, which reveals a fleetingly troubled look on Scottie's ecstatic face, soon becomes the tempestuous whirlwind that accompanies Madeleine Usher's horrific return. When Scottie realizes the dark truth of how he has been duped, he drags Judy up the vortex of circular stairs of the San Juan Batista bell tower. There the torrent of violence comes in the form of Scottie's angry words (Usher's whirlwind is described as "tumultuous shouting") and abusive coercion. And finally, atop the tower, torn between attraction and repulsion of Judy/Madeleine, both hating and loving her, like the narrators of "Morella," Berenice," and "Ligeia," he seemingly wills Judy/Madeleine's death for psychological survival. Like the narrator of "Man of the Crowd," Scottie is stunned, unable to comprehend the dark depths of his experience, which "does not permit itself to be read" (308). Transcending the complexity of the murder plot and the coincidence of finding Judy are his reeling emotions as he stands on the edge of the abyss, before a knowledge of self that is an abyss. More than Poe could in his horror tales, Hitchcock, in more carefully detailing the perspectives of both Scottie and Madeleine, creates a powerful, less solipsistic sense of what this abyss actually is. The inexplicable predicament of living on this earth—that our deepest longings are themselves dangerously deceptive—makes *Vertigo* Hitchcock's most accomplished artistic statement. Like Scottie on the edge of the bell tower (and the "Raven" narrator caught evermore beneath the shadow of his darkest fears and longings), critics endlessly peer into the deep emotional, psychological, and ironic abysses of this film. Hitchcock's pattern of playful borrowing from Poe extends the depths to be plumbed.

Notes

1. Kenneth Silverman, *Edgar A. Poe: Mournful and Never-Ending Remembrance* (New York: Harper Perennial, 1991), 76–77.

2. Marie Bonaparte, *The Life and Works of Edgar Allan Poe: A Psycho-Analytic Interpretation* (London: Imago, 1949), assumes Poe was chaste, perhaps impotent, out of fidelity to his mother (77–89); Hervey Allan, *Israfel: The Life and Times of Edgar Allan Poe* (London: Brentano's, 1927), thought his impotence came from his opium habit (370); Joseph Wood Krutch, *Edgar Allan Poe: A Study in Genius* (New York: Russell & Russell, 1954), noting evidence that his marriage was chaste, seems to assume the explanation that Poe was impotent, psychologically at least (51–57). Vincent Buranelli, *Edgar Allan Poe* (New York: Twayne, 1961), 36; Kenneth Silverman, *Edgar A. Poe: Mournful and Never-ending Remembrance* (New York: Harper Perennial, 1991), 124.

3. Thomas Ollive Mabbott, ed., *Collected Works of Edgar Allan Poe: Poems*, vol. 1 (Cambridge: Harvard University Press, 1969). "The Lake" is found on pages 85–86 of this edition. All others of Poe's poems cited in this chapter are from this edition and will be noted by page number parenthetically in the text.

4. Donald Spoto, *The Dark Side of Genius: The Life of Alfred Hitchcock* (New York: Ballantine, 1983), 306.

5. See Spoto's *Dark Side of Genius* (229) for one source. Here he notes that as early as 1940 when he arrived in California, by Hitchcock's own admission, "his relationship [with Alma] had already become strictly chaste."

6. Robin Wood, *Hitchcock's Films Revisited* (New York: Columbia University Press, 1989), 361.

7. See Margaret M. Horwitz's excellent "The Birds: A Mother's Love," in *A Hitchcock Reader*, eds. Marshall Deutelbaum and Leland Pogue (Ames: Iowa State University Press, 1986), 279–87.

8. Kenneth Silverman, in *Edgar A. Poe*, describes Poe's "copulative endings" in these tales, in which the elements of the sentences are linked by *ands* that "call attention to each element" (113). This technique also adds rotary speed to the vortex of images that lead to the final revelation of Berenice's teeth, Morella's empty tomb, and Ligeia's possession of Rowena.

9. See Daniel Hoffmann, *Poe, Poe, Poe, Poe, Poe, Poe, Poe* (New York: Avon, 1972), 229–58.

10. This also becomes the narrative structure for Whitman's "Out of the Cradle Endlessly Rocking," in which the mature poet looks back at an experience he had as a child.

11. This part of Poe's letter is quoted in Arthur Hobson Quinn, *Edgar Allan Poe: A Critical Biography* (New York: D. Appleton-Century, 1941), 271 n. 11.

12. Silverman, in his biography of Poe, notes that the narrator's building of his dream bower is his simultaneous desire to forget and remember Ligeia (139).

13. *Vertigo* is the only Hitchcock film to make the top ten list in *Sight and Sound*. See *Sight and Sound*, Autumn 1982, 243.

14. The potential for a catastrophic fall is a common motif in several Poe and Hitchcock stories, including "The Assignation," "The Angel of the Odd," "The City in the Sea," "Maelstrom," and "Pit and the Pendulum" for Poe; and *Number Seventeen*, *Rebecca*, *Foreign Correspondent*, *Suspicion*, *Saboteur*, *Shadow of a Doubt*, *Spellbound*, *Strangers on a Train*, *Rear Window*, *North by Northwest*, and *Psycho* for Hitchcock.

15. Madeleine Elster's "beautiful phony trances" (like Berenice's) also mirror Usher's long trancelike reveries. At the same time, her trances resemble Scottie's catatonic state following Madeleine's death. Such female trances (and sometimes male, as in *Spellbound*), are common in Hitchcock: Manny's wife in *The Wrong Man*, Marnie on her honeymoon, and Melanie following the final bird attack. A phony trance appears in *Family Plot* as Madame Blanche cons her gullible customers.

16. Such doublings of men and women occurs in Poe's Psyche figures (in "Ulalume" and "To Helen"), in Hitchcock's *Shadow of a Doubt*, and, even more importantly for the mother theme, in *Psycho*.

17. Quoted in Peter Wollen, "Compulsion," *Sight and Sound*, March 1997, 16. While Poe's tales are generally dreamlike, Hitchcock often uses dreams (*Rebecca*, *Spellbound*, and *Marnie*) and surrealistic mis-en-scène, particularly in emphasizing artificiality in his backdrops (*Rope*, *Marnie*, and *The Birds*).

18. Occasions of shattered overconfidence are quite common in both Poe and Hitchcock, from Poe's Prospero, Minister D——, and William Wilson, to Hitchcock's Rupert Cadell, Eddie Shoebridge, Mark Rutland, and Phillip Vandamm.

~

CHAPTER NINE

Humor and Horror:
Collapsing into Unity

Sly Comedians: The Legacy of Humor and Horror

Among the most obvious but least studied aspects of Poe or Hitchcock is humor, yet the art of both depends on a sense of the comic as much as the horrific. Two of their projects connect Poe and Hitchcock in terms of the priority of humor and its function. Poe wrote roughly as many comic pieces as horror tales. His 1833 plan for *The Tales of the Folio Club* has a comic framework. The supposed writers of the tales, with names like Mr. Convolvulus Gondola and Mr. Solomon Seadrift, are used to create a bizarre and whimsical context for the volume. Hitchcock devised a similar comic context for the often dark tales of his television programs, *Alfred Hitchcock Presents* and *The Alfred Hitchcock Hour* (1955–1965). His droll gallows humor perfectly sets off a mix of horror, mystery, fantastic, and suspense tales, many of which also include humorous elements and end with surprising twists ("there is nothing quite so good as burial at sea. It is simple, tidy, and not very incriminating"). In addition, Hitchcock's comic trailers for *Psycho* and *The Birds* provide hints for how to enjoy his brand of horror. For both Poe and Hitchcock, the comic is clearly inseparable from the horrific.[1] But how are they unique and similar? Unlike Kubrick in *Dr. Strangelove* (1964), for example, who mixes the horrific with the predominantly

satiric, Poe and Hitchcock mix the comic in the predominantly horrific. Although Kubrick's film is a black comedy, neither "The Black
Cat" nor *Strangers on a Train* can be described as one, though both employ humor as part of the overall effect. Like the tension between attractive and repulsive forces in *Eureka*, the tension between humor and
horror in Poe and Hitchcock creates much of the energy in their work.
However, the more overtly humorous stories like "Loss of Breath" and
The Trouble with Harry can be called black comedy. This chapter focuses on the dark tale woven with subtle comic elements.

The cyclical last phase of the *Eureka* cycle is represented in this chapter as analogous to the comic spirit, bringing us full circle to the more
positive spirit of Poe's and Hitchcock's tales and films of ratiocination.
Both mystery and humor represent the assertion of positive over negative forces; ratiocination represents the phase of original unity, and humor represents the process of returning to "original Unity." Just as the
humorous persistently frames the work of Poe and Hitchcock, so this
study begins and ends with the dominance of their often undervalued,
but crucial, positive phases. The comic has been present in most of the
works examined so far, but it has not been emphasized in the exploration of other thematic convergences. For Poe and Hitchcock, whose
humor is often highly ironic and almost subtextual, humor and horror
are simultaneous and inseparable aspects of their art, not merely two
ends of a continuum.[2] For example, in the ostensibly serious *The Birds*
(1963) the horror is fed by a subtle black humor, such as the odd series
of jump cuts melodramatically recording Melanie's horror at the fire trail
leading to a gas pump. Even the horrifying attack on the children's
birthday party is qualified by the mechanical foot kicking of the prostrate girl being assaulted by a large bird. Contrariwise, Hitchcock's
solemnly paced romantic comedy at the beginning of the film suggests
dark subtexts that go against the 1930s screwball tradition he seems to
be quoting. Similarly, in "The Tell-Tale Heart" Poe's narrator absurdly
qualifies and enhances the terror we experience. Humor in Poe and
Hitchcock is virtually an element of style, like accented speech or a peculiar mode of phrasing sentences. The particular energy in these works
originates in their instability of tone: "a double minded man [or film] is
unstable in all his ways" (James 1:8). The dark is always conditioned by
the light, creating a shade of provocative and volatile gray.

This chapter locates itself in the process of collapse, as the tension between positive and negative forces becomes analogous to the tension between comic and horrific forces in the narratives of Poe and Hitchcock. We will particularly examine how the humorous charge asserts its dominance. In describing the return of the universe to its original unity in *Eureka*, Poe notes that this "is an idea, in fact, which belongs to the class of the *excessively obvious*" (*Eureka*, 125). It is obvious because Poe links the cycles of *Eureka* to the unfolding of God's "perfect plot," one in which the denouement springs "out of the bosom of the thesis—out of the heart of the ruling idea . . . as inseparable and inevitable part and parcel of the fundamental conception of the book" (*Eureka*, 129). The universe is organized, by analogy, like the parts of a text, which Poe describes in "Philosophy of Composition": "it is only with the denouement constantly in view that we can give a plot its indispensable air of consequence, or causation, by making the incidents and especially the tone at all points, tend to the development of the intention."[3] Just as the parts of a story must all relate to and support one another, so the parts of the universe, despite its diffuse state, are composed of clusters (solar systems, galaxies, nebulae) that suggest "incipient stages of consolidation" (*Eureka*, 90–91). Thus the last phase of the *Eureka* cycle, "progressive collapse" toward original unity, is the natural outcome of all that came before. As Poe notes, the symmetry of these universal cycles make it "the most sublime of poems" (*Eureka*, 124). Since this collapse is caused by gravity, the progressive collapse increasingly speeds toward a "vortical indrawing" (*Eureka*, 129) on an invisible center. When all of the diffuse parts of the universe are absorbed into this center, matter actually ceases to exist, since matter only exists as both negative and positive charges.

Likening humor to the end of the *Eureka* cycle complicates the claim of many critics that the humor of both Poe and Hitchcock is hostile to their audiences. Stephen Mooney, for example, asserts that Poe's humor is essentially hostile to the reader, being "allied to vaudeville and farce, and is directed toward the exposure of a society in which heroes and rulers are shown to be deluded or irresponsible and their subjects a dehumanized, sycophantic mass."[4] Bryant adds that "nowhere in Poe do we find the good-natured, integrative, redemptive, or transcendent urgings of amiable humor."[5] Robert Regan finds Poe's humor "hostile" to a mass audience he considers pedestrian, and doubts "that any of us who traverses that perilous ground can escape unscarred."[6] Hitchcock too is accused of hostile humor. Some of this goes back to Spoto's biography, provocatively entitled *The Dark Side of Genius* (1983), in which he interprets Hitchcock's toilet humor, practical jokes, and shock statements (actors are like cattle) to assert the director's general nastiness. Pointing to Hitchcock's image as a hostile humorist, Susan Smith equates Brandon's talk of murder as "an art" in *Rope* with Hitchcock's own cinematic art of murder, even claiming that *Rope* is about Hitchcock's humor.[7] Others say that Hitchcock's humor does not grow out of a sustaining community[8] or is "less black than blank," a "cold laughter that fails to nourish."[9] Some of these charges seem irrelevant, since creating warm feelings is clearly outside the realm of Hitchcock's purposes. Going back to Kubrick's *Dr. Strangelove*, it would be rather off the mark to worry about the humor being cold or unregenerative, since Kubrick's satire is meant to be subversive. Such approaches to Hitchcock's humor support the often negative perspectives that cultural critics see in the apolitical Hitchcock. From this standpoint, pure form does not justify genius. Even writers who do not condemn the humor of Poe and Hitchcock offer it little praise. Hitchcock's humor has not been the subject of much analysis.

Although there is a negative side to the humor of these artists, there is more. As noted above, *Eureka* helps adjust the balance of evidence, particularly in Poe's case, presenting a kinder, gentler soul. Poe ends his cosmic romance treatise as Whitman might have, extolling the unity, equality, and divinity of all: "a novel Universe swelling into existence, and then subsiding into nothingness, at every throb of the Heart Divine? And now—this Heart Divine—what is it? *It is our own*" (*Eureka*, 134). He ultimately concludes on a note of benevolence, "no soul is inferior to another" (*Eureka*, 135), and that this view of the universe is comforting and reconciling, making the idea of evil "intelligible" and "endurable" (*Eureka*, 136). If Poe does not feel superior to the souls of others, how is it that his humor seems to be a hostile attack on the reader?[10] Obviously Poe contains both the superior egotistical "tomahawk man" and the furtively benevolent philosopher of his fellow beings. Daniel Hoffmann's identification of the seven different Poes is easily ignored in the heat of analyzing any one of them.[11] But an awareness

of the other Poes, even the multiple comic Poes with their poses, produces a more balanced assessment of what his comedy is up to. Poe essays so many different comic styles that variety of approach and message
is among the hallmarks of his humor. His style includes the absurd ("Angel of the Odd"), the conundrum ("Three Sundays in a Week"), the ex-
travagantly supernatural ("Bon Bon"), the frontier humor ("Diddling"),
satire ("The Man That Was Used Up"), self-parody ("How to Write a
Blackwood Article"), and, yes, hostility ("Four Beasts in One").

As for Hitchcock, Thomas Leitch provides perspective on Hitchcock's humor in his analysis of the director's cameos—a point I find relevant to Poe as well. Refuting claims that the cameos either show
Hitchcock "trapped as an object of a film process" or remind viewers of
the artificiality of film, Leitch responds that neither these nor other
"serious" conclusions account for the inescapable wittiness of the
cameos. He notes about the cameos, as well as other Hitchcock strategies, that the point is to give the audience pleasure: "In short, Hitchcock treats films as objects of pleasure rather than as objects of knowledge."[12] While Leitch is not specifically discussing Hitchcock's sense of
humor, his point is refreshing in this era of critical specialization and
thus myopia. Just as it would be absurd to claim that playing Monopoly
is primarily hostile (making other players pay astronomical rent on our
hotels!), so Hitchcock's gallows humor is not primarily hostile. But in
its very outrageousness it succeeds in giving pleasure by making audiences laugh or gasp, or both. Balancing Spoto's view of Hitchcock as an
exclusively dark genius, Lesley Brill detects a benevolent Hitchcock
behind the films: "I would guess that Hitchcock, far from being an exotic sadist, was deeply conventional, thoughtful, and rather soft-
hearted."[13] I see Hitchcock as demonstrating what both Spoto and Brill
claim. To critics who take him so seriously and analyze him with such
careful biographical and psychological anxiety, Hitchcock might say, as
he once reminded a frustrated Ingrid Bergman, "It's only a movie." For
him, whatever factors may lie behind the creation of a film, its ostensi-
ble purpose is to entertain. Thus both balance and restraint are important for understanding the complex purposes of Poe and Hitchcock.

But there is a caveat. Anthony Lane pointed out that Hitchcock's
sardonic and sadistic wit is an outrageous "con trick" that is "somehow
. . . construed as benevolent" and, more importantly, that "it is a rule of

Hitchcock's cautionary tales that no pleasure can be wholly harmless—
that the more needling the harm, the more pointedly the pleasure will be
pricked into a thrill."[14] For Hitchcock, who compared the experience of
watching his films to riding a roller coaster, the jokes increase the thrill
much like an unexpected drop. He wants us to laugh during his films just
as the carnival owner wants us to laugh on his amusement rides. As
Hitchcock notes about his primary lesson when reading Poe, "fear . . . is a
feeling that people like to feel when they are certain of being in safety."[15]
Both Poe and Hitchcock, therefore, are primarily concerned with satisfy-
ing a certain type of audience hunger for narrative pleasure. There isn't
necessarily a contradiction between an awareness of human flaws and the
intention of entertaining an audience, as Mark Twain demonstrates.[16]

   That said, the many points of comic convergence in the works of
Poe and Hitchcock are prodigious. Some types of humor they share,
such as deadpan (*Trouble with Harry* and "The Predicament"), practical
jokes (*Psycho* [killing off the star—and early] and "Hop Frog"), irony
(*Family Plot* [the thief avoiding his inheritance] and "Cask of Amontillado"), misadventure (*North by Northwest* and "Loss of Breath"), situation comedy (*Murder* [Sir John invaded by children in his bed] and
"The Spectacles"), comic choking (*Strangers on a Train* and "The
Thousand-and-Second Tale of Scheherazade"), and macabre hubris
(*Rope* and "Cask of Amontillado"). At times their stories have the
same underlying joke. In *Spellbound* and "The System of Dr. Tarr and
Prof. Fether," for example, the underlying gag has the patients running
the insane asylum. Among their most evident convergences are found
self-reference and self-parody. Numerous Hitchcock cameos, as well as
his television appearances, parody his size (such as the *Lifeboat* reducing ad) and slowness (missing the bus in *North by Northwest*). Poe also
mocks himself and his profession as a magazine writer and editor in
tales such as "X-ing a Paragrab" and "How to Write a *Blackwood* Article." He also liked to write humorous as well as "serious" versions of the
same subjects, another form of self-reference and parody: "King Pest"
and "Masque of the Red Death," "The Angel of the Odd" and "The
Imp of the Perverse," "The Man That Was Used Up" and "Ligeia," and
"The Predicament" and "Pit and the Pendulum."

   The rest of this chapter will comparatively explore two fairly typical
tales—Poe's "Ligeia" and Hitchcock's *The 39 Steps*—in terms of the

function of humor in relation to terror. These tales are riddled with humor that comes from many directions, often at once. I have already analyzed "Ligeia" from a more serious perspective, which makes it an ideal test case. Many of the same passages will be quoted to demonstrate the multiple perspectives the tale contains. Poe's and Hitchcock's perspective is infused with humor that is inseparable from the terror. With this in mind, four approaches to humor are examined: (1) humor as multileveled, (2) humor as a hoax on characters and audiences simultaneously, leading to (3) the difficulty in interpreting these works made unstable in the mix of humor and horror, and (4) obscure jokes.

"Ligeia" and *The 39 Steps*

While G. R. Thompson discusses the ironic overtones in "Ligeia," the tale's humor, with its obscure jokes and other satirical elements, is multileveled, including a central ambivalence that tempts readers not to take the story or the narration seriously.[17] In "Ligeia" the greatest offense to credulity is the narrator himself. Students in my classes find a narrator weirdly funny who remembers neither Ligeia's surname nor the city in which he met her. Additionally, the narrator's opening tone of exasperation is comical, as if he had been trying hard to remember something just before beginning the narration but finally gives up with a sigh: "I cannot, for my soul, remember how, when, or even precisely where, I first became acquainted with the lady Ligeia."[18] A wholly serious intention would not emphasize such lapses, which direct our attention to the narrator rather than the intended subject: "the *person* of Ligeia." Further intensifying humor along these lines are feeble attempts by the narrator to explain why he can't remember the biographical contexts of his marriage: "Was it a playful charge on the part of my Ligeia? or was it a test of my strength of affection, that I should institute no inquiries upon this point? or was it rather a caprice of my own—a wildly romantic offering on the shrine of the most passionate devotion?" (311)

Perhaps the other obvious reason readers are tempted not to take the story seriously is evidence that Ligeia never existed. This explains the vagueness of the narrator's recollections. First, that she "came and departed as a shadow," and that he was "never made aware of her entrance . . . save by the dear music of her 'low sweet voice,'" suggest inhuman indefiniteness. The narrator's use of dreamlike diction associated with descriptions of Ligeia hint that she is a dream: "opium-dream," "spirit-lifting vision," and "more wildly divine than the phantasies which hovered about the slumbering souls of the daughters of Delos" (311). The language associated with his descriptions of her eyes inadvertently testify of their unreality: "the beauty of beings either above or apart from the earth," "strangeness," "word of no meaning," "incomprehensible anomalies," "something long forgotten," and "strangest mystery of all" (313–14). Finally, her résumé—the most beautiful, the most perfectly educated, and most devotedly loving woman who ever existed—is hardly creditable. Presented with such evidence, readers find themselves situated between the earnestness and absurdity of the narrator's story. Ligeia is clearly the product of wishful thinking, a dream ideal perhaps symbolizing the narrator's psyche, making alert readers derisively skeptical.

In addition to the narration, Poe includes obscure jokes and other satirical elements in the tale. Few critics note a joke in the Glanvill epigraph, which is quoted repeatedly in the tale. That it has never been found and verified as a true quotation from Glanvill after over 160 years, despite our knowledge of Poe's sources and available editions at the time, suggests that the quote is a hoax. The perfect voice for Poe (Glanvill hoped that all truth could be mastered and predicted eventual flights to the moon), the epigraph is in keeping with his daring and imaginative philosophy. Glanvill seems to reinforce the Eurekan perspective on God as a "great will pervading all things," including man, foreshadowing the focus in "Ligeia" on man's attempts to override the feebleness of the human will during the diffusive phase of the universe. Such coherence between Poe and Glanvill has sent scholars on a futile mission to scour the sources, a situation that would no doubt delight Hoffmann's hoaxy Poe.

Another source of obscure jokes in "Ligeia" is the "circle of analogies" between specific descriptions and their relevance to the tale itself. For example, many descriptive comments about Ligeia refer equally to the tale, in part because her name is also the name of the tale. When he describes the "*strangeness* of proportion" in Ligeia's beautiful features, he can just as plausibly be referring to the construction of the tale itself, with its *strange* narrator and his equally strange experience. This strangeness, though not wholly accountable, seems to spring from a combination of madness and opium. This leads to the second example, in which the narrator refers to Ligeia's beauty as "the radiance of an opium-dream" (311). Again, this inexplicable tale, told by an opium addict, also emits the radiant light of a drug-induced dream vision. Such double meanings become a self-reflexive parody, with Poe mocking the oblivious narrator. Such a tension anticipates the way Hitchcock's camera is often at odds with a character's point of view. Further along these lines, when the narrator describes the effect of the leaden glass in the bridal bower, which cast "a ghastly lustre on the objects within," he equally describes the effect of his narration on the details of the tales. Like the leaden-hued window, which lets in limited light, so the amnesia and madness of the narrator similarly selects only the most ghastly details to narrate.

Finally, humor in "Ligeia" also derives from various satires, particularly a general scorn of metaphysics in general, and transcendentalism in particular, which the narrator refers to as "the wild words which [Ligeia] habitually uttered" (316). That the "many mysteries of transcendentalism" are made "vividly luminous" (316) only when Ligeia is hovering over him satirizes transcendentalism in that ephemeral intangibles make sense only fleetingly, soon vanishing like a dream from the rational mind. Like Ligeia herself, these evanescent insights come and go "as a shadow." Poe takes another satirical dig at the transitory truths of transcendentalism, noting that it is "a wisdom too divinely precious not to be forbidden" (316). Thus in addition to being transitory, transcendentalism is ultimately unknowable. In addition, Ligeia's self-reliance, inspired by Glanvill's statement, is surely a knock at transcendental optimism taken over the top. The narrator's dual obsessions with transcendentalism and Ligeia create another subtle satire—the idolatry of the learned. In his previous tales, "Lionizing" and "Mystification," Poe satirizes how easily the elite (out of pride) and the masses (out of ignorance) are taken in by intellectual rigmarole. His later "Cask of Amontillado," in the character of Fortunato, also demonstrates the nearsighted and foolish confidence of the expert. Ligeia's husband, who claims that like a child he abandoned himself to Ligeia's intellectual guidance, certainly joins the ranks of the deceived who childishly put aside their own reason for that of a celebrated other.

Another satire seems to be of narration itself. Tellingly, Poe wrote "How to Write a *Blackwood* Article" and "The Predicament" in 1838, the same year as "Ligeia." Satirizing the tale of sensation characteristic of the British *Blackwood's*, Poe finds a mad narrator to be the perfect combination for introducing humor and horror simultaneously into a text. With the mad narrator he can satirize the narrator of sensation on a level of artistry far beyond the hack writers associated with that style. The exaggerations of the tale of sensation nearly makes "Ligeia" a metaphysical poem in prose, the narrator's manic style being to standard storytelling what conceit is to metaphor. Hence, like a metaphysical poem, the story perpetually hovers between the ridiculous and the sublime. The narrator's overstatements of wisdom "too divinely precious not to be forbidden" (316) or "assumptions and aspirations which mortality had never before known" (317) deconstruct themselves. This becomes increasingly characteristic of Poe's style, evident in his late poem, "The Raven," when the distraught student speaks of "dreaming dreams no mortal ever dared to dream before." Being taken to the limit of our imagination, we simultaneously delight in the wonder of the impossible conception and laugh at its exaggerated obscurity. Poe's use of such hysterical prose (in both senses of the words) captures the narrator's madness and arrests the reader in the middle ground between reason and dream, humor and horror.

Putting the reader in a bind between the two responses to "Ligeia" makes the story itself "changeable in aspect" and ultimately beyond rational, analytical reconstructions. Like the eclectic furnishings, moving curtains, and back-and-forth living and dying of Rowena and Ligeia, we are left without stable footing on which to negotiate the meaning in the tale. As a result, Poe more completely controls the audience, manipulating through various modes of response, placing us in a state of mind analogous to the unstable inexplicabilities of a dream. Humor, then, is Poe's means of duplicating his characters' confusing experiences in his readers. A careful reader, analogously to the narrator, seems forced to say—with a sigh—that he or she "can't for my soul determine how, when, or even precisely where humor and horror begin and end." "Ligeia" succeeds in increasing pleasure in the increased complexity and wonder in our response. We, like the narrator concerning Ligeia, are both "delighted and appalled" by the tale's irony and horror, which prevents our gaining control over it. Is this a hoax on the reader? Yes, but one born of a desire to entertain, not merely assault.

Humor in *The 39 Steps*, as in "Ligeia," is multileveled and intricate. It is a serious spy story, with harrowing life-and-death situations as well as a national threat. This is essentially the serious tone of John Buchan's novel on which the film is based. Hitchcock envisions a more humorous film version of the novel as it naturally grows out of fearful and suspenseful situations. His approach, here as elsewhere, makes the story almost a dark situational comedy, combining delight and terror in a sublime cocktail meant to entertain from several directions simultaneously.

The audience of *The 39 Steps*, like readers of "Ligeia," are placed in a complex position full of irreconcilable opposites. The opening score reveals this double aspect of the film, Mr. Memory's lighthearted theme juxtaposed with the more ominous "spy" themes in the score. This contradictory impression is reinforced by the opening scenes, which combine the ordinary music hall setting with unusual and unsettling canted camera angles at the ticket counter. Together with the score, these opening shots make the mood uncertain, though because of the setting, we reflect Hannay's inability to take the proceedings very seriously. Mr. Memory's act is also presented from a double perspective: while he means the act to be impressive (he memorizes fifty new facts a day and has willed his brain to the British Museum), he is taken as a joke by the rowdy audience who derisively cheer at his forthcoming donation. Further, he is assailed by silly questions ("Where's my old man been since last Saturday?") and has a difficult time maintaining order. Such chaos, though presented as a joke, hints at other dark forces at work in the film. Even in a music hall, life is precarious and uncertain.

The mood of rowdy humor becomes suddenly terrifying when a gunshot starts a stampede exit from the music hall. This appropriately initiates the spy story as agent Annabella Smith, who had fired the gun, "picks up" Hannay in order to find protection in his flat. Even here, a double perspective surrounds these scenes in the two characters' opposing attitudes. While Annabella is deadly serious, Hannay takes it all as a joke—"It's your funeral," he comments about their one-night stand. (This dark joke, of course, proves prophetic.) In the audience, we find ourselves torn between their attitudes, particularly since her earnest precautions not to be seen in the flat seem so theatrical. This is

Hitchcock's benign hoax on his audiences, as well as on Hannay. Just as Hitchcock always tried to stay ahead of his audiences, making sure they can't anticipate what is coming, his characters too must be kept in the dark. In this way his characters and audiences are doubles of each other. Hitchcock disarms any who might dismiss the film as just another formula story by parodying the form through Hannay's cynicism ("It sounds like a spy story"). This perfectly sets up his, and our, sincere terror later when we realize that none of this is a joke. Hannay's attitude begins to change when he sees Smith's pursuers on the street, though he continues to make jokes. When Smith warns him of a man with no top joint on his little finger, Hannay flippantly says he'll "make a note of it." Later that night, when Smith staggers into his room with a knife in her back, terror seems to replace humor as the chase begins. Her death is performed in a theatrical way—staggering, choking, coughing—so that while Hannay is terrorized, the audience is made uneasy by the obvious artificiality of the scene, perhaps even tempted to smile.

This struggle between humor and terror with terror becoming dominant sums up the first half of the film—the gunshot ending the light music hall scene and Smith's death ending the dalliance between her and Hannay. Other such scenes include the scream that becomes a train whistle as the charwoman discovers Smith's body and Hannay makes a panicky exit from the crofter's house. Later, all seems well when he finds the professor—until he sees his diminished pinkie. But what terrifies Hannay, amuses us, as the professor banters about leading Hannay up "or down" the garden path and preparations are made to serve lunch. However, we are shocked that this villainous spy has a family and social respectability. When the professor shoots Hannay, we feel Hannay's surprise and terror. The mood continues to go back and forth between humor and terror. We are surprised again with the constable's uproarious laughter, Hannay being saved when the bullet lodged in a hymnbook: "Some of those hymns are terrible hard to get through." The mood switches again when other policemen arrive and the apparently sympathetic constable turns on Hannay, ordering him arrested. Such mood switches keep audiences, like Hannay, unable to find a comfortable place in the film.

To survive Hitchcock's hoax on him, Hannay must keep switching roles for new audiences. He plays the philanderer for the milkman, the milkman for the spies, the mechanic for the crofter, the politician for the crowd at the rally, a murderer for Pamela, and a honeymooner for the innkeepers. The motif of theatricality initiated here is the basis for many of Hitchcock's wrong-man/double-chase thrillers like *Foreign Correspondent*, *Saboteur*, and *North by Northwest*. Like Hannay in *The 39 Steps*, we are also caught in a theatrical maelstrom, quickly changing our own reactions—terror to laughter to surprise—to suit the ever changing and surprising demands of the film. This pattern of ending humorous scenes with terror is finally reversed once Pamela sides with Hannay. The few long scenes remaining in the film end positively.

As in Poe's "Ligeia," Hitchcock's multilevel approach in *The 39 Steps* includes satires and obscure jokes, creating a constant undercurrent of humor. Among the targets of his light satire are religion, women's fashions, and politics. Religion is hit from several angles. First, religious prudery is represented by a shocked priest who is sitting in a train car where a traveling salesman is displaying and discussing women's undergarments. The priest makes a hurried and embarrassed exit. Another similarly light jest at religion comes with the constable's comic remark about how hard it is to get through some of the hymns. On the darker side of religious satire is the puritanically cruel crofter. As a suspicious tightwad (a side dig at the Scots) and an abusive husband whose life is austerely drab by choice, the crofter represents the antithesis of virtues associated with Christianity. Women, their fashions and attitudes, are lampooned in a number of ways, beginning with the undergarment salesman. As the salesman holds up an old-fashioned girdle, another man cringes, "my wife!" The silliness of women's underclothes are further exploited when Pamela tries to remove her wet nylons while handcuffed to Hannay. His dangling hand and her attempts to maintain modesty (and his offer to help) make for a brilliantly comic moment. (Similar jabs at the problems of women's clothing in difficult circumstances occur when Dulcie wriggles frantically into her dress in *Murder*, Eve breaks a heel on Mount Rushmore, and Melanie blithely boards a motorboat in her expensive but inappropriate high fashion outfit in *The Birds*.) The mood is touchingly satirical when the crofter's wife asks Hannay about city women, and whether they paint their toenails. Finally, the emptiness of political rhetoric is satirized as it is all too easily invented and passed on by Hannay to the ignorant citizens who are supposedly up on current affairs. Significantly, the audience at the music hall and the political rally are mirror images of each other—rowdy, intolerant, and easily manipulated. Together, these satirical elements are more playful than biting, meant more for fun than as serious commentary on the human condition.

Underneath the satire are obscure, subtextual jokes that Hitchcock seemingly prepared for himself and for anyone who can spot them. His meticulous inclusion of subtle comedy mirrors his obsessive concern with other details of costume, set, and color. Hitchcock clearly believes in the importance of making the film's visual and verbal fabric a tight weave. He loves to make fun of the police whenever he can. Sometimes these obscure jokes are visual puns, such as one of the policeman who falls into the river while chasing Hannay in the Scottish Highlands. He is all wet physically, as well as "all wet" about Hannay's guilt. The police are also the subject of a visual and aural joke as they excitedly chase Hannay through several train cars. In the baggage car they are confronted by several barking dogs, the perfect objective correlative to their own mindless hunt of Hannay, like hounds after the fox.[19] Another type of subtle pun is Hannay's inability to remember the source of Mr. Memory's theme song. Finally, the fact that the entire film takes place during "crazy month" at the Palladium comments on the action of the film as well as the film itself.

"The Fall of the House of Usher" and *Psycho*

Poe's "Usher" and Hitchcock's *Psycho* build their brand of delicate and refined ironic humor around nothing at all. In fact, that itself is a major part of the joke, both on characters and audiences. In these tales the oppositions shift slightly from appearance versus reality to existence versus nonexistence, taking the theme of inexplicability to a new and more strangely humorous level of the MacGuffin. In these stories the MacGuffin is no longer a mysterious plot point that in itself is irrelevant to the story, but it becomes the center of the plot itself. The several patterns these stories have in common, including the doubling of the female and male pair in a mysterious house, are examples of the MacGuffin (though Norman and Mrs. Bates are admittedly a unique pair). The male protagonists in both these stories are nervously insane and practice their separate arts—Usher does painting and music, Norman does taxidermy. In both stories a woman is killed by her male counterpart but comes back, and both women are associated with the cellar. Again, however, Hitchcock makes a twist in *Psycho* when Mrs. Bates only comes back in Norman's mind (while this is left ambiguous in Poe's "Usher"). The mysterious houses in both settings are in the vicinity of a tarn or bog, both stories prominently feature a storm, both are filled with inexplicable situations, and finally both conclude as the male is "estranged" by his more powerful female counterpart.

I begin my look at "Usher" by confessing a certain vulnerability to T. O. Mabbott's accusation that the "reference to opium is, as always in Poe, a suggestion that unimaginative readers may consider the whole story hallucination" (*Edgar Allan Poe*, 418). But I would qualify my confession as an unimaginative reader by agreeing with Thompson's view that "it is misleading to conceive of the meaning of ["Usher"] as devolving solely upon any single and fixed subject. . . . The tale is a concatenation of [several subjects] and not an either/or question" (*Poe's Fiction* 88). I would amplify Thompson's idea further to note that Poe's tales can have more than one potential organizational principle (or narrative framework) as well as several potential themes. As Floyd Stovall notes, while Poe may produce "in the mind of the reader a single impression or effect," he can arrive there through various narrative interpretive frameworks.[20] My reading of "Usher" is that the tale is a dream or vision that begins as the narrator looks down into the tarn and ends as he imagines the house sinking into it. Thus the rest of the tale is itself a MacGuffin, a reading that is well supported by the text and produces a level of ironic humor perhaps available only to Mabbott's "unimaginative" readers.

On first reading "Usher," we feel its terror and mystery in the foreboding sense Usher himself has that something horrific will inevitably happen. The narrator seems mostly transparent, reacting to external realities in a seemingly reasonable way. Initial readings can reduce the importance of his instability—that the story is about his perceptions. As critical students of the tale prove, subsequent readings make us more aware of hints that he is creating the reality we are inclined to take for granted. His statement about a "bitter lapse into every-day life" provides an important insight into a man who prefers dreams to reality, whether opium or sleep induced. The narrator's own lack of self-awareness of the possible influence of his opium habit on his perceptions introduces an ironic disconnection which continues throughout the tale. His gloomy surreal reactions to seeing the house, and the very words he uses, are suspiciously echoed later by Usher, who also believes that the house and grounds have an atmosphere peculiar to themselves. Linking his and Usher's perspectives further, he refers to Usher's views as "superstition," a term he uses to describe his own feelings. The narrator seems mostly unaware of these similarities until the end of the story, when he notes that Usher's "condition terrified . . . it infected me" (411). While these examples provide clues to the seasoned reader of the story, the narrator's experience looking down into the tarn most clearly hints at the tale's dream framework. Seeing the strange homestead inversely reflected in the tarn gives him a "shudder even more thrilling than before" (400), causing his "superstition" to "accelerate" and oppressing him with terror.

At this point in "Usher," and this is the clue to a major narrative shift, the narrator notes that this effect "*must* have been a dream" (398). A further hint occurs when he wonders if he only dreamed Usher's "wild improvisations." While it is not significant whether he dreams the rest of the story, awaking as the house sinks into the tarn, his dream—or insanity, if you prefer—nicely accounts for the ironic narrative structure of projection and MacGuffin that follows. This interpretation also links the tale as a dream narrative of no real meaning with his narration of individual events in the story. Viewing the tale from this point of view, readers are aware of a cosmic irony in the narrator's constant unconscious projection of himself, as dreamer, of supposedly external events and people. With this background, a source of humor is immediately evident on second sight when the narrator notes that Usher called him for the "cheerfulness of my society," an idea certainly not borne out by the text.

Nearly everything the narrator observes from this point on seems an ironic reflection of him and his tale. His dream narration, like the crumbling structure of the mansion, for example, has "the specious totality of old woodwork which has rotted for long years" (400).

Describing Usher's life and art, the narrator states that "an excited and highly distempered ideality threw a sulphureous lustre over all"

(405). In invoking idealism—existence being in the idea and not in external reality—Poe provides a major clue that the narrator is creating his tale within the "distempered" perspectives of a dream. This suggests, for example, that the "mystic current" of the meaning in "The Haunted Palace," in which all move to a "discordant melody," is certainly the narrator's mad dream. Tellingly, he "easily remembered" the words of the song. He even foreshadows his own escape from the sinking house in the end: "Through the pale door/ A hideous throng rush out forever" (407). The narrator is creating and projecting his own reality as Usher's tale becomes a joke on Usher and the narrator (and, we realize, on us) in the discussion of "the sentience of all vegetable things," which Usher takes a level further to the sentience of all things. As we perceive that this pervasive "sentience" is part of the dream, the words at the end of the discussion make more sense: "The result was discoverable, he added, in that silent yet importunate and terrible influence which for centuries had moulded the destinies of his family, and which made *him* what I now saw him—what he was" (408). Since the narrator, therefore, is indeed dream-shaping the destinies of the Ushers, his final comment on Usher's theories becomes ironically comical: "Such opinions need no comment, and I will make none." Usher is thus sensing that he is part of a dream without being able to consciously comprehend or articulate it. Usher's perception becomes his fear of an impending disaster, the inevitable moment that the dreamer awakes. Thus the relationship between the narrator, Roderick, Madeleine, and the house itself becomes a mad tryst indeed.

Another dimension, and giveaway, to the underlying joke being played out in this tale is the meaninglessness of so much of what is said and the coincidence of actions. In the end we are left with the same question: What is really going on in the house of Usher? As the tale winds toward its conclusion, its dream character is suggested more and more, particularly by a series of magical coincidences. The first, of course, is that the narrator sees Madeleine just at the moment Usher first mentions her. Next is a fantastic storm that conveniently sets the stage for Madeleine's horrific emergence from the tomb. Finally comes the series of coincident sound effects for "The Mad Tryst" made by Madeleine's movements. These coincidences are Usher's prophetic anticipations that he will die a terrifying death and that Madeleine is not really dead. Doubling Usher, the narrator anticipates something horrible about Madeleine, noting that on seeing her, he felt "utter astonishment not unmingled with dread" (404).

These perspectives as well as the narrative details suggest that the entire tale of "Usher" is a MacGuffin. The narrator often hints at some meaning or revelation that is never forthcoming, which cannot be spoken (as the experience in "The Man of the Crowd" could not be read). For example, in describing how he and Usher filled their time, he says he "shall ever bear about me a memory of the many solemn hours I thus spent alone with the master of the House of Usher" (405). But in the next sentence he confesses that he would "fail in any attempt to convey an idea of the exact character of the studies, or of the occupations, in which he involved me." Many such linguistic MacGuffins occur throughout the tale. As the narrator first passes through the house, he observes that "much that I encountered on the way contributed, I know not how, to heighten the vague sentiments of which I have already spoken" (400). Such is certainly characteristic of the uncertainties of dreams and becomes an important element of both the frustrating ironies of the tale and the atmosphere of vague dread.

If we haven't gotten the joke at this point, Poe clearly alludes to his comically ironic purposes in the list of books the narrator and Usher "pored together over" (408). Nearly all are in some way comic or absurd. "Vervet et Chartruse" is mocking burlesque poetry with satirical aspects; "Belphegor" is a humorous tale of wives causing the damnation of their husbands; and "Journey into the Blue Distance" blends romance and satire. More absurd are "Subterranean Voyage of Nicholas Klimm," concerning walking and talking trees, and "Civitus Solis," describing the inhabitants of the sun. Relating to our theme of the indiscernible nature of reality, Pomponius Mela writes of the society of pans and satyrs that seem both there and not there to outsiders.[21] In this case we are the outsiders and can't discuss what is and is not real. Finally, Poe jabs us in the ribs about his comic purposes as the narrator reports that now "Usher would sit dreaming for hours" over Mela. Not only is Usher merely a dream himself, but he dreams of nothingness. This tale anticipates and embodies Poe's later poem, "A Dream within a Dream."

"Usher" ends where it began, the narrator staring down at the tarn as the House of Usher sinks. Unable to goad his imagination into torturing anything "ought of the sublime" out of the Usher homestead, the narrator has sought and found the sublime by creating his tarn dream-vision. This dream approach to narrative resembles several other works in which Poe's characters use some object as a screen to launch a vision, including "The Raven," "To Helen," "The Black Cat," "The Tell-Tale Heart," "Ulalume," and "The Lake." The last poem, written years before "Usher," particularly anticipates the functions of the tarn in "Usher." Like the narrator of "Usher," the poet of "The Lake" notes that the terrors of the lake come only at night. Further, like the tarn for the house, there was "death . . . in that poisonous wave,/ And in its gulf a fitting grave." Finally, the lake is a place of "lone imagining" and "solace" in which one finds "that terror was not fright,/ But a tremulous delight." Such a narrative scam is itself sublime, initially creating terror but concluding with delight for the reader. As a test case of how humor functions in Poe, it is clear that Poe does not like his gothic horror straight up. He qualifies it with various forms of humor and irony. Readers are made to question what is meant to be funny, what horrific, what is delight and what is terror, since most of the events in the story can be taken from both perspectives. Such complexities within the narrative structure certainly appealed to Hitchcock since they are often reflected in his films.

If love is "lovelier the second time around," Hitchcock is funnier. Like Poe, Hitchcock complicates the terror of *Psycho* with obscure intellectual delights that can only be enjoyed upon successive viewings. In terms of the film's humor, the most obvious source is the dialogue. When Norman says that his mother is "not herself today," his real (if unintentional) meaning only reveals itself the second time through. Similarly, when Norman notes that it is a "dirty night" on first meeting Marion, that his mother is as harmless as a "stuffed bird," or that we all go "a little mad" sometimes, the film's initiates laugh. Another dimension of humor the second time around includes clues indicating that Norman is the murderer, which are at first invisible. This fact becomes clear as we connect Marion's association with birds and Norman's hobby as a taxidermist. Marion's last name is Crane and she "eats like a bird," according to Norman. In addition to owning stuffed predatory birds, Norman knocks over a framed picture of a bird when he enters Marion's cabin and finds her murdered. The humor here is in the very fact of the clues, the recognition of one of "Hitchcock's games." Finally, it is darkly amusing, at subsequent screenings of the film, to know that it is Norman's voice speaking for his mother's. The earnest theatricality of madness can be entertaining.

Like "Usher," *Psycho* is full of seeming significance the first time through, most of which proves to be a narrative dead end. As the film progresses we find ourselves playing "where's the MacGuffin," particularly as we begin to see so many counterfeit plot points up to the murder of Marion—that her boss sees her leaving town, that a cop follows her, that she buys a new car, that she hides the money in the newspaper, that she finds wisdom during her conversation with Norman, and that she steals the money in the first place. All these plot twists prove to be steps down the garden path in order to provide the audience with *the* cinematic thunderbolt of the twentieth century. Ironically, even after the shower murder, which virtually proves the film's duplicity, the audience continues to find insignificant scenes full of suspense (as Hitchcock knew they would). Even on a microcosmic level, nothingness abounds. For example, during the shower murder itself, no apparent cuts, other than the camera, are recorded, no face is evident for the killer, there is nothing for Marion to grab as she reaches out blankly, and nothing for her dead eye to see. Another set of microcosmic nothings are the little fictions that the characters keep inventing. These scenarios, like the "Usher" narrator's tarn dream, provide sublimity and meaning their dull lives cannot provide. Sam suggests Marion lie to her boss so she can stay in the hotel longer, Marion and Sam create fantasies about what a suitable dinner date at her house would mean, Cassidy imagines picking up Marion as his mistress, Lila and Sam pretend to be married, and most poignantly Norman pretends his mother is alive.

Other seemingly significant details are revealed that make it difficult to know where things are going on a first viewing. When Arbogast, Lila, and Sam involve themselves in the detective process, we know this plot twist is a MacGuffin, since Marion is already dead. When Lila finds the slip of paper with $40,000 written on it, we know it will get her nowhere. On the other hand, some seemingly meaningful incidents after the shower murder pull us in but later turn out to be MacGuffins. One example of this is when Sam and Lila report that Norman's mother has been seen at the window and that Norman behaved as if she were alive. The sheriff's question about who is buried in Greenlawn Cemetery provides a momentary tingle at the back of the neck but goes nowhere since Mrs. Bates is dead, the coffin empty (although on another level half of Norman's life is buried in her coffin).

Hitchcock is a one-man Penn and Teller, the comic magicians who show you how they are going to work a magic trick and then still surprise, shock, and amuse you. For instance, another famous Hitchcock scam on the audience, noticed by nearly all later, is the sinking of Marion's car in the bog behind the motel. Seeing it the first time, we find ourselves rooting for Norman, noble protector of his mother, anxiously hoping the car will finish sinking. As we learn the truth about Norman, we can't help but smile at the way the scene draws us in, making it a representative moment in the film and a tribute to Hitchcock's genius for manipulating audiences. Even after the shower murder puts the lie to everything that has gone before, we still can't help trusting what we see, assuming Norman's innocence and good intentions. Norman is such an everyman—he is nervous, he stutters, and he is awkward around women—all attributes with which we can identify. Again, however, as with the clues that he is Marion's killer, we should know better, or at least be suspicious. That we don't understand Norman as well as we think is finally hinted at as Lila opens a book with no title in his room. Like the book, Norman is a mystery. At the same time, this incident is prophetic of his "mother's" taking over, virtually ending Norman's existence.

Hitchcock's "little joke," as he described the film, is revealed most clearly in the comic trailer in which he stars. A mirror reflection of the film itself, the trailer involves Hitchcock taking us on a tour of the motel and house, showing us places that will be significant during the film, ending up at the shower. During the leisurely tour his words are backed by a score that alternates between comic and suspenseful music, perfectly foreshadowing first and subsequent viewings of it. His tone, like his television persona's, is blandly humorous, particularly as he continually stops just short of revealing anything about the plot at each significant location. In fact, he cuts himself off midsentence several times. However, the final stop on the tour, the bathroom, ends with a shock as he pulls back the shower curtain to reveal a screaming Janet Leigh.

Like the film itself, Hitchcock presents obvious clues, mixes the tone between humor and horror, and goes at a slow, deliberate pace that lulls one into complacency, preparing his audience for the shock of its life. But the film's secret joke, its "mystic current," allows the audience, at later viewings, to be in on the joke.

I claim that self-parody is an important aspect of humor in Poe and Hitchcock, and someone who argues that they are hostile to their audiences must also argue that they are hostile toward themselves. The humor in Poe and Hitchcock functions as an important part of the total experience of the horror thrill ride. Thompson's study of Poe's fiction inadvertently levels the playing field between Poe and Hitchcock, enabling us to link their humor to their horror. Thompson deftly demonstrates how the canny Poe, master of the various styles of storytelling in his day, never played straight with his readers. As the diffusive phases of *Eureka* corroborate, the universe is basically perverse, or ironic, leading Poe to center his tales on the misperception and irrationality inherent in human experience. Consequently, rather than serious gothic tales, Poe's stories include ironic jokes and hoaxes on readers and characters both, with humor cutting several ways. Like Hitchcock's movies, Poe's tales are never completely straight, involving the reader in unexpected levels of pleasure based on a sophisticated and ironic worldview in which black humor rules. This is the concept called "Hitchcockian," an adjective that conjures a particular range of cinematic pleasures. It is no coincidence that Poe invented the detective story, a form that centers its pleasures on someone's death. This is also the supreme black joke underlying Hitchcock's films—the trouble with Harry is that he's dead! Since neither Poe nor Hitchcock is primarily interested in social criticism or realism, each expected (and ultimately received from his fans) the high degree of "willing suspension of disbelief" necessary for playing his dark games. The reward for alert participants is pleasure in an environment as consciously artificial as the game Clue (now marketed in a Hitchcock variation). The idea is to have fun—of a complex, highly interactive nature.

Notes

1. For both, explicitly humorous pieces are their least successful works. Hitchcock's *Mr. and Mrs. Smith* (1941) and *The Trouble with Harry* (1955) were

critical and popular flops. As for Poe, his obscure and extravagant comic satires are the works least appreciated by readers and critics.

2. Paul Lewis, "Poe's Humor: A Psychological Analysis," *Studies in Short Fiction* 26, no. 4 (1989): 531–46, suggests helpfully that the difference between horror and humor in Poe is a matter of degree, not kind.

3. Arthur Hobson Quinn and Edward H. O'Neill, *The Complete Poems and Stories of Edgar Allan Poe* (New York: Knopf, 1973), 978.

4. "The Comic in Poe's Fiction," *American Literature* 33, no. 4 (1962): 434.

5. John Bryant, "Poe's Ape of UnReason: Humor, Ritual, and Culture," *Nineteenth-Century Literature* 51, no. 1 (1996): 16.

6. "Hawthorne's 'Plagiary'; Poe's Duplicity," in *The Naiad Voice: Essays on Poe's Satiric Hoaxing* (Port Washington, N.Y.: Associated Faculty Press, 1983), 86.

7. Susan Smith, *Suspense, Humor, and Tone* (London: BFI, 2000), 58–59.

8. William Rothman, *Hitchcock: The Murderous Gaze* (Cambridge: Harvard University Press, 1982), 171.

9. Terry Teachout, "The Genius of Pure Effect," *Civilization* 5, no. 1 (1999): 10.

10. In terms of the criticism of such comic satirical pieces, the hostility charge has been strengthened by two points: (1) these tales aren't really very funny and (2) they are frustratingly difficult to comprehend—perhaps leaving the critics feeling hostile and put upon.

11. Daniel Hoffman, *Poe, Poe, Poe, Poe, Poe, Poe, Poe* (New York: Avon, 1972).

12. Thomas Leitch, *Find the Director and Other Hitchcock Games* (Athens: University of Georgia Press, 1991), 7.

13. Lesley Brill, *The Hitchcock Romance* (Princeton: Princeton University Press, 1988), xiii.

14. Anthony Lane, "In Love with Fear," *New Yorker*, August 16, 1990, 80.

15. Sidney Gottlieb, ed., *Hitchcock on Hitchcock: Selected Writings and Interviews* (Berkeley: University of California Press, 1995), 143.

16. Poe is often compared with Mark Twain in discussions of his humor. See Henig Cohen, "A Comic Mode of the Romantic Imagination: Poe, Hawthorne, Melville," in *The Comic Imagination in American Literature*, ed. Louis D. Rubin Jr. (New Brunswick, N.J.: Rutgers University Press, 1973), 86; James W. Gargano, "The Distorted Perception of Poe's Comic Narrators," *Topic* 30 (1976): 33; Eugene R. Kanjo, "'The Imp of the Perverse': Poe's Dark Comedy of Art and Death," *Poe Newsletter*, October 1969, 41; Tom Quirk, "What If Poe's Humorous Tales Were Funny? Poe's 'X-ing a Paragrab' and Twain's 'Journalism in Tennessee,'" *Studies in American Humor* 3, no. 1 (1995): 36–48.

17. G. R. Thompson, *Poe's Fiction: Romantic Irony in the Gothic Tales* (Madison: University of Wisconsin Press, 1973), 86–87.

18. Thomas Ollive Mabbott, ed., *Collected Works of Edgar Allan Poe: Poems*, vol. 1 (Cambridge: Harvard University Press, 1969), 310.

19. But again he presents them both comically and seriously. On the serious side are the ominous policemen of *The Wrong Man* and *Psycho*. On the more humorous side are the inept country cops of *The Trouble with Harry* and *The Birds*, the amusingly named Sergeant Emile Klinker in *North by Northwest* and the mama's boy detective in *Spellbound*.

20. On one level, the myriad readings of a tale like "Usher," which is infinitely suggestive, proves the point. This is really a variation of the principle of the one in the many. As in my example from "Tell-Tale Heart," which can either be a dream he is telling his doctor or a confession to us before his death. Both structures work.

21. See details on these allusions in Mabbott's *Edgar Allan Poe: Sketches and Tales* (Urbana: University of Illinois Press, 1978), 1:419–21.

~

Annotated Bibliography of Poe and Hitchcock Connections

This annotated bibliography cites scholarship that in some way links the work of Edgar Allan Poe and Alfred Hitchcock, with articles ranging from passing mentions to detailed examinations of particular thematic or theoretical connections. These comments and criticisms were written between 1957 and 2000, with many having been published during the 1990s. Hitchcock scholars have become increasingly aware of Poe's importance in Hitchcock's creative imagination.

Parts of this bibliography are reprinted by the kind permission of *Hitchcock Annual* (2000–2001) and *Poe Studies Newsletter* (Fall 1999).

Allen, Richard. "Message from the Conference Director." *Program notes to "Hitchcock: A Centenary Celebration."* New York: New York University, 1999. In his welcome to the Hitchcock centenary conference, Allen notes that "dual traditions . . . inspired Hitchcock's work" that "continue to frame our reception and interpretation of it." These are the comic thriller and the darker side, "his links to Poe, Baudelaire, and expressionism, where all that is solid in human relationships seems to melt in the air."

Auiler, Dan. *Vertigo: The Making of a Hitchcock Classic.* New York: St. Martin's Griffin, 1998. After reprinting Hitchcock's early short fiction, "Gas," Auiler notes that the "nineteen-year-old Hitchcock certainly demonstrated his love for Poe, whose combination of melodrama and dark comedy he imitated wryly" (p. 7).

Barr, Charles. *English Hitchcock: A Movie Book*. London: Cameron & Hollis, 1999. In discussing influences on the Hitchcock of the British period, Barr notes in passing that Edgar Allan Poe is "clearly important," though the British films are marked more by the influence of John Buchan and Marie Belloc Lowndes.

Brand, Dana. "Rear-View Mirror: Hitchcock, Poe, and the Flaneur in America." In *Hitchcock's America*, edited by Jonathan Freedman and Richard Millington, 123–34. New York: Oxford University Press, 1999. Brand introduces a number of general connections between Poe and Hitchcock, including several interactions between specific tales and films, stating that "some of Hitchcock's best work in America is clearly influenced by Poe." The heart of the chapter draws comparisons between the image of the flaneur in "The Man of the Crowd," "The Murders in the Rue Morgue," and *Rear Window*. During the analysis Brand suggests that some of Hitchcock's understanding of Poe came indirectly from Baudelaire's translations into French and the influence his views had on the biographers Hitchcock may have read.

Breitwieser, Mitchell. "Jazz Fractures: F. Scott Fitzgerald and Epochal Representation." *American Literary History* 12, no. 3 (2000): 373–74. Breitwieser notes that in *The Last Tycoon* Monroe Stahr's obsession with Kathleen, a woman who resembles his dead wife, "recalls Edgar Allan Poe's 'Ligeia' (1838) and anticipates Alfred Hitchcock's *Vertigo* (1958)." He goes on to note how Fitzgerald ultimately handles the story differently.

Brown, Royal S. "Back from among the Dead: The Restoration of Alfred Hitchcock's *Vertigo*." *Cineaste* 23 (1997): 8. In discussing *Vertigo* as an Orpheus tale, Brown notes that Scottie is an Orpheus "in the most morbid and misogynistic tradition of the Edgar Allan Poe esthetic" in which the dead woman is "momentarily brought back to life" to act "out her own demise before it really happens."

———. "*Vertigo* as Orphic Tragedy." In *Perspectives on Alfred Hitchcock*, edited by David Boyd, 114. New York: G. K. Hall, 1995. Scottie is compared with Poe's artist husband in "The Oval Portrait" as one who "sucks the life" out of his artistic creation.

Conrad, Peter. *The Hitchcock Murders*. London: Faber & Faber, 2000. Poe is invoked in a discussion of *Rope*: "Edgar Allan Poe thought that the detective should train himself to be a physiognomist of the domestic interior, and in *Rope*, following the procedure recommended by Poe, James Stewart incriminates the furniture" (p. 337).

Godard, Jean-Luc. "Alfred Hitchcock est Mort." In *Jean-Luc Godard par Jean-Luc Godard*. Editions de l'Etoile-Cahiers du Cinema, 1985. In assessing

Hitchcock's work and career, Godard states that Hitchcock belongs to the moralist Anglo-Saxon tradition that includes Nathaniel Hawthorne and Edgar Allan Poe, coloring the way we view the films (p. 414).

Goldhurst, William. "Self-Reflective Fiction by Poe: Three Tales." *Modern Language Studies* 16 (1986): 5. Goldhurst notes in passing that Poe's "practice of introducing intricate self-reflective elements" into his work "represents whimsical intrusions of the creator into his creation (in the manner of the late Alfred Hitchcock's customary walk-on part in each of his films)."

Gunning, Tom. "From the Kaleidoscope to the X-Ray: Urban Spectatorship, Poe, Benjamin, and *Traffic in Souls* (1913)." *Wide Angle*, October 1997, 25–61. Hitchcock is mentioned as part of a tradition of paranoid urban thrillers characterized by "apparent knowledge and actual impotence" inaugurated in Poe's "The Man of the Crowd."

Hardy Phil, ed. *The Overlook Film Encyclopedia: Horror.* Woodstock, N.Y.: Overlook, 1995. In assessing *The Tomb of Ligeia* (1965), this reference compares it to *Vertigo*, featuring "different kinds of obsession and possession" (p. 167).

Hitchcock, Alfred. Foreword to *Edgar Allan Poe: Sallsamma historier.* Stockholm: Raben & Sjogren, 1964. A reprint of Hitchcock's remarks about Poe's influence on him (see next citation) used as a foreword to a Swedish edition of Poe's tales. Hitchcock's remarks on Poe were widely used. This edition is possibly a Swedish translation of a 1960 Paris edition of Poe's tales (*Hitstoires extraordinaires*) that also used the Hitchcock introduction. Of special interest are the sentences added to introduce these remarks: "For a good many years I have been called the 'King of the Thriller.' It is probably for this reason that I have been asked to write a foreword to Edgar Allan Poe's *Bizarre Tales.* I am greatly flattered for I must acknowledge that this renowned author is the genre's undisputed genius" (pp. 7–10).

———. "Why I Am Afraid of the Dark." In *Hitchcock on Hitchcock: Selected Writings and Interviews,* edited by Sidney Gottlieb, 99–101, 142–45. Berkeley: University of California Press, 1995. Translated by Claire Marrone from the original in *Arts: Lettres, Spectacles,* June 1–7, 1960, 1, 7. Hitchcock's lengthy discussion of Poe's effect on him (and a bit of commentary by Sid Gottlieb), with his revealing confession that "it's because I liked Edgar Allan Poe's stories so much that I began to make suspense films." In introducing Hitchcock's discussion of Poe's influence, Gottlieb suggests that "Hitchcock and Poe are both profound realists and surrealists, adventurers in the linked realms of imagination and terror, and, as Hitchcock ruefully admits, prisoners of as well as experts in their genre."

Hoffman, Daniel. *Poe Poe Poe Poe Poe Poe Poe.* New York: Avon, 1972. Introducing his discussion of the detective tales, Hoffman states in passing that when he first read "The Purloined Letter," "I had just seen the original movie of *The Thirty-Nine Steps*" (p. 116).

Leonard, Garry. "Keeping Our Selves in Suspense: The Imagined Gaze and Fictional Constructions of the Self in Alfred Hitchcock and Edgar Allan Poe." In *Suspense: Conceptualizations, Theoretical Analyses, and Empirical Explorations*, edited by Peter Vorderer, Hans J. Wulff, and Mike Friedrichsen, 19–35. Mahwah, N.J.: Erlbaum, 1996. A Freudian and a Lacanian discuss readers' and audiences' feelings of both anxiety and relief through suspense as they "insert [them]selves into the symbolic register" of the work in a process of self-construction. Leonard cites examples of how Poe and Hitchcock manipulate audience experience through suspense techniques that raise basic questions about the self. As Leonard's title suggests, he doesn't claim broader connections or influence between the two.

McGilligan, Patrick. "Alfred Hitchcock: Before the Flickers." *Film Comment*, July–August 1999, 22–31. In this section from his upcoming biography of Hitchcock, McGilligan refutes Spoto's claim that Hitchcock's short story "Gas" is only "a sophomoric Poe imitation" (p. 26). He cites the story's humor and twist ending as evidence that he didn't have Poe in mind as sole source.

Miller, Gabriel. "Beyond the Frame: Hitchcock, Art, and the Ideal." *Post Script*, Winter 1986, 36. In passing, Miller notes that Hitchcock's houses, like those in Poe's work, reflect their inhabitants.

Mogg, Kenneth. *The Alfred Hitchcock Story*. London: Titan, 1999, 146, 149. Moog points to a passage in the Boileau-Narcejac novel that was the basis for *Vertigo* (*The Living and the Dead*) "that might have come from Poe, describing Scottie's guilt-feelings after Madeleine's death: 'It was will-power he lacked . . . He would have had to pour out far more vitality than he possessed to keep her in this world'" (pp. 146, 149). Moog later notes about the film's ending that Scottie lacks the vitality needed to keep Madeleine in this world.

———. "The Fragments of the Mirror: *Vertigo* and Its Sources." *MacGuffin* 25 (1998): 13–26. In discussing various cinematic and literary sources for Hitchcock's *Vertigo*, Moog finds "Ligeia" to be the "most relevant" of the Poe sources for the film. The key connection seems to be that Poe's narrator and Scottie view their ideal women as means of "escaping, or explaining, life's cruel enigmas." According to Moog, both works explore questions of the limits of human volition.

Morris, Christopher D. "Rope." *Film Criticism*, Winter 1999–2000, 17–40. Morris notes that Poe's "The Purloined Letter" is "a text that informs *Rope*" in two ways: (1) incriminating evidence is placed so prominently "as to be undiscoverable by traditional rationality" and (2) like Dupin, "Rupert is linked with Oedipus" in his compulsive "need to determine reason."

Naremore, James. "Hitchcock at the Margins of Noir." In *Alfred Hitchcock: Centenary Essays*, edited by Richard Allen and S. Ishii Gonzales, 275–76. London: British Film Institute, 1999. Naremore makes specific links between Poe and *Vertigo*, suggesting that the film seems a mixture of Dashiell Hammett and Edgar Allan Poe. He also notes that the "spirit of Poe dominates the film" and points out various links between it and "Usher," "Annabel Lee," and "The Philosophy of Composition." In his conclusion Naremore discusses other broader ties between the two artists, including their similarly "quasi-scientific approach" and mass appeal.

Paglia, Camille. *The Birds*. London: BFI Film Classics, 1998. Comparing the film to du Maurier's original story, she notes that hers, "unlike Hithcock's, ends in intimations of catastrophe as sweeping as the carnage wrought by Poe's Red Death" (p. 10).

Pelko, Stojan. "Punctum Caecum, or, Of Insight and Blindness." In *Everything You Always Wanted to Know about Lacan (But Were Afraid to Ask Hitchcock)*, edited by Slavoj Zizek, 114. London: Verso, 1992. In this and a later chapter by Zizek (p. 215), reference is made to Hitchcock's use of ideas from Poe's "The Purloined Letter" in the charity ball scene from *Saboteur*, in which "the simultaneous omnipotence and radical impotence of gaze as developed by Poe" is played out.

Perez, Gilberto. "The Woman and the Fiend: Hitchcock's *Shadow of a Doubt* and Murnau's *Nosferatu*." Paper presented at *Hitchcock: A Centenary Celebration*, New York, October 1999. Perez compares the doubling of Charlie and Uncle Charlie to the doubling of Roderick and Madeleine Usher as partaking of the same gothic tradition that invokes a fear of incest.

Perry, Dennis R. "Imps of the Perverse: Discovering the Poe/Hitchcock Connection." *Literature/Film Quarterly* 24 (1996): 393–99. Perry introduces the idea of a major aesthetic affinity between Poe and Hitchcock, citing their common themes, personal obsessions, and strong emphasis on technical craftsmanship. Discusses how Hitchcock changed Narcejac and Boileau's *The Living and the Dead* (1957) into the more Poe-esque *Vertigo* with its "Usher" and "Ligeia" themes and situations. "For Hitchcock, Poe's craftsmanship became the impetus for developing his own theories and style."

Price, Theodore. *Hitchcock and Homosexuality: His 50-Year Obsession with Jack the Ripper and the Superbitch Prostitute: A Psychoanalytic View*. Metuchen, N.J.: Scarecrow, 1992. In developing a psychoanalytic reading of Hitchcock, Price refers to how Freud's family romance themes in the films are hidden in the open as in Poe's "Purloined Letter." He also refers to Bonaparte's study of Poe in discussing the psychoanalytic view of crime and its relation to Hitchcock.

Railton, Stephen. *Authorship and Audience: Literary Performance in the American Renaissance*. Princeton, N.J.: Princeton University Press, 1991. Notes that Hitchcock's films are "lineally descended" from Poe, for whom "'elevating' the soul was a purely secular, rhetorical display of his own manipulatory skills" (p. 138).

Rohmer, Eric, and Claude Chabrol. *Hitchcock: The First Forty-Four Films*. Translated by Stanley Hochman. Rev. ed. New York: Frederick Ungar, 1979. In this first book-length study of Hitchcock (first published in 1957), the authors note a number of connections between two of their French culture heroes in discussions of *Strangers on a Train* and *Rear Window*. Rohmer and Chabrol are obviously steeped in Poe and use their knowledge as a convenient means of explaining Hitchcock's techniques and themes. In addition, they make specific comparisons between works, such as the runaway carousel in *Strangers* and Poe's maelstrom.

Rowe, Thomas M. "The Dark Fire: Poe's Links to Hitchcock." *Poe Messenger*, Autumn 1985, 4–10. In this heavily biographical comparison Rowe claims that Hitchcock essentially modernizes Poe, putting on film the same chaotic forces found in the tales. Relying on Spoto's biographical analysis of Hitchcock to show Poe's personal similarities to the director, Rowe also looks briefly at the theme of the double and the common use of audience manipulation.

Ryall, Tom. *Alfred Hitchcock and the British Cinema*. Urbana: University of Illinois Press, 1986. Ryall traces Hitchcock's version of the "spy thriller" back to the mystery and violence pioneered by Poe and other writers like Doyle and Collins who were influenced by him.

Samuels, Charles Thomas. "Hitchcock." *American Scholar* 39 (1970): 297. In an article essentially criticizing Hitchcock's artistic shortcomings, Poe is slighted by association: "Like Poe, the writer he most resembles, Hitchcock is obsessed by a small stock of situations which we can mistake for themes; but, as in Poe's case, these 'themes' are only emotional stimuli born from the primitive stage of indiscriminate terror."

Sarris, Andrew. "Hitch and Me: A Case of *Vertigo*." *New York Observer*, April 19, 1999, C1. In reviewing the history of critical reaction to Hitchcock, particularly his own, Sarris suggests that no one can claim to have discovered Hitchcock: "he was always there close to the surface of our comprehension like Edgar Allan Poe's purloined letter."

Sered, Jean. "The Dark Side." *Armchair Detective* 22 (1989): 118, 246–48. In this long article demonstrating similarities between Hitchcock and Cornell Woolrich, "Rear Window" author Sered notes that both were "strongly influenced by the writings of Edgar Allan Poe." Sered suggests as an example that both Hitchcock and Woolrich, like Poe, used themes or images of claustrophobia in their work.

Simper, DeLoy. "Poe, Hitchcock, and the Well-Wrought Effect." *Literature/Film Quarterly* 3, no. 3 (1975): 226–31. An apologia that defends Hitchcock as a careful craftsman by comparing his project with Poe's in terms of similar "theories of composition." The bulk of the paper is devoted to an analysis of *The Birds* that demonstrates its artistic integrity and validity.

Skal, David J. *The Monster Show: A Cultural History of Horror*. New York: Norton, 1993. Skal links the styles of Poe and Hitchcock through their similarity to a third writer, stating that Grand Guignol playwright, Andre de Lorde, "was a conscious technician of terror, who enjoyed extravagant comparisons to Poe in the popular press, and who, in many respects, prefigured the methods of Alfred Hitchcock" (p. 57).

Smith, Don G. *The Poe Cinema: A Critical Filmography Based on the Works of Edgar Allan Poe*. Jefferson, N.C.: McFarland, 1999. Smith makes passing mention of Hitchcock throughout the book. In the afterword he suggests that Hitchcock is the most visible film director influenced by Poe.

Spoto, Donald. *The Art of Alfred Hitchcock: Fifty Years of His Motion Pictures*. New York: Hopkinson & Blake, 1976. Spoto notes in discussing *Suspicion* that Hitchcock shares his interest in the theme of the power of the dead to affect the living with Poe and James. Later, in discussing *Shadow of a Doubt*, he suggests that Hitchcock is in tune with his adopted American literary roots, paralleling his criticism of Puritanism in Santa Rosa with that found in Melville, Hawthorne, and Poe.

———. *The Art of Alfred Hitchcock: Fifty Years of His Motion Pictures*. 2d ed. New York: Anchor, 1992. In his revised edition Spoto adds a passing reference to "William Wilson" in explaining the theme of the double in *Strangers on a Train*.

———. *The Dark Side of Genius: The Life of Alfred Hitchcock*. New York: Ballantine, 1984. In this major biography of Hitchcock, Spoto notes several Poe connections to individual films and quotes Hitchcock's 1960 statements about Poe's influence at length (see Gottlieb above). Spoto refers to the youthful Hitchcock's Poe-inspired short tale, "Gas," which "shows the young Hitchcock's instinctive grasp of the mechanics of reader manipulation and the evocation of fear."

Sterritt, David. *The Films of Alfred Hitchcock*. Cambridge: Cambridge University Press, 1993. Sterritt notes that Marian Crane hides her stolen money in the Bates' motel in plain sight "a la Poe's 'The Purloined Letter.'"

Taylor, John Russell. *Hitch: The Life and Times of Alfred Hitchcock*. New York: Berkley, 1985. Describes an interview with Hitchcock when he first arrived in America in which he "held forth about the possibilities of enterprising B-features as a field for experiment, using offbeat stories by writers such as O. Henry or Edgar Allan Poe—a curious anticipation of what he was going to do with his television series years later" (p. 142).

Toles, George. "'If Thine Eye Offend Thee . . .': Psycho and the Art of Infection." *New Literary History*, Spring 1984, 631–51. In this study of disturbing visions in *Psycho*, Toles notes that "Hitchcock resembles Poe in his relentless preoccupation with repressed material." He also states that "*Psycho* properly belongs in the company of . . . Edgar Allan Poe's 'Berenice' . . . achieving their respective forms of pornographic intensity by impersonally rendered shocks, also attaching the same obsessive significance to the eye as metaphor."

Truffaut, Francois. *Hitchcock*. New York: Touchstone, 1967. In the introduction to his lengthy series of interviews with Hitchcock, Truffaut states that "Hitchcock belongs—and why classify him at all?—among such artists of anxiety as Kafka, Dostoyevsky, and Poe" (p. 15).

Wollen, Peter. "*Rope*: Three Hypotheses." *Alfred Hitchcock: Centenary Essays*, edited by Richard Allen and S. Ishii-Gonzales, 83. London: British Film Institute, 1999. This article suggests that in *Rope* Hitchcock brings together two of his favorite literary texts, one of which is "Edgar Allan Poe's *Tales of the Grotesque and Arabesque*, particularly 'The Pit and the Pendulum,' which vividly portrayed the terror of confinement."

———. "Compulsion." *Sight and Sound*, March 1997, 14, 17–18. Mention is made that Boileau-Narcejac "invoked Edgar Allan Poe and the Surrealists as models" and Wollen reviews Hitchcock's statement on Poe, for whom he had a "life-long admiration."

Wood, Michael. "Fearful Cemetery." *Hitchcock's America*, edited by Jonathan Freedman and Richard Millington, 174. New York: Oxford University Press, 1999. In his article about *Family Plot*, Wood sees a similarity between the "resurrection" of Arthur Adamson and "those characters in Poe who scarcely ever manage to stay in their graves."

Zayed, Georges. *The Genius of Edgar Allan Poe*. Cambridge: Schenkman, 1985. Zayed defends Poe from the old problem of being identified with his mad narrators by suggesting that "it is as though we identified, for instance, Alfred Hitchcock . . . with (his) characters and attributed to (him) the misdeeds (he) describes in (his) stories" (p. 10).

Zizek, Slavoj. "Hitchcock." *October* 38 (1986): 103. Lacanian analysis of death and the family romance in Hitchcock, focusing mainly on *The Birds*. In passing Zizek notes that Lacan's reference to numerical logic of accidental and random series of triads in examining Poe's "Purloined Letter" has application to classifying Hitchcock's films in groups of threes according to themes and periods.

Index

~

About the Author

Dennis R. Perry is associate professor of English at Brigham Young University, where he teaches courses in American literature, literature and film, and writing. He has published articles on Poe and Hitchcock and various early American texts. He and his wife, Mary Lyn Fletcher, are the parents of six children.